AI Agents for Beginners: A Practical Guide to Building and Using Autonomous AI

By John Moses

Table of Contents

Chapter 1: Introduction to AI Agents

Introduction to AI Agents

Autonomous AI agents are at the forefront of technological innovation, driving advancements in various fields, from autonomous vehicles to personalized medicine. By leveraging the power of artificial intelligence, these agents can perform tasks, make decisions, and even learn from their experiences, all without human intervention. This chapter will delve into the definition of AI agents, explore their historical context, underscore their importance in today's tech-heavy environment, and address common misconceptions.

What are AI Agents?

At its core, an AI agent is a computer system capable of performing tasks that would typically require human intelligence. These tasks include learning, reasoning, problem-solving, perception, and understanding language. An AI agent operates within an environment, which can be anything from a digital space to the real world, and acts upon it towards achieving specific goals. The agent's ability to sense its environment through data and act upon that information to achieve its objectives is what distinguishes it from a mere program.

Examples of AI Agents

- Chatbots: Designed to simulate conversation with human users, particularly over the internet.

- Autonomous Vehicles: Vehicles equipped with AI that can navigate and drive without human input.
- Personal Assistants: Such as Siri, Alexa, and Google Assistant, which can perform tasks for users based on voice commands.

Brief History of AI

The journey of AI from a concept to the highly advanced agents we see today is both fascinating and instructive. The term "Artificial Intelligence" was first coined by John McCarthy in 1956, during the Dartmouth Conference. The early days were marked by optimism and grand visions of machines capable of mimicking human intelligence. Over the decades, AI research went through cycles of progress and so-called "AI winters," where funding and interest in AI technology waned due to unmet expectations.

The resurgence of AI in the 21st century can be attributed to advances in computational power, the availability of big data, and breakthroughs in machine learning algorithms, particularly deep learning. These elements have enabled the creation of AI agents that can perform complex tasks, surpassing earlier limitations.

Importance of AI Agents in Modern Technology

AI agents are becoming increasingly integral to our daily lives and the operation of various industries. Their importance can be seen in several key areas:

- Efficiency and Automation: AI agents can automate routine tasks, from sorting emails to managing inventory, freeing humans to focus on more complex problems.
- Personalization: In marketing, entertainment, and e-commerce, AI agents provide personalized

recommendations and experiences based on individual user preferences and behavior.

- Decision Making: In fields like finance and healthcare, AI agents help in making more accurate predictions and decisions by analyzing vast amounts of data.

- Innovation: AI agents are enabling new services and products, from real-time language translation to predictive healthcare, that were unimaginable a few decades ago.

Common Misconceptions about AI Agents

Despite their potential, misconceptions about AI agents abound, often fueled by sensationalist media and science fiction. It's crucial to address these myths for a grounded understanding of AI:

- AI Agents Will Replace All Human Jobs: While AI will automate some tasks, it also creates new jobs and industries, often requiring human-AI collaboration.

- AI Agents Have Their Own Consciousness: Current AI agents operate under a set of rules and cannot think or feel. The concept of consciousness in AI is still a subject of philosophical and scientific debate.

- AI Agents Can Solve Any Problem: AI's effectiveness is limited by the data it's trained on and the specificity of tasks it's designed for. Complex issues requiring broad, general knowledge or human intuition remain challenging for AI.

Building Your First AI Agent

To demystify the process of creating AI agents and make this technology more accessible, we'll walk through building a simple AI agent. This example will use Python, a popular programming language for AI development, due to its simplicity and the powerful libraries available.

Setting Up Your Environment

Before diving into coding, ensure you have Python installed on your computer. You'll also need to install some libraries that are essential for AI development, such as NumPy (for numerical operations) and TensorFlow or PyTorch (for machine learning). You can install these libraries using pip, Python's package installer:

```
pip install numpy tensorflow
```

Creating a Simple AI Agent

For our first project, let's build a basic chatbot AI agent. This chatbot will use a predefined set of responses to answer user queries.

```
import random # Define potential user inputs and the
chatbot's responses user_inputs = ["hello", "how are
you?", "goodbye"] responses = { "hello": ["Hello!",
"Hi there!", "Hey!"], "how are you?": ["I'm an AI,
so I don't have feelings, but thanks for asking!",
"I'm doing well, thanks!"], "goodbye": ["Goodbye!",
"See you later!", "Bye!"] } def chatbot(input_text):
# Lowercase the input to match the dictionary keys
input_text = input_text.lower() if input_text in
user_inputs: # Select a random response return
random.choice(responses[input_text]) else: return
"I'm not sure how to respond to that." # Example
usage print(chatbot("Hello"))
```

This simple example illustrates the basic principle of an AI agent: taking input from its environment (user queries), processing it (matching to known inputs), and acting upon it (returning a response).

AI agents represent a significant leap forward in our ability to automate tasks, make informed decisions, and create more personalized digital experiences. By understanding the basics of how these agents work and starting to engage with their creation, we can demystify AI and harness its potential to solve real-world problems. In the next section, we will delve deeper into the architectures that underpin AI agents, exploring how they can learn and adapt over time to become even more effective at achieving their goals.

Understanding AI Agent Architectures

To fully grasp how autonomous AI agents operate, it's crucial to understand the various architectures that underpin them. These architectures are essentially the blueprints that guide the decision-making processes of AI agents, allowing them to act autonomously in a wide range of environments.

Rule-Based Systems

Rule-based systems are one of the simplest forms of AI architectures. They operate on a set of predefined rules or conditions to make decisions. These rules are often expressed as "if-then" statements that guide the agent's actions in specific situations.

```
# Example of a rule-based system if sensor_input >
threshold: action = 'Turn on' else: action = 'Turn
off'
```

Note: While rule-based systems are straightforward and easy to implement, they lack the flexibility to learn from new data or adapt to unforeseen circumstances.

Machine Learning Models

Machine learning models represent a more advanced architecture for AI agents. Unlike rule-based systems, these models can learn and improve over time based on the data they process. This learning capability enables AI agents to adapt to new situations, even those not explicitly programmed by the developers.

```
# Example of using a machine learning model from
sklearn.ensemble import RandomForestClassifier #
Training the model model = RandomForestClassifier()
model.fit(training_data, training_labels) #
Predicting with the model predictions =
model.predict(new_data)
```

Machine learning models can range from simple linear regressions to complex deep learning networks, depending on the task at hand.

Reinforcement Learning

Reinforcement learning (RL) is a paradigm of machine learning where an agent learns to make decisions by performing actions in an environment to achieve a goal. The agent receives feedback in the form of rewards or punishments, which it uses to learn the best series of actions to accomplish its objective.

```
# Example of a reinforcement learning setup for
episode in range(total_episodes): state =
environment.reset() while not done: action =
agent.choose_action(state) next_state, reward, done,
_ = environment.step(action) agent.learn(state,
action, reward, next_state) state = next_state
```

RL is particularly useful for scenarios where the model needs to make a sequence of decisions that lead to a long-term goal, such as in game playing or autonomous navigation.

Practical Implementation of AI Agents

Building a functional AI agent requires careful planning and implementation. Below are key steps and best practices for developing autonomous AI agents.

Defining the Problem

The first step in creating an AI agent is to clearly define the problem it needs to solve. This involves understanding the environment in which the agent will operate, the tasks it will perform, and the goals it aims to achieve. A well-defined problem statement will guide the choice of architecture and technologies used.

Selecting the Right Architecture

Choosing the appropriate architecture is crucial for the success of an AI agent. The decision should be based on the complexity of the task, the availability of data, and the need for adaptability. For simple decision-making tasks, a rule-based system might suffice. For more complex problems requiring learning and adaptation, machine learning models or reinforcement learning might be more appropriate.

Data Preparation

For AI agents based on machine learning, preparing the data is a critical step. This involves collecting, cleaning, and formatting data in a way that the model can process. It's essential to ensure the data is of high quality and representative of the scenarios the agent will encounter.

Implementation and Testing

With the problem defined, architecture selected, and data prepared, the next step is to implement the AI agent. This involves coding the agent according to the chosen architecture and training it with the prepared data.

```
# Example of training a machine learning model
model.fit(training_data, training_labels)
```

Testing is an ongoing process that should be performed throughout the development cycle. It involves evaluating the agent's performance in controlled environments to ensure it behaves as expected. Testing can help identify and correct issues before deploying the agent in real-world scenarios.

Deployment and Monitoring

Deploying an AI agent involves integrating it into the target environment where it will operate. This can be complex, especially for agents that interact with physical environments, such as robots or autonomous vehicles.

After deployment, it's important to continuously monitor the agent's performance to ensure it adapts to changes in the environment and improves over time. Monitoring can also help identify when the agent encounters situations it was not trained to handle, allowing for further improvements.

Challenges and Best Practices

Handling Uncertainty

One of the biggest challenges in building and deploying AI agents is dealing with uncertainty. Real-world environments are unpredictable, and an AI agent must be able to make decisions under uncertain conditions.

> **Best Practice:** Implementing mechanisms for uncertainty management, such as probabilistic models or contingency planning, can help AI agents remain robust in the face of uncertainty.

Continuous Learning

Ensuring that an AI agent continues to learn and adapt after deployment is crucial for maintaining its effectiveness. This can be challenging due to changes in the environment or the emergence of new data.

> **Best Practice:** Setting up a feedback loop where the agent can learn from its actions and outcomes in the real world is essential for continuous improvement.

Ethical Considerations

As AI agents become more autonomous, ethical considerations become increasingly important. Ensuring that AI agents act in ways that are safe, fair, and respectful of privacy is a significant challenge.

> **Best Practice:** Incorporating ethical guidelines into the design and development process and engaging with stakeholders to understand societal impacts are crucial

steps in addressing these concerns.

Building autonomous AI agents involves navigating a complex landscape of architectural choices, implementation challenges, and ethical considerations. By understanding the principles outlined in this chapter and applying best practices, developers can create AI agents that are not only functional but also adaptable, ethical, and ready to tackle real-world problems.

Implementing AI Agents in Real-World Applications

After understanding the various architectures that underpin AI agents, the next logical step is to explore how these theoretical concepts are applied in real-world scenarios. Implementing AI agents effectively requires not only a solid grasp of the underlying architectures but also an understanding of the practical considerations that come into play when deploying these agents in specific contexts.

Choosing the Right Architecture for Your Application

The choice of architecture for an AI agent is pivotal and should be dictated by the specific requirements and constraints of the application. Here are a few considerations to keep in mind:

- Complexity of the Task. Simpler tasks may be well-suited to rule-based systems, whereas more complex, unpredictable environments might necessitate the use of machine learning models.

- Real-time Decision Making: Applications requiring real-time responses might benefit from lightweight, decision-tree architectures over more computationally intensive neural networks.

- Learning Capability: If the application involves tasks that evolve over time, architectures that support machine learning and adaptation will be necessary.

Example: Customer Service Chatbot

For instance, a customer service chatbot intended to handle a wide array of customer queries can be built using a hybrid architecture. This might involve a rule-based system for common, straightforward queries and a machine learning component for understanding and learning from more nuanced customer interactions.

```
# Example of a simple rule-based response if query
== "What is your return policy?": response = "Our
return policy lasts 30 days. If 30 days have gone by
since your purchase, unfortunately, we can't offer
you a refund or exchange." else: # Invoke machine
learning model for complex queries response =
machine_learning_model.predict(query)
```

Note: The integration of machine learning models requires a dataset of past customer queries and responses for training. The quality and size of this dataset significantly impact the bot's effectiveness.

Real-World Use Cases

AI agents find application across a broad spectrum of fields, each with its unique challenges and requirements.

- Healthcare: AI agents can assist in patient diagnosis by analyzing medical data, identifying patterns that are indicative of specific conditions.

- Finance: In the finance sector, AI agents are used for algorithmic trading, fraud detection, and customer service.
- Smart Homes: AI agents in smart homes learn from the homeowner's preferences and routines to manage lighting, temperature, and security systems efficiently.

Implementing an AI Agent for Algorithmic Trading

Algorithmic trading involves making high-speed trading decisions based on market data analysis. An AI agent in this domain could be designed to learn and adapt its trading strategy in real-time, responding to market fluctuations.

```
# Example of an AI agent for algorithmic trading
class TradingAgent: def __init__(self, model):
self.model = model def analyze_market_data(self,
market_data): prediction =
self.model.predict(market_data) return prediction
def make_trade_decision(self, analysis): if analysis
> 0.5: return "Buy" else: return "Sell"
```

Best Practices and Tips

When implementing AI agents in real-world applications, consider the following best practices:

1. Start Small: Begin with a minimal viable product (MVP) and iterate based on feedback and performance metrics. 2. Data Quality: Ensure the data used for training machine learning models is high quality, diverse, and representative of real-world conditions. 3. Monitoring and Maintenance: Continuous monitoring is crucial to identify and correct any issues or biases in the AI agent's decisions. 4. Ethical Considerations. Be mindful of ethical concerns, including privacy, transparency, and fairness in decision-making.

Addressing Common Challenges

Implementing AI agents is fraught with challenges, ranging from data scarcity and quality issues to ethical dilemmas and integration complexities. Addressing these requires a careful, measured approach, prioritizing transparency, user feedback, and ethical guidelines in the development process.

By understanding the practical aspects of implementing AI agents, developers can better navigate the complexities of bringing these technologies into real-world applications. Through careful planning, ethical consideration, and ongoing refinement, AI agents can be tailored to meet the needs of virtually any application, unlocking new possibilities and enhancing efficiency across industries.

Practical Considerations for AI Agent Deployment

Deploying AI agents in real-world scenarios entails more than just selecting the right architecture. It involves understanding the environment in which the agent will operate, the tasks it will perform, and the challenges it may encounter. Let's delve into some practical considerations that are crucial for the successful deployment of AI agents.

Understanding the Operational Environment

An AI agent's operational environment significantly influences its design and functionality. Whether it's a digital landscape, such as a website for customer service bots, or a physical one, like robots navigating a warehouse, understanding the environment is crucial.

- Digital Environments: For agents operating in digital environments, considerations include the software interfaces they'll interact with, the variability of user inputs, and the need for secure and private data handling.

- Physical Environments: Agents in physical environments must deal with real-world physics, obstacles, and often unpredictable conditions. This requires robust sensory and processing capabilities to navigate and perform tasks effectively.

Example: Navigation AI in Autonomous Vehicles

```
# Pseudocode for basic obstacle detection and
navigation def detect_obstacle(sensor_data): if
sensor_data['distance_to_object'] <
SAFE_DISTANCE_THRESHOLD: return True return False
def navigate(steering, speed, sensor_data): if
detect_obstacle(sensor_data): decrease_speed(speed)
change_direction(steering) else:
maintain_speed(speed)
```

Note: This example simplifies the complex processes involved in autonomous vehicle navigation, emphasizing the need to understand the operational environment and the agent's interaction with it.

Data Acquisition and Processing

AI agents rely on data to learn, make decisions, and perform tasks. The quality, quantity, and relevance of this data are pivotal for the agent's effectiveness.

- Data Quality: Ensure the data is accurate, complete, and free from biases that could lead to flawed decision-making.

- Data Quantity: More data can lead to better learning outcomes, but it's also essential to balance this with the computational resources available.

- Data Processing: Efficient algorithms for processing and analyzing data can significantly enhance the performance of AI agents.

Real-World Use Case: Predictive Maintenance

A manufacturing plant deploys AI agents equipped with machine learning algorithms to predict equipment failures before they occur. By analyzing historical maintenance data and real-time operational metrics, these agents can identify patterns that precede failures, allowing for timely interventions.

Ethical Considerations and Bias Mitigation

AI agents, especially those interacting with users or making autonomous decisions, must be designed with ethical considerations in mind. This includes ensuring privacy, fairness, and transparency in decision-making processes.

- Bias Mitigation: Implement strategies to identify and reduce biases in data and algorithms, promoting fair and unbiased outcomes.

- Transparency: Design AI agents to provide explanations for their decisions, making them understandable to humans, especially in critical applications like healthcare or law enforcement.

Example: Bias Detection Tool

```
# Pseudocode for detecting bias in dataset def
detect_bias(dataset): bias_detected = False #
Algorithm to analyze dataset for signs of bias #
This can include checking for imbalanced classes,
underrepresentation of groups, etc. if
analysis_indicates_bias: bias_detected = True return
bias_detected
```

> **Warning:** Bias in AI can lead to unfair outcomes and discrimination. Regular audits and updates are necessary to ensure AI agents act ethically.

Scaling and Maintenance

As AI agents are deployed and begin to operate, ensuring they can scale to handle increased load and that they're maintained to adapt to new challenges is vital.

- Scalability: Design your AI agents to handle growth, whether it's more users, more data, or more complex tasks.

- Maintenance: Regular updates and maintenance are necessary to keep AI agents performing optimally, including updating data models, refining algorithms, and patching security vulnerabilities.

Deploying AI agents in real-world applications requires careful consideration of the operational environment, data handling practices, ethical implications, and ongoing maintenance needs. By addressing these considerations, developers can create AI agents that are not only effective but also responsible and adaptable to changing conditions.

Chapter 2: Understanding AI: Core Concepts

Basics of Machine Learning

Machine learning (ML) is a subset of artificial intelligence (AI) that gives computers the ability to learn from and make decisions based on data. Unlike traditional programming, where developers explicitly code every decision the computer should make, machine learning algorithms learn patterns from data, enabling them to make predictions or decisions without being explicitly programmed to perform the task.

Types of Machine Learning

There are three main types of machine learning: supervised learning, unsupervised learning, and reinforcement learning.

- Supervised Learning: This involves learning a function that maps an input to an output based on example input-output pairs. It can be thought of as a teacher supervising the learning process: we know the correct answers, and the algorithm iteratively makes predictions and is corrected by the teacher.

```
# Example of supervised learning algorithm: Linear
Regression from sklearn.linear_model import
LinearRegression X = [[0, 1], [5, 1], [15, 2], [25,
5], [35, 11], [45, 15], [55, 34], [60, 35]] y = [4,
5, 20, 14, 32, 22, 38, 43] model =
LinearRegression().fit(X, y)
```

- Unsupervised Learning: In unsupervised learning, the algorithm learns patterns from untagged data. The system tries to learn without a teacher. It's left on its own to find structure in the input data.

```
# Example of unsupervised learning algorithm:
K-means clustering from sklearn.cluster import
KMeans X = [[1, 2], [1, 4], [1, 0], [10, 2], [10,
4], [10, 0]] kmeans = KMeans(n_clusters=2,
random_state=0).fit(X)
```

- Reinforcement Learning: This type is different; the algorithm learns to perform an action from experience. Reinforcement learning is about taking suitable action to maximize reward in a particular situation.

```
# Example of reinforcement learning: Q-learning
import numpy as np # Initialize Q-table with zeros Q
= np.zeros([state_space, action_space]) # Example of
updating the Q-value for a state-action pair
Q[state, action] = Q[state, action] + alpha *
(reward + gamma * np.max(Q[new_state, :]) - Q[state,
action])
```

Challenges in Machine Learning

While machine learning offers powerful tools to solve complex problems, it also presents several challenges:

- Data Quality: The performance of a machine learning model is directly tied to the quality of the data it is trained on. Poor quality data, such as missing values or incorrect labels, can significantly degrade model performance.

- Overfitting and Underfitting: Overfitting occurs when a model learns the detail and noise in the training data to the extent that it performs poorly on new data. Underfitting occurs when a model is too simple to learn the underlying structure of the data.

- Computational Complexity: Some machine learning algorithms require significant computational resources, especially for large datasets or complex models like deep neural networks.

Best Practices

- Data Preprocessing: Spend time cleaning and preprocessing your data. This can include handling missing values, normalizing data, and feature engineering.
- Model Selection: Start with simple models to establish a baseline and gradually move to more complex models.
- Cross-validation: Use cross-validation techniques to assess how your model will generalize to an independent dataset.
- Regularization: Techniques like LASSO and Ridge regression can help prevent overfitting by penalizing large coefficients in your model.

Introduction to Neural Networks

Neural networks are a set of algorithms, modeled loosely after the human brain, that are designed to recognize patterns. They interpret sensory data through a kind of machine perception, labeling, or clustering raw input. Neural networks help us cluster and classify information.

How Neural Networks Work

Neural networks consist of input, hidden, and output layers. The input layer receives the initial data. The hidden layers process the data through weighted connections. The output layer produces the prediction or classification.

```
# Example of a simple neural network with one hidden
layer in Keras from keras.models import Sequential
from keras.layers import Dense model = Sequential([
Dense(units=5, input_shape=(3,), activation='relu'),
Dense(units=1, activation='sigmoid') ])
model.compile(optimizer='sgd',
loss='binary_crossentropy')
```

Training Neural Networks

Training a neural network involves adjusting the weights of the connections in the network based on the difference between the predicted output and the actual output. This process is repeated across many iterations in a process known as backpropagation.

- Backpropagation: This is a key algorithm for training neural networks. It works by computing the gradient of the loss function with respect to each weight by the chain rule, updating the weights in the opposite direction to minimize the loss.

Challenges and Best Practices

- Vanishing and Exploding Gradients: These are common issues when training deep neural networks. They can be mitigated by using proper initialization methods, batch normalization, and careful selection of activation functions.

- Overfitting: Similar to machine learning models, neural networks can overfit to training data. Techniques such as dropout, data augmentation, and regularization can help.

- Choosing the Right Architecture: There's no one size fits all architecture. Experimenting with different numbers of layers and neurons, along with cross-validation, can help find the optimal structure for your specific problem.

Overview of Deep Learning

Deep learning, a subset of machine learning, involves the use of deep neural networks. These networks have many layers (hence "deep") and have shown remarkable success in many fields, including image recognition, natural language processing, and game playing.

Key Components of Deep Learning

- Convolutional Neural Networks (CNNs): Primarily used in image processing, CNNs automatically and adaptively learn spatial hierarchies of features from images.

- Recurrent Neural Networks (RNNs): Used for sequential data, like time series or natural language, RNNs can remember information for long periods, making them effective for tasks like language modeling and machine translation.

- Generative Adversarial Networks (GANs): GANs consist of two networks, a generator and a discriminator, that are trained simultaneously. GANs are particularly known for generating realistic images and videos.

Applications of Deep Learning

Deep learning has been successfully applied in a variety of fields:

- Computer Vision: From facial recognition systems to autonomous vehicles, deep learning models can interpret and understand the visual world.

- Natural Language Processing (NLP): Deep learning has transformed NLP, enabling machines to understand, interpret, and generate human language with high accuracy.

- Healthcare: Deep learning is used in predictive analytics, medical imaging, and understanding genetic patterns, revolutionizing the healthcare industry.

Challenges and Solutions

- Data Requirements: Deep learning models require large amounts of data. Solutions include data augmentation, transfer learning, and synthetic data generation.
- Interpretability: Deep learning models are often seen as "black boxes" due to their complexity. Techniques like feature visualization and attention mechanisms are used to improve model interpretability.
- Computational Resources: Training deep learning models can be resource-intensive. Distributed computing, efficient network architectures, and hardware accelerators like GPUs and TPUs can mitigate these issues.

Understanding the core concepts of AI, including machine learning, neural networks, and deep learning, is crucial for anyone entering the field. These technologies power a wide range of applications, from simple tasks like spam detection to complex systems like self-driving cars. As we continue to advance in these areas, the potential for creating intelligent systems that can learn and adapt to various tasks is virtually limitless.

Introduction to Neural Networks

Neural networks form the backbone of many modern AI systems, simulating the way human brains operate to solve complex problems. At their core, neural networks are composed of layers of interconnected nodes, or "neurons," each designed to perform specific computations. These networks can learn and make decisions by adjusting the connections (weights) between neurons based on the data they process.

How Neural Networks Work

A simple neural network includes an input layer, one or more hidden layers, and an output layer. The input layer receives the data, the hidden layers process the data through various computations, and the output layer produces the final result.

- Input Layer: This is the entry point of the data into the network. Each neuron in the input layer represents a feature of the input data.

- Hidden Layers: These layers perform computations using weighted connections established between the neurons. They can capture complex relationships in the data.

- Output Layer: The final layer that provides the output of the neural network, which can be a classification or a regression value depending on the task.

Example:

Consider a neural network designed to recognize handwritten digits. The input layer receives the pixel values of the image, the hidden layers process these values through a series of computations, and the output layer classifies the image as a digit between 0 and 9.

```
import tensorflow as tf from tensorflow.keras import
layers, models # Define a simple neural network with
1 hidden layer model = models.Sequential()
model.add(layers.Dense(512, activation='relu',
input_shape=(784,))) model.add(layers.Dense(10,
activation='softmax')) # Compile the model
model.compile(optimizer='rmsprop',
loss='categorical_crossentropy',
metrics=['accuracy'])
```

> **Note**: This example uses TensorFlow, a popular library for building neural networks. The network has one hidden layer with 512 neurons and uses the ReLU activation function. The output layer has 10 neurons corresponding to the 10 possible digits and uses the softmax activation function for classification.

Training Neural Networks

Training a neural network involves adjusting the weights of the connections between neurons to minimize the difference between the predicted output and the actual output. This process is typically done using a method called backpropagation combined with an optimization algorithm like stochastic gradient descent.

1. Forward Pass: The data is passed through the network from the input to the output layer, and a prediction is made. 2. Loss Calculation: The difference between the prediction and the actual output is calculated using a loss function. 3. Backward Pass (Backpropagation): The gradient of the loss function is calculated for each weight in the network, and the weights are adjusted in the direction that minimizes the loss. 4. Repeat: This process is repeated for many iterations over the training dataset until the network's predictions are sufficiently accurate.

Example:

```
# Assuming X_train and y_train are the training data
and labels, respectively model.fit(X_train, y_train,
epochs=10, batch_size=32)
```

This code snippet trains the model on the training data (x_train and y_train) for 10 epochs, with a batch size of 32. An epoch is a complete pass through the entire training dataset.

Overview of Deep Learning

Deep Learning is a subset of machine learning that utilizes deep neural networks. The "deep" in deep learning refers to the use of multiple hidden layers in neural networks, enabling the model to learn complex patterns and perform tasks with unprecedented accuracy, such as image and speech recognition, natural language processing, and more.

Characteristics of Deep Learning

- Ability to Process Large Datasets: Deep learning models excel at handling vast amounts of data, learning more intricate patterns as the dataset size increases.

- Automatic Feature Extraction: Unlike traditional machine learning models that require manual feature selection, deep learning models are capable of automatically discovering useful features from the data.

- Highly Versatile: Deep learning models can be applied to a wide range of tasks and data types, making them highly adaptable to new challenges.

Real-World Applications

- Image Recognition: Deep learning models can identify objects within images with high accuracy, used in applications from medical imaging to security surveillance.

- Natural Language Processing (NLP): These models understand, interpret, and generate human language, powering virtual assistants and translation services.

- Autonomous Vehicles: Deep learning enables self-driving cars to make sense of their surroundings and navigate safely.

Challenges and Considerations

- Computational Resources: Training deep learning models requires significant computational power, often necessitating the use of GPUs or distributed computing environments.

- Overfitting: Due to their complexity, deep learning models are prone to overfitting, where the model performs well on the training data but poorly on new, unseen data. Techniques such as dropout and data augmentation are used to mitigate this risk.

Example: Image Recognition with Convolutional Neural Networks (CNNs)

```
model = models.Sequential()
model.add(layers.Conv2D(32, (3, 3),
activation='relu', input_shape=(28, 28, 1)))
model.add(layers.MaxPooling2D((2, 2)))
model.add(layers.Conv2D(64, (3, 3),
activation='relu'))
model.add(layers.MaxPooling2D((2, 2)))
model.add(layers.Conv2D(64, (3, 3),
activation='relu')) model.add(layers.Flatten())
model.add(layers.Dense(64, activation='relu'))
model.add(layers.Dense(10, activation='softmax')) #
The model is then compiled and trained similarly to
the previous examples
```

This example demonstrates a basic Convolutional Neural Network (CNN) for image recognition. CNNs are particularly well-suited for processing grid-like data, such as images. This network includes convolutional layers, which automatically learn spatial hierarchies of features, and pooling layers, which reduce the dimensionality of the data to make the neural network more efficient.

Tip: When working with deep learning models, it's crucial to experiment with different architectures and parameters to find the best solution for your specific problem.

Deep learning has transformed the field of artificial intelligence, enabling computers to solve problems that were once considered beyond reach. As computational resources become more accessible and datasets grow, the potential applications of deep learning continue to expand, promising to revolutionize a wide array of industries.

Overview of Deep Learning

Deep learning is a subset of machine learning that utilizes networks capable of learning from data in a way that mimics the human brain. This section delves into the fundamentals of deep learning, its distinctions from traditional machine learning, and its real-world applications.

What is Deep Learning?

Deep learning is an advanced form of machine learning involving neural networks with many layers, hence the term "deep." These deep neural networks are adept at processing vast amounts of data, recognizing patterns, and making decisions. Deep learning models can automatically learn and improve from experience without being explicitly programmed for specific tasks.

Deep Learning vs. Traditional Machine Learning

While both deep learning and traditional machine learning fall under the broad umbrella of AI, there are key differences:

- Data Handling: Deep learning algorithms excel with large datasets, whereas traditional machine learning can perform well with smaller datasets.

- Feature Extraction: In traditional machine learning, features need to be manually specified and extracted. Deep learning, on the other hand, automatically discovers the best features to use for a given task.

- Computational Resources: Deep learning generally requires more computational power and data than traditional machine learning.

```
# Sample Python code comparing traditional ML and
deep learning model initialization # Traditional ML:
Decision Tree Classifier from sklearn.tree import
DecisionTreeClassifier clf =
DecisionTreeClassifier() # Deep Learning: Using
TensorFlow and Keras for a simple neural network
from tensorflow.keras.models import Sequential from
tensorflow.keras.layers import Dense model =
Sequential([ Dense(128, activation='relu'),
Dense(10, activation='softmax') ])
```

Real-World Applications of Deep Learning

Deep learning has been revolutionary in several domains, including:

- Image Recognition: Deep learning models can identify objects, faces, and scenes in images with remarkable accuracy.

- Natural Language Processing (NLP): From translation services to chatbots, deep learning has significantly advanced the understanding and generation of human language by machines.

- Autonomous Vehicles: Deep learning algorithms process the massive amounts of data from sensors in real-time, enabling self-driving cars to make safe navigation decisions.

Note: While deep learning offers tremendous benefits, it also requires careful consideration regarding the quality and quantity of the training data, as well as the computational resources available.

Key AI Terminology

Understanding the vocabulary used in AI is crucial for anyone looking to delve deeper into the field. Below are some of the essential terms and their definitions:

Algorithms

An algorithm is a set of rules or instructions designed to perform a specific task. In AI, algorithms are used to process data, learn from it, and make decisions or predictions based on that learning.

Data Mining

Data mining involves examining large datasets to discover patterns, correlations, and trends. It's a critical process in AI for understanding and preparing data for training models.

Supervised Learning

Supervised learning is a type of machine learning where models are trained on labeled data. The model learns to make predictions based on input-output pairs.

Unsupervised Learning

Unsupervised learning, in contrast to supervised learning, involves training models on data without explicit instructions on what to do with it. The model tries to identify patterns and relationships within the data itself.

Reinforcement Learning

Reinforcement learning is an area of machine learning where an agent learns to make decisions by taking actions in an environment to achieve some goals. The agent learns from the consequences of its actions, rather than from direct instruction.

Understanding these core concepts of AI is crucial for building a solid foundation in the field. As we move forward, we will explore how to apply these concepts practically to develop intelligent systems capable of autonomous operation.

Key AI Terminology

Understanding the language of AI is crucial for anyone looking to delve into this field. This section introduces essential terms and concepts that form the foundation of AI technology. By familiarizing yourself with these terms, you'll be better equipped to understand how AI agents are built and how they function.

Machine Learning Algorithms

At the core of many AI systems are machine learning algorithms. These algorithms enable computers to learn from data, improving their accuracy over time without being explicitly programmed to do so.

- Supervised Learning: This involves training a model on a labeled dataset, which means that each training example is paired with an output label. Supervised learning algorithms include regression and classification models.

```
from sklearn.datasets import load_iris from
sklearn.tree import DecisionTreeClassifier # Load
the dataset iris = load_iris() X, y = iris.data,
iris.target # Initialize and train the classifier
classifier = DecisionTreeClassifier()
classifier.fit(X, y)
```

- Unsupervised Learning: In contrast, unsupervised learning algorithms are trained using information that is neither classified nor labeled. Clustering and association are common unsupervised learning methods.

```
from sklearn.cluster import KMeans from
sklearn.datasets import load_iris # Load the dataset
iris = load_iris() X = iris.data # Clustering kmeans
= KMeans(n_clusters=3) kmeans.fit(X)
```

- Reinforcement Learning: This type of learning uses a system of rewards and penalties to compel the computer to solve a problem by itself. Its goal is to find a strategy that maximizes the sum of the rewards.

```
import gym env = gym.make('CartPole-v1') observation
= env.reset() for _ in range(1000): action =
env.action_space.sample() # your agent here
observation, reward, done, info = env.step(action)
if done: observation = env.reset() env.close()
```

Neural Networks and Deep Learning

- Neural Networks: At a high level, neural networks are algorithms intended to recognize patterns. They interpret sensory data through a kind of machine perception, labeling, or clustering raw input.

- Deep Learning: Deep learning is a subset of machine learning that employs deep neural networks. It's particularly useful for processing large amounts of complex data, such as images and speech.

```
from keras.models import Sequential from
keras.layers import Dense # Define the model model =
Sequential([ Dense(32, activation='relu',
input_shape=(784,)), Dense(10,
activation='softmax'), ]) # Compile the model
model.compile(optimizer='adam',
loss='categorical_crossentropy',
metrics=['accuracy'])
```

Note: When working with neural networks and deep learning, it's essential to have a solid understanding of the data you're using. Preprocessing and feature selection play critical roles in the performance of your models.

Best Practices and Challenges

- Data Quality: The quality of your data is paramount. Ensure your datasets are clean and relevant to the task at hand.

- Model Complexity: While complex models can capture intricate patterns, they also risk overfitting. Balance complexity with the necessity.

- Computational Resources: Deep learning models, in particular, require significant computational power. Plan your resources accordingly.

These key terms and concepts form the backbone of AI technology. As you progress in your AI journey, you'll encounter these and many more. Understanding them is the first step toward mastering AI.

Chapter 3: Architecture of AI Agents

Reactive AI Agents

Introduction to Reactive Agents

Reactive AI agents are designed to respond to their environment or stimuli without the necessity of an internal model of the world. This architecture is based on the concept of stimulus-response, where the agent perceives its environment and immediately reacts to it. The simplicity of reactive agents makes them fast and efficient for specific tasks where a deep understanding of the environment is not required.

Key Characteristics

- Simplicity: Reactive agents operate without the need for complex data structures or algorithms to model their environment, making them less resource-intensive.

- Speed: Due to their straightforward nature, reactive agents can make decisions quickly, which is crucial in time-sensitive applications.

- Scalability: These agents can easily be scaled to handle larger systems or more complex environments by adding more simple agents rather than by enhancing their individual complexity.

Examples in Real-World Applications

1. Robotic Vacuum Cleaners: These devices navigate and clean floors by reacting to physical obstacles and dirt sensors without mapping the entire house. 2. Traffic Management Systems: Reactive signals adjust to real-time traffic conditions, optimizing flow without predicting future traffic states.

```
# Example of a simple reactive agent algorithm for a
robotic vacuum cleaner def
react_to_obstacle(sensor_input): if sensor_input ==
'obstacle': return 'turn' else: return
'move_forward' def react_to_dirt(sensor_input): if
sensor_input == 'dirty': return 'clean' else: return
'continue'
```

Note: Reactive agents are best suited for environments where the agent's tasks are straightforward and the environment is relatively static or predictable.

Best Practices

- Keep it Simple: Design your reactive agents to perform specific tasks. Avoid overcomplicating their decision-making processes.

- Modularity: Build your system with small, purpose-focused agents that can work independently. This enhances system reliability and ease of maintenance.

- Environment Interaction: Design your agents to have robust and sensitive interaction mechanisms with their environment to improve their responsiveness.

Common Challenges and Solutions

- Limited Flexibility: Reactive agents might struggle in environments that require long-term planning or strategy.

Combining reactive agents with other types of agents can sometimes mitigate this limitation.

- Environmental Complexity: As the complexity of the environment increases, the number of rules required for the agent to function effectively can become unmanageable. To address this, focus on the most critical interactions and simplify the environmental model as much as possible.

Cognitive AI Agents

Understanding Cognitive Agents

Cognitive AI agents are designed to simulate human-like understanding and reasoning. They possess the ability to build and maintain a model of the world, which they use to make informed decisions. This type of agent relies on more complex algorithms, including machine learning and logic, to process and interpret data.

Key Characteristics

- World Modeling: Cognitive agents create a representation of their environment, allowing them to make predictions and plan actions.

- Learning Ability: These agents can improve their performance over time through learning from past experiences.

- Decision Making: With the help of artificial intelligence techniques, cognitive agents can evaluate multiple potential actions and choose the most appropriate one based on their goals.

Examples in Real-World Applications

1. Personal Assistants: Devices like smartphones and smart speakers use cognitive AI to understand user queries and provide relevant information or actions. 2. Autonomous Vehicles: These vehicles use complex models of their surroundings, including other vehicles, pedestrians, and road conditions, to navigate safely.

```
# Pseudocode example of a cognitive agent making a
decision class CognitiveAgent: def __init__(self,
knowledge_base): self.knowledge_base =
knowledge_base def make_decision(self,
environment_data): world_model =
self.build_world_model(environment_data)
possible_actions =
self.evaluate_possible_actions(world_model)
best_action =
self.choose_best_action(possible_actions) return
best_action # Methods to build world model, evaluate
possible actions, and choose the best action # would
be implemented here.
```

Warning: Cognitive agents require significant computational resources due to their complex data processing and decision-making algorithms. Ensure adequate resources are available for your application.

Best Practices

- Continuous Learning: Implement mechanisms for your cognitive agents to learn from new data and experiences to improve their decision-making over time.

- Error Handling: Plan for and manage errors or unexpected inputs gracefully to maintain the robustness of your agent.

- Ethical Considerations: Ensure that the decision-making processes of your cognitive agents align with ethical guidelines, especially in applications with significant social impact.

Common Challenges and Solutions

- Data Quality and Availability: Cognitive agents depend on high-quality data to learn and make decisions. Ensure your data pipelines are reliable and your data is of high quality.

- Complexity Management: As cognitive agents learn and evolve, managing their complexity becomes challenging. Regularly review and refactor your agents' learning and decision-making processes to maintain understandability and efficiency.

Choosing the Right Architecture

Factors to Consider

- Task Complexity: Simple, repetitive tasks might be best suited to reactive agents, while tasks requiring understanding and decision-making might require cognitive agents.

- Environmental Predictability: In highly dynamic or unpredictable environments, cognitive agents' ability to adapt and learn can be advantageous.

- Resource Availability: Reactive agents are less resource-intensive than cognitive agents, making them suitable for applications with limited computational power or energy availability.

Making the Decision

Choosing between reactive, cognitive, and hybrid architectures depends on balancing the needs of your application with the capabilities of each type of agent. In some cases, a hybrid approach that combines the simplicity and speed of reactive agents with the adaptability and intelligence of cognitive agents may offer the best solution.

> **Tip:** Experiment with different architectures in a controlled setting to understand their strengths and weaknesses in the context of your specific application.

In the next section, we will explore hybrid AI agents in more detail, examining how they integrate the benefits of both reactive and cognitive approaches to create versatile and effective AI solutions.

Cognitive AI Agents

Understanding Cognitive Agents

Cognitive AI agents represent a more sophisticated approach to artificial intelligence, designed to simulate human-like thinking and reasoning. Unlike reactive agents, which operate purely on the stimulus-response principle, cognitive agents possess the capability to understand, learn from, and act upon the world using knowledge and reasoning. This type of AI involves more complex processes such as perception, memory, learning, and problem-solving.

Key Components

The architecture of cognitive agents typically involves several key components:

- Knowledge Base: A repository of facts and information that the agent uses to make decisions.
- Inference Engine: The logic that applies rules to the knowledge base to derive conclusions or make predictions.
- Learning Module: Enables the agent to learn from past actions and improve its performance over time.
- Perception: The ability to sense the environment. This could involve processing data from sensors or interpreting input data to form a representation of the world.

Example: A Smart Home Assistant

Consider a smart home assistant designed as a cognitive AI agent. It possesses a knowledge base containing information about the homeowner's preferences, schedules, and routines. The inference engine applies rules to this knowledge base to make decisions, such as adjusting the thermostat or suggesting a departure time to avoid traffic based on the homeowner's schedule and current traffic conditions. The learning module allows the assistant to adapt to changes in the homeowner's preferences or routines, improving its suggestions over time.

```
class SmartHomeAssistant: def __init__(self,
knowledge_base, rules): self.knowledge_base =
knowledge_base self.rules = rules def
make_decision(self, input_data): # Apply rules to
knowledge base and input data to make a decision
pass def learn(self, new_data): # Update knowledge
base with new information pass
```

Note: The complexity of cognitive agents means they require more computational resources than reactive agents, and their development can be more time-consuming and challenging.

Advantages and Challenges

Cognitive agents offer the advantage of handling complex and ambiguous situations by applying reasoning and learning from past experiences. However, developing these agents involves challenges such as ensuring the accuracy and relevancy of the knowledge base and designing effective learning algorithms.

Hybrid AI Agents

The Best of Both Worlds

Hybrid AI agents combine the immediacy and efficiency of reactive agents with the thoughtful, knowledge-driven approach of cognitive agents. The goal of a hybrid agent is to leverage the strengths of both architectures to create systems that are both efficient and intelligent.

Architecture Overview

A typical hybrid agent architecture might include:

- Reactive Layer: Handles immediate responses to the environment, ensuring fast and efficient action.

- Cognitive Layer: Manages complex decision-making based on knowledge, reasoning, and learning.

- Interface Layer: Serves as a mediator between the reactive and cognitive layers, ensuring that the system's overall behavior is coherent and effective.

Example: Autonomous Vehicles

An autonomous vehicle is a prime example of a hybrid AI agent. The reactive layer allows the vehicle to respond instantly to obstacles, traffic signals, and other immediate environmental stimuli. Meanwhile, the cognitive layer processes more complex data, such as mapping routes, optimizing fuel consumption, or planning around traffic jams, based on a comprehensive understanding of the road network and the vehicle's current status.

```
class AutonomousVehicle: def __init__(self, sensors,
knowledge_base): self.sensors = sensors
self.knowledge_base = knowledge_base def
navigate(self, destination): # Use reactive layer
for immediate responses # Use cognitive layer for
complex decision making pass
```

Warning: Designing hybrid AI agents requires careful planning to ensure that the reactive and cognitive layers work in harmony, without one layer overshadowing the effectiveness of the other.

Choosing the Right Architecture

Selecting the appropriate architecture for an AI agent depends on several factors, including the complexity of the task, the need for learning and adaptation, and the resources available for development and operation. While reactive agents are suited for simple, well-defined tasks, cognitive and hybrid agents are better for applications requiring complex decision-making and adaptability.

Summary

Understanding the differences between reactive, cognitive, and hybrid AI agents is crucial for designing effective autonomous systems. Each architecture offers unique advantages and comes with its own set of challenges. By carefully considering the needs of the application and the capabilities of each type of agent, developers can choose the most appropriate architecture to achieve their goals. Whether building a simple reactive agent for a specific task or a sophisticated hybrid agent capable of navigating the complexities of the real world, the key is to align the agent's design with its intended function.

Hybrid AI Agents

Understanding Hybrid Agents

Hybrid AI agents combine the best features of both reactive and cognitive architectures, creating a more versatile and efficient system. These agents are designed to handle a wide range of tasks, from simple, reflexive responses to complex, thought-driven actions. The hybrid approach allows for the rapid response of reactive agents while still maintaining the depth of understanding and learning capabilities of cognitive agents.

How Hybrid Agents Work

A typical hybrid AI agent operates by utilizing a layered architecture, where different layers are responsible for different types of processing:

- Reactive Layer: This is the most basic level, handling immediate responses to stimuli without the need for deliberation or memory.
- Cognitive Layer: Above the reactive layer, this component deals with more complex decision-making processes, utilizing memory, learning, and reasoning to make informed decisions.
- Deliberative Layer: This optional layer can exist in more advanced agents, incorporating long-term planning and strategy into the agent's actions.

This structure allows hybrid agents to act quickly in situations that require immediate action, while also being capable of more thoughtful analysis when necessary.

Implementing Hybrid Agents

Implementing a hybrid AI agent requires careful planning and a deep understanding of both reactive and cognitive architectures. Here's a basic outline for creating a simple hybrid agent:

1. Design the Reactive Layer: Start by defining the basic behaviors your agent will need to respond to instantly. These should be simple, stimulus-response pairs.

2. Develop the Cognitive Layer: Identify the more complex tasks your agent needs to perform that require learning, memory, or reasoning. Implement algorithms suited for these tasks, such as machine learning models or rule-based systems.

3. Integrate the Layers: Ensure that the reactive layer can operate independently but also feed information into the

cognitive layer when necessary. This might involve the cognitive layer overriding reactive behaviors when a more sophisticated response is needed.

```
# Example: Hybrid Agent Structure (Pseudocode) class
HybridAgent: def __init__(self):
self.reactive_component = ReactiveComponent()
self.cognitive_component = CognitiveComponent() def
perceive(self, environment): # Perception logic pass
def act(self): immediate_response =
self.reactive_component.check_for_stimuli() if
immediate_response: return immediate_response else:
return self.cognitive_component.make_decision()
```

Note: This is a simplified example. The complexity of the components and their interactions can vary greatly based on the specific requirements of the agent.

Best Practices and Tips

- Balance is Key: Ensure a balance between reactive and cognitive processing. Too much reliance on one can lead to inefficiencies or bottlenecks.

- Optimize for Speed and Efficiency: While integrating, optimize the reactive layer for speed and the cognitive layer for efficiency and accuracy.

- Continuous Testing and Evaluation: Hybrid agents can become complex. Regular testing and evaluation are crucial to maintain performance and identify areas for improvement.

Real-World Use Cases

Hybrid AI agents have a wide range of applications:

- Autonomous Vehicles: Combining rapid reactions to immediate hazards with complex navigation and decision-making.

- Healthcare Robotics: Providing instant assistance or feedback while also being capable of complex patient care planning.

- Smart Home Systems: Managing simple tasks and responses to environmental changes, alongside more complex decision-making regarding energy efficiency and user preferences.

Common Challenges

- Integration Complexity: Ensuring smooth communication and priority handling between layers can be challenging.

- Resource Management: Hybrid agents can be resource-intensive, requiring careful management of computational resources.

- Adaptability: Maintaining adaptability and learning capabilities in a hybrid system can be more complex than in purely cognitive systems.

Hybrid AI agents represent a powerful approach to building versatile and efficient AI systems. By combining the strengths of reactive and cognitive architectures, these agents can handle a wide spectrum of tasks, from simple reflex actions to complex decision-making processes. Despite the challenges in integration and resource management, the potential applications of hybrid agents in fields like autonomous driving, healthcare, and smart homes are vast and promising.

Choosing the Right Architecture

Selecting the appropriate architecture for your AI agent is a critical decision that can significantly impact the performance and effectiveness of your application. This section will guide you through the considerations and practicalities of choosing between reactive, cognitive, and hybrid architectures for your AI agent.

Factors to Consider

When deciding on an architecture for your AI agent, several key factors come into play:

- Complexity of the Task: The nature and complexity of the tasks you expect your AI agent to perform are perhaps the most significant determinants. Simple, repetitive tasks may only require the straightforward, rule-based logic of reactive agents, while more complex and dynamic problems might benefit from the depth and adaptability of cognitive agents.

- Real-time Performance Needs: If your application demands rapid, real-time responses, the lean and efficient design of reactive agents might be more suitable. In contrast, applications that can tolerate slight delays for more thoughtful analysis or learning may leverage cognitive architectures.

- Learning and Adaptation: Consider whether your AI agent needs to learn from its experiences and improve over time. Cognitive and hybrid agents are designed with learning capabilities at their core, unlike reactive agents, which do not learn from past actions.

- Resource Constraints: The computational resources available for your project can also influence your choice. Cognitive agents, with their more complex algorithms, typically require more processing power and memory than simpler reactive agents.

Practical Implementation

Implementing the chosen architecture involves a series of practical steps, tailored to the specific requirements of your project.

Reactive Agents

For a reactive agent, you might start by defining a set of rules or behaviors triggered by specific environmental conditions. For example, a reactive agent in a home automation system could be programmed as follows:

```
def control_lights(sensor_data): if
sensor_data['light_level'] < 20: return
'turn_on_lights' else: return 'turn_off_lights'
```

This simple rule-based approach allows the agent to react immediately to changes in light levels without the need for complex processing.

Cognitive Agents

Building a cognitive agent, on the other hand, typically involves developing or utilizing machine learning models that enable the agent to understand and interpret data at a deeper level. For instance, a cognitive agent designed for customer service might be implemented using a natural language processing (NLP) model:

```
from transformers import pipeline nlp =
pipeline("sentiment-analysis") feedback = "The
service was outstanding and the staff was incredibly
helpful." print(nlp(feedback))
```

This snippet demonstrates how a cognitive agent could analyze customer feedback sentiment, a task that requires understanding context and nuance beyond simple rule-based logic.

Hybrid Agents

For hybrid agents, implementation might involve integrating both reactive and cognitive components. A hybrid agent in an autonomous vehicle could use reactive mechanisms for immediate obstacle avoidance while simultaneously processing complex sensor data through cognitive models for navigation and decision-making:

```
def avoid_obstacle(distance_to_object): if
distance_to_object < 1: # meters return
'execute_evasive_maneuver' else: return
'continue_course' # Cognitive component for
navigation might be more complex and involve machine
learning models
```

Best Practices and Tips

Regardless of the architecture chosen, there are several best practices to follow:

- Modularity: Design your agent with clear, modular components. This approach enhances maintainability and allows for easier upgrades or changes to individual parts of the system.

- Testing: Rigorously test your AI agent in a variety of scenarios to ensure it behaves as expected under different conditions.

- Performance Monitoring: Implement logging and monitoring to track your agent's performance and identify areas for improvement.

- Ethical Considerations: Always consider the ethical implications of your AI agent, especially in applications that significantly impact human lives.

Choosing between reactive, cognitive, and hybrid architectures requires careful consideration of your project's needs, the tasks at hand, and the resources available. By understanding the strengths and limitations of each architecture, you can make an informed decision that best suits your objectives, ensuring your AI agent is both efficient and effective in its operations.

Chapter 4: Essential Tools and Frameworks

Python and Essential Libraries

Python stands as the lingua franca of AI development due to its simplicity, versatility, and the vast ecosystem of libraries and frameworks it supports. For anyone embarking on the journey of building AI agents, a solid grasp of Python and its essential libraries is indispensable.

Why Python?

Python's syntax is clean and intuitive, making it an excellent choice for beginners and experienced developers alike. Its interpretive nature allows for rapid testing and iteration, which is crucial during the development of complex AI models. Moreover, the extensive support from the community and the rich repository of documentation and tutorials make Python an unrivaled choice for AI development.

Core Libraries for AI

- NumPy: NumPy is the foundational library for scientific computing in Python. It provides support for large, multi-dimensional arrays and matrices, along with a collection of mathematical functions to operate on these arrays. Understanding NumPy is essential for handling data processing tasks in AI.

```
import numpy as np # Creating a 2D array array_2d =
np.array([[1, 2, 3], [4, 5, 6]]) print(array_2d)
```

- Pandas: Pandas is a library offering high-level data structures and tools for effective data manipulation and analysis. It is particularly useful for handling and analyzing input data before feeding it into an AI model.

```
import pandas as pd # Creating a DataFrame from a
dictionary data = {'Name': ['John', 'Anna'], 'Age':
[28, 22]} df = pd.DataFrame(data) print(df)
```

- Matplotlib: Visualization is key in understanding the datasets you work with and the performance of your AI models. Matplotlib is a plotting library that provides a solid foundation for constructing visualizations in Python.

```
import matplotlib.pyplot as plt # Plotting a simple
line graph plt.plot([1, 2, 3], [2, 4, 6]) plt.show()
```

- Scikit-learn: For machine learning tasks, scikit-learn is the go-to library. It features various algorithms for classification, regression, clustering, and dimensionality reduction. It is also designed to work seamlessly with NumPy and Pandas.

```
from sklearn.model_selection import train_test_split
from sklearn.linear_model import LogisticRegression
from sklearn import datasets # Load dataset iris =
datasets.load_iris() X_train, X_test, y_train,
y_test = train_test_split(iris.data, iris.target,
test_size=0.4, random_state=0) # Create and train a
model model = LogisticRegression()
model.fit(X_train, y_train) # Model accuracy
print("Model accuracy:", model.score(X_test,
y_test))
```

- TensorFlow and PyTorch: For deep learning tasks, TensorFlow and PyTorch are the two leading libraries. Both provide comprehensive tools and libraries for creating deep learning models, with support for powerful computations that can scale across CPUs, GPUs, and even TPUs.

```
# TensorFlow example import tensorflow as tf #
Define a simple Sequential model model =
tf.keras.Sequential([ tf.keras.layers.Dense(10,
activation='relu', input_shape=(784,)),
tf.keras.layers.Dense(10, activation='softmax') ])
model.compile(optimizer='adam',
loss='sparse_categorical_crossentropy',
metrics=['accuracy']) # PyTorch example import torch
import torch.nn as nn # Define a simple neural
network class SimpleNN(nn.Module): def
__init__(self): super(SimpleNN, self).__init__()
self.layer1 = nn.Linear(784, 128) self.layer2 =
nn.Linear(128, 10) def forward(self, x): x =
torch.relu(self.layer1(x)) x = self.layer2(x) return
x model = SimpleNN()
```

Note: Choosing between TensorFlow and PyTorch often comes down to personal preference and the specific requirements of the project. TensorFlow is known for its production-ready tools and broader ecosystem, while PyTorch is praised for its ease of use and dynamic computation graph.

AI Development Frameworks

While Python libraries provide the building blocks for machine learning and deep learning, AI development frameworks offer a higher level of abstraction, making the development of complex AI agents more manageable.

- Keras: Initially developed as an interface for TensorFlow, Keras has since evolved into a standalone framework that can run on top of TensorFlow, Theano, or Microsoft Cognitive Toolkit. Its API is designed for human beings, not machines, making it accessible to beginners.

- FastAI: Built on top of PyTorch, FastAI simplifies the process of training fast and accurate neural nets using modern best practices. It's particularly useful for practitioners looking to dive into deep learning without getting bogged down by the underlying complexities.

- OpenAI Gym: For those interested in reinforcement learning, OpenAI Gym provides a toolkit for developing and comparing reinforcement learning algorithms. It offers a wide variety of environments, from simple text-based games to complex 3D simulations, to test and train your AI agents.

```
import gym env = gym.make('CartPole-v1') observation
= env.reset() for _ in range(1000): env.render()
action = env.action_space.sample() # your agent here
(this takes random actions) observation, reward,
done, info = env.step(action) if done: observation =
env.reset() env.close()
```

Warning: Reinforcement learning can be computationally intensive and may require powerful hardware, especially for complex environments. Cloud platforms and GPUs are often used to speed up the training process.

Cloud Platforms for AI

Leveraging cloud platforms can significantly accelerate the development and deployment of AI models. These platforms offer scalable compute resources, managed AI services, and pre-built models that can be customized to fit specific needs.

- Google Cloud AI Platform: Offers a mix of pre-trained models and a platform to generate your own tailored models. It supports a wide range of AI tasks, from vision and natural language processing to decision making and translation.

- AWS SageMaker: A fully managed service that provides every developer and data scientist with the ability to build, train, and deploy machine learning models quickly. SageMaker offers broad framework support, automatic model tuning, and scalable deployment options.

- Azure Machine Learning: Microsoft's offering emphasizes ease of use and efficiency in model creation and deployment. It supports various machine learning frameworks, provides tools for automating machine learning pipelines, and offers enterprise-grade security.

Using cloud platforms can not only speed up the development cycle but also enable the deployment of AI agents at scale, making them accessible to a wider audience without the need for substantial upfront investment in hardware.

> **Tip**: While cloud platforms offer significant advantages, it's important to consider cost, privacy, and data security. Always review the terms of service and pricing models to ensure they align with your project's needs and budget.

Development Environments

Choosing the right development environment can enhance productivity and make the process of coding, testing, and debugging AI agents more efficient.

- Jupyter Notebooks: Ideal for prototyping and exploratory analysis, Jupyter Notebooks support interactive coding sessions and can display plots and graphs inline. They're widely used in the data science community and are supported by most cloud AI platforms.

- Visual Studio Code (VS Code): A lightweight but powerful source code editor that supports Python and many other languages. Its vast array of extensions, including those for machine learning and AI, make it a versatile tool for developers.

- PyCharm: Specifically designed for Python development, PyCharm offers advanced code navigation, debugging tools, and support for web development frameworks. Its professional version also includes support for scientific tools, including Jupyter Notebooks and Anaconda.

Choosing the right tools and frameworks is crucial for the efficient development of AI agents. From the foundational libraries in Python to sophisticated AI development frameworks and cloud platforms, the ecosystem provides developers with a vast array of resources. In the next section, we'll delve into practical implementation details, including setting up your development environment, working with data, and deploying your first AI agent.

AI Development Frameworks

Building AI agents requires more than just a programming language; it necessitates a suite of tools designed to streamline the development process. AI development frameworks offer pre-built functions and structures that help in the design, training, and deployment of AI models. Let's delve into some of the most popular frameworks that are essential for AI agent development.

TensorFlow

TensorFlow, developed by Google, is one of the most widely used open-source frameworks for machine learning and deep learning. It provides a comprehensive, flexible ecosystem of tools, libraries, and community resources that allows researchers to push the state-of-the-art in ML, and developers to easily build and deploy ML-powered applications.

Key Features:

- Flexibility and Portability: TensorFlow models can run on multiple CPUs or GPUs and even on mobile operating systems.
- Scalability: It can scale the complexity of tasks from a single node to thousands of computations.
- Visualization: Integration with TensorBoard for visualization of network architecture, optimization processes, and more.

```
import tensorflow as tf # Define a simple sequential
model model = tf.keras.Sequential([
tf.keras.layers.Flatten(input_shape=(28, 28)),
tf.keras.layers.Dense(128, activation='relu'),
tf.keras.layers.Dropout(0.2),
tf.keras.layers.Dense(10) ])
model.compile(optimizer='adam', loss=tf.losses.Spars
eCategoricalCrossentropy(from_logits=True),
metrics=['accuracy'])
```

Note: TensorFlow is highly versatile but can be overwhelming for beginners due to its complexity and breadth of functionality.

PyTorch

PyTorch, developed by Facebook's AI Research lab, has gained popularity for its ease of use, efficiency, and dynamic computational graph that provides flexibility in building complex models.

Key Features:

- Dynamic Computation Graphs: Allows for modifications to the graph on-the-fly and is intuitive to work with.

- Pythonic Nature: Integrates seamlessly with the Python data science stack, making it easier to learn and use.

- Strong GPU Acceleration: Efficiently utilizes GPU hardware for faster computation and training.

```
import torch import torch.nn as nn import
torch.nn.functional as F class SimpleNN(nn.Module):
def __init__(self): super(SimpleNN, self).__init__()
self.layer1 = nn.Linear(28 * 28, 128) self.layer2 =
nn.Linear(128, 10) def forward(self, x): x =
F.relu(self.layer1(x)) x = self.layer2(x) return x
model = SimpleNN()
```

Tip: PyTorch is particularly favored for research and prototyping due to its dynamic nature and ease of use.

Keras

Keras, now integrated into TensorFlow as `tf.keras`, is an open-source neural network library written in Python. It is designed to enable fast experimentation with deep neural networks.

Key Features:

- User-Friendly: Keras has a simple, consistent interface optimized for common use cases.

- Modular and Composable: Keras models are made by connecting configurable building blocks together, with few restrictions.

- Easy to Extend: Write custom building blocks, new layers, loss functions, etc. in pure Python.

```
from tensorflow import keras from tensorflow.keras
import layers model = keras.Sequential([
layers.Dense(64, activation='relu',
input_shape=(784,)), layers.Dense(64,
activation='relu'), layers.Dense(10,
activation='softmax') ])
model.compile(optimizer=keras.optimizers.Adam(),
loss=keras.losses.CategoricalCrossentropy(),
metrics=['accuracy'])
```

Best Practice: Use Keras for its simplicity and ease
of use, especially if you are new to AI development or if
your project requires rapid prototyping.

Cloud Platforms for AI

The computational demands of training AI models,
especially those involving deep learning, can be substantial.
Cloud platforms offer powerful, scalable computing resources
that can significantly accelerate the development and
deployment of AI agents.

AWS SageMaker

Amazon Web Services (AWS) provides SageMaker, a fully
managed service that enables data scientists and developers to
quickly and easily build, train, and deploy machine learning
models at any scale.

Advantages:

• Fully Managed: AWS handles much of the heavy lifting of
  model development, such as server management and
  scaling.

- Integrated Jupyter Notebooks: Allows for easy data exploration and analysis.
- Broad Algorithm Support: Comes pre-built with many popular algorithms and supports bringing your own.

Google Cloud AI Platform

Google Cloud AI Platform is a suite of services designed to help AI developers work more efficiently and scale their ML models. It supports both custom model development and the use of pre-trained models.

Advantages:

- Seamless Integration: Works well with other Google services and products.
- State-of-the-Art Tools: Access to cutting-edge Google AI technology, including AutoML and TensorFlow.
- Scalable Infrastructure: Google's infrastructure can scale to meet the needs of any project.

Microsoft Azure Machine Learning

Azure Machine Learning is a cloud-based service for building, training, and deploying machine learning models. It simplifies the machine learning process with an end-to-end platform that streamlines every step of the development cycle.

Advantages:

- Drag-and-Drop ML Model Building: Offers a visual interface in addition to coding environments.
- MLOps: Supports best practices in machine learning operations, making it easier to deploy and manage models.
- Diverse Compute Options: Provides a wide range of computing options, from CPUs to GPUs to FPGAs.

Development Environments

Choosing the right development environment can enhance productivity and make the process of building AI agents more enjoyable. Integrated Development Environments (IDEs) like PyCharm and Visual Studio Code offer powerful features for Python development, including code completion, debugging, and version control integration. Jupyter Notebooks are particularly popular for AI development due to their interactive nature, allowing developers to run code blocks sequentially and visualize results inline.

Jupyter Notebooks:

- Interactive Coding: Facilitates the iterative process of model development and testing.
- Documentation and Sharing: Notebooks can be easily shared with others, containing both the code and its output.
- Integration: Supports integration with data sources and visualization libraries.

The landscape of tools and frameworks for AI agent development is both broad and deep, offering options for developers of all skill levels. From powerful frameworks like TensorFlow and PyTorch to comprehensive cloud platforms and user-friendly development environments, the resources available today make building AI agents more accessible than ever. By selecting the right tools for your project and leveraging the strengths of each, you can streamline the development process and focus on creating innovative AI solutions.

Cloud Platforms for AI

When building AI agents, the computational requirements can quickly escalate beyond the capabilities of local machines, especially for training large models. Cloud platforms provide scalable, flexible, and powerful computing resources, making them an indispensable part of the AI development toolkit.

Amazon Web Services (AWS)

Amazon Web Services offers a broad array of tools for AI developers under the umbrella of AWS Machine Learning. Services like Amazon SageMaker simplify the process of building, training, and deploying machine learning models at scale.

```
import sagemaker from sagemaker.tensorflow import
TensorFlow # Define your TensorFlow model model =
TensorFlow(entry_point='your_model.py',
role='SageMakerRole', instance_count=1,
instance_type='ml.p2.xlarge',
framework_version='2.3.0') # Train your model
model.fit('s3://your-bucket/your-data/')
```

Note: Always consider the cost implications of using cloud resources. AWS, like other cloud platforms, charges based on the resources consumed, so keep an eye on your usage.

Google Cloud Platform (GCP)

Google Cloud Platform is another major player in cloud computing, with AI and machine learning services that rival AWS. Google AI Platform provides a suite of tools that supports the entire machine learning lifecycle from data preparation to model training and deployment.

For instance, you can use Google's AI Platform Training to train your machine learning models at scale using their managed services.

```
gcloud ai-platform jobs submit training job_name \
--job-dir=gs://your-bucket/job-dir \
--runtime-version=2.3 \ --python-version=3.7 \
--scale-tier=BASIC_GPU \ --module-name=trainer.task
\ --package-path=./trainer \ --region=us-central1
```

This command line utility from GCP allows you to easily deploy training jobs to the cloud, leveraging Google's robust infrastructure.

Microsoft Azure

Microsoft Azure provides a comprehensive set of AI services with Azure Machine Learning being the cornerstone for developers looking to build and deploy AI models. Azure's approach focuses on both code-first and low-code solutions, making it accessible to developers and non-developers alike.

Azure Machine Learning Studio is a drag-and-drop tool that can be used to build complex models without writing a single line of code. For more advanced users, the Azure Machine Learning SDK for Python offers full control over the machine learning process.

```
from azureml.core import Workspace, Experiment,
Environment, ScriptRunConfig ws =
Workspace.create(name='myworkspace',
subscription_id='your-subscription-id',
resource_group='your-resource-group') exp =
Experiment(workspace=ws, name='myexperiment') config
= ScriptRunConfig(source_directory='./src',
script='train.py', compute_target='cpu-cluster', env
ironment=Environment.from_conda_specification(name='
myenv', file_path='./environment.yml')) run =
exp.submit(config)
```

This snippet demonstrates how to set up a workspace, create an experiment, and submit a training job using the Azure ML SDK.

Best Practices and Tips

When working with cloud platforms, there are several best practices to keep in mind:

- Cost Management: Always monitor your usage and costs. Utilize budget alerts and cost management tools provided by the cloud platforms to avoid unexpected charges.

- Security: Ensure that your cloud resources are secure. Use identity and access management (IAM) policies to control access to your resources.

- Scalability: Design your AI applications with scalability in mind. Take advantage of cloud services that automatically scale based on demand.

- Data Privacy: Be mindful of data privacy regulations and ensure that your applications comply with relevant laws, especially when handling sensitive information.

Cloud platforms play a crucial role in the AI development process by providing the necessary computational power and scalability. AWS, GCP, and Azure each offer unique services that cater to different needs within the AI development lifecycle. By leveraging these platforms, developers can accelerate the development and deployment of AI agents while managing costs and maintaining scalability.

Development Environments for AI

Selecting an appropriate development environment is crucial for efficient AI agent development. This section explores popular Integrated Development Environments (IDEs) and code editors that can significantly enhance productivity by offering robust tools and features designed for AI programming.

Visual Studio Code (VS Code)

Visual Studio Code, a free, open-source IDE developed by Microsoft, is widely favored among AI developers for its versatility, extensive library of extensions, and support for Python, the most commonly used programming language in AI development.

- Key Features:
- IntelliSense for code completion and error detection
- Integrated Git control
- Debugging support
- Extensible with extensions for Python, Jupyter Notebooks, and more
- Practical Example: To set up a Python development environment in VS Code for AI projects, install the Python extension from the marketplace, configure the interpreter, and you are ready to start writing Python code. For AI-specific tasks, extensions like `Python for VSCode` and `Jupyter` can be invaluable.

```
# Install Python Extension for VS Code 1. Open
Extensions sidebar panel 2. Search for 'Python' 3.
Click Install
```

Note: Always ensure your development environment is configured with the correct version of Python and the necessary libraries for your AI project.

Jupyter Notebooks

Jupyter Notebooks offer an interactive computing environment that is perfect for exploratory data analysis, visualization, and machine learning. They are especially useful for AI agents' development due to their ability to combine executable code, rich text, and visualizations in a single document.

- Key Features:

- Supports over 40 programming languages, including Python

- Shareable notebooks with live code, equations, and visualizations

- Integration with big data tools and frameworks

- Practical Example: Jupyter Notebooks are ideal for prototyping AI models. You can iteratively develop and test your model by running individual code cells, visualize the results immediately, and make adjustments as needed.

```
# Sample code to plot data in Jupyter Notebook
import matplotlib.pyplot as plt plt.plot([1, 2, 3,
4]) plt.ylabel('Sample Numbers') plt.show()
```

PyCharm

PyCharm is another popular IDE among AI developers, offering a rich set of features specifically designed for Python development. It provides intelligent code assistance, debugging, and testing, making it a robust tool for AI projects.

- Key Features:

- Smart code completion

- Code inspections

- Integrated debugger and test runner

- Supports web development with Django

- Practical Example: PyCharm's intelligent code completion and on-the-fly error checking can significantly speed up the development of AI agents by catching errors early and suggesting fixes.

```
# To get started with PyCharm 1. Download and
install PyCharm 2. Configure your Python interpreter
3. Create a new project and start coding
```

Best Practices and Tips

When working with AI development environments, consider the following best practices:

- Choose the Right Tool for the Job: Select an IDE or code editor that best fits your project's needs and your personal coding preferences.

- Customize Your Environment: Take advantage of extensions, plugins, and customization options to tailor your development environment to AI development.

- Stay Organized: AI projects can become complex; use features like project management and version control integrations to keep your codebase manageable.

- Invest in Learning: Spend time learning the shortcuts and advanced features of your chosen development environment to boost your productivity.

By carefully selecting and customizing your development environment, you can streamline the development process for AI agents and focus more on innovation and less on configuration and troubleshooting.

Chapter 5: Building Your First AI Agent

Setting up the Development Environment

Before diving into the construction of your first AI agent, it's crucial to prepare the development environment. This setup will ensure that you have all the necessary tools and libraries to build, test, and debug your AI agent effectively.

Choosing the Right IDE

An Integrated Development Environment (IDE) is essential for efficient coding, testing, and debugging. For Python, which is our language of choice for building AI agents, there are several popular IDEs:

- PyCharm: Offers a rich set of features including code analysis, graphical debugger, integrated unit tester, and supports web development with Django.

- Visual Studio Code (VS Code): A lightweight but powerful source code editor that runs on your desktop. It comes with built-in support for Python and an extensive ecosystem of extensions for other languages (like C++, C#, Java, JavaScript, Node.js, and more).

- Jupyter Notebook: Ideal for prototyping and data analysis, Jupyter Notebooks support live code, equations, visualizations, and narrative text.

For beginners, Visual Studio Code is highly recommended due to its simplicity, extensibility, and support for Python

69

development.

Installing Python

Python is the backbone of many AI projects due to its simplicity and the vast availability of libraries and frameworks. To install Python:

1. Visit the official Python website at https://www.python.org/. 2. Download the latest version of Python for your operating system. 3. Follow the installation instructions, ensuring that you check the box to Add Python to PATH during installation.

Setting Up a Virtual Environment

Using a virtual environment for your project is best practice. It allows you to manage dependencies for your project without affecting global Python packages. To set up a virtual environment:

```
# Install virtualenv if you haven't already pip
install virtualenv # Navigate to your project
directory cd path/to/your-project # Create a virtual
environment virtualenv venv # Activate the virtual
environment # On Windows venv\Scripts\activate # On
Mac/Linux source venv/bin/activate
```

Installing Necessary Libraries

For AI development, certain libraries are indispensable. You can install these using `pip`, Python's package installer. Some of the essential libraries include:

- NumPy: For numerical computations and handling arrays.
- Pandas: For data manipulation and analysis.
- Matplotlib: For creating static, interactive, and animated visualizations.
- Scikit-learn: For machine learning, including various classification, regression, and clustering algorithms.
- TensorFlow or PyTorch: For deep learning applications.

To install these libraries, use the following command:

```
pip install numpy pandas matplotlib scikit-learn tensorflow
```

Or, if you prefer PyTorch over TensorFlow:

```
pip install numpy pandas matplotlib scikit-learn torch
```

Designing the Agent Architecture

Before coding your AI agent, it's essential to understand and design its architecture. An AI agent typically consists of three main components:

- Perception: How the agent receives data from its environment.
- Decision Making: The process of deciding what actions to take based on the perceived data.
- Action: Executing the decided actions to affect the environment.

Understanding the Environment

The environment is anything outside the agent that it interacts with. It could be a physical environment (like a robot navigating a room) or a virtual environment (like an AI playing a video game).

Deciding on the Agent Type

AI agents can be broadly categorized into two types:

- Reactive Agents: These agents don't have any memory of past actions and decide what to do solely based on the current perception of the environment.
- Stateful Agents: These agents remember past actions or states and use this memory to make future decisions.

For beginners, building a reactive agent is a good starting point as it involves simpler logic and fewer components.

Example: A Simple Reactive AI Agent

Imagine we want to build a reactive AI agent that navigates a simple grid environment. The agent perceives whether the adjacent cells are free or blocked and moves to a free cell.

Coding Your First AI Agent

With the development environment set up and the agent architecture designed, it's time to start coding.

Implementing Perception

The agent's perception function can be implemented as follows:

```
def perceive_environment(current_position,
environment): # Assume environment is a 2D list
where 0 represents a free cell and 1 represents a
blocked cell free_cells = [] directions = [(0,1),
(1,0), (0,-1), (-1,0)] # Representing right, down,
left, up for direction in directions: new_position =
(current_position[0] + direction[0],
current_position[1] + direction[1]) if
environment[new_position[0]][new_position[1]] == 0:
free_cells.append(new_position) return free_cells
```

Decision Making

A simple decision-making function that randomly chooses one of the free cells can be coded as:

```
import random def decide_move(free_cells): return
random.choice(free_cells)
```

Taking Action

The action function to move the agent to the new position could look like this:

```
def move_agent(new_position): # This function would
include code to move the agent to the new position
print(f"Moving agent to position {new_position}")
```

Putting It All Together

Finally, you can create a simple loop to simulate the agent's behavior in the environment:

```
current_position = (0, 0) # Starting position
environment = [[0, 1, 0, 0], [0, 0, 1, 0], [1, 0, 0,
1], [0, 0, 0, 0]] # 0 is free, 1 is blocked for _ in
range(10): # Simulate 10 moves free_cells =
perceive_environment(current_position, environment)
if not free_cells: print("No free cells. Agent is
stuck.") break new_position =
decide_move(free_cells) move_agent(new_position)
current_position = new_position
```

This basic example demonstrates the core concepts of building an AI agent: perceiving the environment, making decisions, and taking actions. As you progress, you can add more complexity by incorporating stateful behavior, learning mechanisms, or more sophisticated decision-making algorithms.

Testing and Debugging

Once your AI agent is up and running, testing and debugging are crucial steps to ensure it behaves as expected. Here are some tips for effective testing and debugging:

- Unit Testing: Write unit tests for individual components of your agent (e.g., perception, decision-making) to ensure they function correctly in isolation.

- Logging: Implement logging throughout your agent's code to track its decisions, actions, and perceptions. This information is invaluable for debugging.

- Visualization: If possible, create visual representations of your agent's environment and its movements. Visual feedback can help identify issues that may not be obvious from code or logs alone.

> **Note**: Always start with simple environments and scenarios when testing your AI agent. Once it performs well in simple cases, gradually increase complexity.

By following these steps, you'll have a solid foundation for building and improving your AI agent. Remember, building AI agents is an iterative process. Don't be discouraged by initial failures; each iteration is a learning opportunity that brings you closer to a fully functional AI agent.

Designing the Agent Architecture

Designing the architecture of your AI agent is a critical step in the development process. This procedure involves deciding how your agent will perceive its environment, make decisions, and act upon those decisions. An effective architecture is modular, scalable, and adaptable to changes.

Understanding Agent Components

At its core, an AI agent consists of three main components: Perception, Decision Making, and Action. Let's break down each component:

- Perception: This is how the agent receives information about its environment. It could be through sensors in a physical robot or data input in a software program.

- Decision Making: Once the agent has perceived its environment, it needs to decide what to do. This involves algorithms that process the input and make decisions based on it.

- Action: After deciding, the agent must act. This could be moving a robot, displaying information, or executing a program command.

Choosing the Right Model

For our simple AI agent, we will use a model based on state machines. A state machine is a concept used in computer science to describe a system that can be in one of a few different states. It changes states based on inputs (in our case, perceptions) and has defined actions for each state.

```
class AIAgent: def __init__(self): self.state =
'initial' def perceive_environment(self, input): #
Update state based on input pass def
decide_action(self): # Decide action based on state
pass def act(self): # Perform action pass
```

This structure allows our agent to be simple yet flexible. We can define different states and corresponding actions without making the system overly complex.

Implementing Perception

Perception can be implemented in numerous ways, depending on your agent's environment. For a software agent that processes text data, perception might involve reading and interpreting text.

```
def perceive_environment(self, text): if "hello" in
text.lower(): self.state = 'greeted' else:
self.state = 'default'
```

This method updates the agent's state based on whether the text includes a greeting.

Coding Your First AI Agent

With the architecture designed, it's time to start coding your AI agent. We'll build on the structure outlined in the previous sections.

Decision Making and Action

Let's expand our `AIAgent` class to include decision making and actions. For simplicity, our agent will greet if greeted or otherwise stay idle.

```
def decide_action(self): if self.state == 'greeted':
return 'greet_back' return 'idle' def act(self,
action): if action == 'greet_back': print("Hello
there!") elif action == 'idle': pass # Do nothing
```

Putting It All Together

Now, we integrate all the components. Our agent will perceive input, decide on an action, and act accordingly.

```
def run(self, input):
self.perceive_environment(input) action =
self.decide_action() self.act(action) agent =
AIAgent() agent.run("hello")
```

This simple agent perceives a greeting and decides to greet back. Extend this by adding more states and actions to make your agent more complex and interesting.

Testing and Debugging

After coding your agent, it's essential to test and debug it to ensure it behaves as expected.

Unit Testing

Unit testing involves testing individual parts of your agent's code. You can use Python's `unittest` framework to automate this. Create tests for each component (perception, decision making, action) to ensure they work correctly in isolation.

```
import unittest class
TestAIAgent(unittest.TestCase): def
test_perceive_environment(self): agent = AIAgent()
agent.perceive_environment("hello")
self.assertEqual(agent.state, 'greeted') # Add more
tests for decision making and action if __name__ ==
'__main__': unittest.main()
```

Debugging

When your agent does not behave as expected, debugging is necessary. Use logging to track your agent's state changes and decisions. Python's `logging` module can be very helpful.

```
import logging
logging.basicConfig(level=logging.DEBUG) def
perceive_environment(self, text):
logging.debug(f"Received input: {text}") #
Perception logic logging.debug(f"State changed to:
{self.state}")
```

This will help you understand how your agent is processing inputs and changing states.

Best Practices and Tips

- Start Simple: Begin with a basic agent and incrementally add complexity.
- Modular Design: Keep your code organized and modular. This makes it easier to debug and extend.
- Logging: Make extensive use of logging to help with debugging.
- Unit Testing: Regularly test your code to catch errors early.

Challenges

1. Extend the Agent: Add more states and actions to your agent. For example, make it respond differently to questions and statements. 2. Implement a GUI: Create a simple graphical user interface (GUI) for your agent, allowing users to interact with it visually.

Building your first AI agent is an exciting journey. With the basics covered, you can now explore more complex agent architectures and applications. Remember, experimentation and practice are key to mastering AI development.

Coding Your First AI Agent

With a solid understanding of the architecture behind an AI agent, the next step is to dive into coding. For this purpose, Python, given its wide range of libraries and straightforward syntax, is an ideal choice. In this section, we'll walk through the process of coding a basic AI agent capable of navigating a simple environment.

Setting Up Your Development Environment

Before coding, ensure your development environment is properly set up. Python 3.x should be installed on your system, along with pip, Python's package installer. This will allow you to easily add libraries necessary for AI development, such as NumPy for numerical operations and Matplotlib for visualization.

```
# Check Python version python --version # Install
NumPy and Matplotlib pip install numpy matplotlib
```

Implementing Perception

The first component to code is perception. Our AI agent will perceive its environment through a simplified grid system. Each cell in the grid can either be empty or contain an obstacle. The agent needs to understand its surroundings to make informed decisions.

```
import numpy as np # Environment setup grid_size =
(5, 5) environment = np.zeros(grid_size) # Adding an
obstacle environment[2][2] = 1 # Marking cell at row
2, column 2 as an obstacle def
perceive_environment(agent_position): # Returns the
status of adjacent cells x, y = agent_position
surroundings = {'left': environment[x, max(y-1, 0)],
'right': environment[x, min(y+1, grid_size[1]-1)],
'up': environment[max(x-1, 0), y], 'down':
environment[min(x+1, grid_size[0]-1), y]} return
```

```
surroundings
```

Coding Decision Making

The decision-making process involves evaluating the agent's perceptions and deciding the next move. For simplicity, our agent will move towards an empty cell while avoiding obstacles.

```
def decide_move(surroundings): # Simple
decision-making algorithm to move towards an empty
cell for direction, status in surroundings.items():
if status == 0: # If cell is empty return direction
return 'stay' # Stay in place if all adjacent cells
are blocked
```

Implementing Action

The action component translates the agent's decision into movement within the environment. This involves updating the agent's position based on the decision made.

```
def move_agent(agent_position, decision): x, y =
agent_position if decision == 'left' and y > 0: y -=
1 elif decision == 'right' and y < grid_size[1] - 1:
y += 1 elif decision == 'up' and x > 0: x -= 1 elif
decision == 'down' and x < grid_size[0] - 1: x += 1
return x, y
```

Bringing It All Together

With the perception, decision-making, and action components in place, we can now define a simple loop to simulate the AI agent's behavior in the environment.

```
# Initial agent position agent_position = (0, 0) for
_ in range(10): # Simulate 10 steps surroundings =
perceive_environment(agent_position) decision =
decide_move(surroundings) agent_position =
move_agent(agent_position, decision) print(f"Moved
to {agent_position}")
```

Note: This example is highly simplified and serves as a conceptual foundation. Real-world applications would require more sophisticated perception, decision-making algorithms, and action mechanisms.

Best Practices and Tips

- Start Simple: Begin with a straightforward implementation and gradually add complexity.
- Modular Code: Keep your code organized into functions or classes for clarity and maintainability.
- Test and Debug: Regularly test your code to catch errors early and understand the agent's behavior.

Common Challenges and Troubleshooting

When coding your AI agent, you may encounter several challenges:

- Infinite Loops: Ensure your decision-making algorithm always has a condition to break out of loops.
- Unintended Behaviors: Test your agent in various scenarios to catch and correct unexpected behaviors.

- Performance Issues: Optimize your code by profiling and identifying bottlenecks.

By following these steps and guidelines, you'll have laid the foundation for your first AI agent, ready for further development and complexity.

Testing and Debugging

After coding your first AI agent, the next crucial steps involve testing and debugging to ensure its functionality and efficiency. Testing is an integral part of developing AI agents as it helps in identifying any discrepancies, errors, or unwanted behaviors that deviate from the expected outcomes. Debugging, on the other hand, involves pinpointing the root cause of these issues and fixing them. This section covers essential strategies and tips for effectively testing and debugging your AI agent.

Unit Testing

Unit testing involves testing individual components or functions of your AI agent to ensure they work as intended. For our Python-based AI agent, we can use the `unittest` framework, which is built into Python, to create and run unit tests.

Example of Unit Test

Let's say you have a function `navigate()` in your AI agent, which calculates the next move based on the current position and target. You can write a unit test to verify that `navigate()` correctly calculates the next move.

```
import unittest from your_ai_agent import navigate
class TestNavigation(unittest.TestCase): def
```

```
test_navigate(self): current_position = (0, 0)
target_position = (1, 1) expected_next_move = (0, 1)
# Assuming the agent moves vertically first
self.assertEqual(navigate(current_position,
target_position), expected_next_move) if __name__ ==
'__main__': unittest.main()
```

Note: Replace `your_ai_agent` and the expected
behavior based on your specific implementation details.

Integration Testing

While unit testing focuses on individual components,
integration testing assesses how different parts of your AI agent
work together. This is crucial for identifying issues that may not
surface during unit testing, especially in the interactions
between your agent's components.

For integration testing, you can create tests that simulate
more complex scenarios or environments where multiple
functions interact. For instance, you could simulate a small
maze for your agent to navigate through, checking if it can reach
the target without errors.

Debugging Tips

Debugging is an art that requires patience and practice.
Here are some strategies to make debugging your AI agent
more effective:

- Use Print Statements: Strategically placed print statements
  can help trace the flow of execution and the state of
  variables at different points.

- Leverage Debugging Tools: Most IDEs come with built-in debugging tools that allow you to step through your code, inspect variables, and evaluate expressions at runtime.

- Simplify and Isolate: When facing a complex bug, try to simplify the scenario or isolate the component causing the issue. This can often make it easier to identify the root cause.

Handling Common Challenges

When testing and debugging AI agents, you may encounter specific challenges such as non-deterministic behaviors or performance issues. To address these:

- For Non-deterministic Behaviors: Ensure your tests account for different outcomes if your agent has elements of randomness or probabilistic decision-making.

- For Performance Issues: Profile your agent to identify bottlenecks. Optimization may involve algorithmic improvements, code refactoring, or leveraging more efficient data structures.

Practical Exercise

1. Write Unit Tests: Create at least three unit tests for different components of your AI agent. 2. Perform Integration Testing: Simulate a complex scenario that requires multiple components of your agent to work together. Analyze the results for any discrepancies. 3. Debugging Challenge: Introduce a deliberate bug in one of your agent's components. Practice using print statements and a debugger to locate and fix the issue.

By thoroughly testing and debugging your AI agent, you can significantly improve its reliability and performance, making it better equipped to handle real-world tasks. This iterative process of development, testing, and refinement is fundamental to building robust and efficient AI systems.

Chapter 6: Natural Language Processing for Agents

Introduction to Natural Language Processing (NLP)

Natural Language Processing, or NLP, is a critical field in artificial intelligence that focuses on the interaction between computers and humans through natural language. The goal of NLP is to enable computers to understand, interpret, and generate human languages in a way that is both valuable and meaningful. This capability is paramount for building AI agents that can communicate effectively with users, understand their requests, and provide helpful responses.

Why is NLP Important for AI Agents?

NLP allows AI agents to break down and comprehend the vast nuances of human language, including slang, idioms, and regional dialects. This comprehension is crucial for tasks such as answering questions, making recommendations, or even detecting the sentiment behind a user's message. By equipping AI agents with NLP capabilities, developers can create more interactive, responsive, and engaging experiences for users.

Text Processing Basics

Before diving into complex NLP tasks, it's essential to understand the basics of text processing. This foundation is critical for preparing and manipulating text data for further analysis and interpretation by AI agents.

Tokenization

Tokenization is the process of breaking down text into smaller units, such as words or sentences. This step is fundamental in NLP because it turns unstructured text into a format that's easier for algorithms to process.

```
# Example of word tokenization from nltk.tokenize
import word_tokenize text = "Hello, AI enthusiasts!
Welcome to NLP." words = word_tokenize(text)
print(words)
```

Stop Words Removal

Stop words are common words like "is", "and", "the", etc., that are often removed from the text because they contribute little to the meaning of the data for analysis.

```
from nltk.corpus import stopwords stop_words =
set(stopwords.words('english')) filtered_words =
[word for word in words if not word in stop_words]
print(filtered_words)
```

Stemming and Lemmatization

Both stemming and lemmatization are techniques used to reduce words to their base or root form. Stemming might chop off the ends of words hoping to achieve this goal often leading to incorrect meanings and spelling. Lemmatization, on the other hand, considers the context and converts the word to its meaningful base form.

```
from nltk.stem import WordNetLemmatizer lemmatizer =
WordNetLemmatizer() lemmatized_words =
[lemmatizer.lemmatize(word) for word in
filtered_words] print(lemmatized_words)
```

> **Note:** It's crucial to preprocess your text data through these steps before feeding it into more complex NLP models or tasks. This preprocessing improves the performance and accuracy of your AI agents.

Language Models and Transformers

With the basics of text processing covered, let's delve into more advanced NLP concepts, such as language models and transformers. These technologies have revolutionized the field of NLP by enabling unprecedented accuracy and flexibility in language understanding and generation.

Understanding Language Models

A language model is a statistical model that determines the probability of a sequence of words appearing in a given language. Traditional language models were often based on n-grams or sequences of 'n' words and their likelihood of occurrence. However, these models were limited by their inability to capture long-term dependencies or the context beyond their fixed window size.

The Rise of Transformers

Transformers have emerged as a groundbreaking innovation in NLP, primarily introduced by the paper "Attention is All You Need" in 2017. Unlike previous models, transformers use a mechanism called "attention" to weigh the influence of different words in the sentence, regardless of their position. This approach allows transformers to capture more nuanced interpretations of text by understanding the context and relationships between words more effectively.

```
from transformers import pipeline # Using a
pre-trained transformer model for sentiment analysis
classifier = pipeline('sentiment-analysis') result =
classifier("I love natural language processing.")
print(result)
```

Sentiment Analysis

Sentiment analysis is a common NLP task that involves determining the emotional tone behind a body of text. This is incredibly useful for AI agents tasked with monitoring social media, customer reviews, or any platform where understanding human emotion is beneficial.

Implementing Sentiment Analysis

Using the transformers library, one can easily implement sentiment analysis with pre-trained models. These models have been trained on vast datasets and can accurately gauge the sentiment of a sentence or paragraph.

```
# Example of sentiment analysis sentiment =
classifier("Unfortunately, the product didn't meet
```

```
my expectations.") print(sentiment)
```

> **Warning:** While pre-trained models offer convenience and robustness, it's important to evaluate their performance on your specific dataset or domain, as biases in training data can lead to inaccurate predictions.

Conversation Handling

For AI agents to interact effectively with users, they must be capable of managing conversations. This includes understanding the user's intent, maintaining the context of the conversation, and generating appropriate responses.

Building a Simple Chatbot

One of the simplest forms of conversation handling is a rule-based chatbot. These bots follow predefined pathways or rules to respond to user inputs. However, for more advanced and natural interactions, AI agents rely on machine learning and deep learning models to parse and respond to user queries.

```python
# Rule-based chatbot example def
respond_to_greeting(input_text): greetings = ["hi",
"hello", "hey"] responses = ["Hello there!", "Hi,
how can I help you?", "Hey!"] if input_text.lower()
in greetings: return random.choice(responses) else:
return "I'm not sure how to respond to that."
print(respond_to_greeting("hi"))
```

Utilizing Context in Conversations

To maintain a coherent conversation, AI agents must remember the context of the interaction. Advanced models and techniques, such as memory networks or context-aware transformers, are employed to achieve this. These models can keep track of previous exchanges and use this information to inform their responses, making conversations with AI agents more fluid and natural.

Best Practices and Tips

- Preprocess Text Data: Always clean and preprocess your text data before feeding it into NLP models. This step can significantly enhance your model's performance.

- Choose the Right Model: Evaluate different models to find the one best suited for your task. Transformers are powerful for a wide range of NLP tasks but consider your specific needs and constraints.

- Beware of Biases: AI models can inherit biases from their training data. Be mindful of this when implementing NLP solutions, especially for sensitive applications.

- Iterate and Improve: NLP is a rapidly evolving field. Continuously test, evaluate, and improve your AI agents based on user feedback and new research findings.

In this section, we've explored the fundamentals of Natural Language Processing, covering everything from text processing basics to advanced concepts like transformers and sentiment analysis. These tools and techniques are essential for building AI agents capable of understanding and interacting with human language. As we've seen, NLP enables a wide range of applications, from simple chatbots to sophisticated AI systems capable of analyzing sentiment or managing complex conversations. By applying the best practices and tips discussed, you can enhance the capabilities of your AI agents and create more engaging, effective, and human-like interactions.

Text Processing Basics

Before diving into the more advanced topics of NLP, it's essential to understand the basics of text processing. Text processing involves several steps that prepare raw text data for analysis and interpretation by AI agents. These steps include tokenization, normalization, stemming, and lemmatization.

Tokenization

Tokenization is the process of breaking down a text into smaller units called tokens. Tokens can be words, phrases, or symbols depending on the granularity required for the task. For example, the sentence "AI agents are intelligent" can be tokenized into words: ["AI", "agents", "are", "intelligent"].

```
from nltk.tokenize import word_tokenize text = "AI
agents are intelligent" tokens = word_tokenize(text)
print(tokens)
```

Normalization

Normalization involves converting text into a uniform format. This can include converting all characters to lowercase to ensure that words like "Hello," "hello," and "HELLO" are treated the same.

```
tokens = ["AI", "agents", "are", "Intelligent"]
normalized_tokens = [token.lower() for token in
tokens] print(normalized_tokens)
```

Stemming and Lemmatization

Stemming and lemmatization are techniques used to reduce words to their root form. While stemming cuts off prefixes and suffixes (often leading to incorrect spelling), lemmatization considers the context and converts the word to its meaningful base form.

```
from nltk.stem import PorterStemmer from nltk.stem
import WordNetLemmatizer stemmer = PorterStemmer()
lemmatizer = WordNetLemmatizer() word = "running"
print("Stemmed:", stemmer.stem(word))
print("Lemmatized:", lemmatizer.lemmatize(word,
pos='v'))
```

Note: Lemmatization usually provides better results for further processing since it preserves the semantic meaning of the base word.

Language Models and Transformers

With a solid foundation in text processing, we can move on to understanding language models and transformers, which are at the heart of modern NLP.

Language Models

A language model predicts the likelihood of a sequence of words. This capability is fundamental in many NLP applications, such as autocomplete features, spell checkers, and AI conversation agents. Traditional language models were based on statistical methods, but recent advances have shifted towards neural network-based models for their superior performance.

Transformers

Transformers are a type of neural network architecture that has revolutionized NLP. Unlike their predecessors, transformers can process entire sequences of text simultaneously, making them significantly faster and more efficient for tasks like translation, summarization, and question-answering.

```
from transformers import pipeline # Using a
pre-trained transformer model for sentiment analysis
sentiment_pipeline = pipeline("sentiment-analysis")
result = sentiment_pipeline("I love learning about
AI!") print(result)
```

Sentiment Analysis

Sentiment analysis is the process of determining the sentiment expressed in a piece of text. It's a powerful tool for AI agents, enabling them to understand user feedback, social media comments, and more.

Implementing Sentiment Analysis

Most sentiment analysis models classify text into categories like positive, negative, and neutral. Using pre-trained models from libraries such as Hugging Face's Transformers makes it easy to add sentiment analysis capabilities to your AI agent.

```
result = sentiment_pipeline("This chapter on NLP is
incredibly informative and well-written.")
print(result)
```

Real-World Use Cases

Sentiment analysis has a wide range of applications, from monitoring brand sentiment on social media to analyzing customer reviews. AI agents equipped with sentiment analysis can provide valuable insights into user opinions and trends.

Conversation Handling

The ultimate goal of many NLP systems is to enable AI agents to handle conversations with humans in a natural and seamless manner. This involves understanding context, managing dialogue states, and generating appropriate responses.

Dialogue Management

Dialogue management is crucial for maintaining a coherent conversation. It involves tracking the conversation's state and deciding the next best response based on the user's input and the conversation history.

Generating Responses

Modern AI agents often use techniques like sequence-to-sequence models or transformers to generate human-like responses. These models can be fine-tuned on specific domains or tasks to improve their relevance and accuracy.

```
from transformers import GPT2LMHeadModel,
GPT2Tokenizer tokenizer =
GPT2Tokenizer.from_pretrained("gpt2") model =
GPT2LMHeadModel.from_pretrained("gpt2") input_text =
"What is the weather like today?" input_ids =
tokenizer.encode(input_text, return_tensors='pt')
output = model.generate(input_ids, max_length=50)
print(tokenizer.decode(output[0],
skip_special_tokens=True))
```

Best Practices and Tips

When implementing NLP capabilities in AI agents, consider the following best practices:

- Always pre-process text data to improve the quality of the input for your models.

- Leverage pre-trained models and fine-tune them on your data to save time and resources.

- Pay attention to the ethical implications of NLP, such as bias in language models.

- Continuously evaluate and update your models to adapt to new languages and dialects.

Understanding and implementing NLP capabilities are crucial for developing AI agents that can interact effectively with humans. By mastering text processing, leveraging modern language models like transformers, and applying techniques such as sentiment analysis and conversation handling, developers can create sophisticated and responsive AI agents.

Language Models and Transformers

After establishing a solid foundation in text processing, the next significant step in NLP for AI agents involves understanding and implementing language models, with a particular focus on transformers. Language models are algorithms that use statistical methods to predict the next word in a sentence based on the words that precede it. Transformers, introduced in the paper "Attention Is All You Need" in 2017, have revolutionized the way we approach language models by enabling more complex and nuanced understanding and generation of text.

Understanding Language Models

A language model is trained on a large corpus of text data and learns the probability distribution of word sequences. This allows it to predict the likelihood of a sequence of words appearing together, which is fundamental in tasks such as text completion, translation, and summarization.

```
# Pseudo-code for a simple language model prediction
predicted_word =
language_model.predict_next_word("The quick brown
fox jumps over the") print(predicted_word) # Likely
outputs: "lazy", "fence", etc.
```

The Rise of Transformers

Transformers are a type of deep learning model that rely on self-attention mechanisms to weigh the relevance of different parts of the input data differently. This is particularly useful in understanding the context and relationships between words in a sentence, outperforming previous models that processed text linearly.

```
# Pseudo-code to illustrate transformer usage
transformer_model = TransformerModel.load_pretrained
('bert-base-uncased') sentence_embedding =
transformer_model.encode("The quick brown fox jumps
over the lazy dog") print(sentence_embedding) #
Outputs a vector representation of the sentence
```

Note: The real power of transformers lies in their ability to handle long-range dependencies in text, making them ideal for complex NLP tasks.

Practical Implementation

To implement a transformer model in an AI agent, one can leverage pre-trained models available through libraries such as Hugging Face's Transformers. These models can be fine-tuned on domain-specific data to enhance their performance on tasks like question answering or sentiment analysis.

```
from transformers import pipeline # Load a
pre-trained transformer model for sentiment analysis
sentiment_pipeline = pipeline('sentiment-analysis')
result = sentiment_pipeline("I love natural language
processing!") print(result) # Outputs: [{'label':
'POSITIVE', 'score': 0.99987}]
```

Real-World Use Cases

- Chatbots and Virtual Assistants: By understanding and generating human-like responses, AI agents can provide more effective and natural customer service.

- Content Generation: From news articles to creative stories, AI agents can produce coherent and contextually relevant text.

- Language Translation: Transformers have significantly improved the quality and speed of machine translation services.

Best Practices and Tips

- Dataset Quality: The performance of a language model is highly dependent on the quality and diversity of the training data. Ensure your dataset is large and representative of the task at hand.

- Compute Resources: Training transformers from scratch requires significant computational resources. Whenever possible, start with pre-trained models and perform fine-tuning to meet your specific needs.

- Ethical Considerations: Be mindful of bias in your training data and the potential for misuse of generative text models. Implementing safeguards and monitoring outputs is crucial.

Common Challenges and Solutions

Implementing transformers in AI agents is not without its challenges. Here are some common issues and how to address them:

- Model Interpretability: Transformers are complex and their decision-making process can be opaque. Techniques such as attention visualization can help in understanding how models arrive at their predictions.

- Resource Intensiveness: Fine-tuning and deploying transformers can be resource-heavy. Utilizing cloud-based solutions and optimizing models for inference can mitigate these issues.

- Data Privacy: When working with sensitive information, ensure that data is handled securely and in compliance with relevant regulations. Techniques like federated learning can be beneficial in privacy-preserving scenarios.

Actionable Steps

1. Explore pre-trained models: Familiarize yourself with the range of pre-trained NLP models available and select one that aligns with your project's needs. 2. Fine-tune on specific data: Customize the model by fine-tuning it on a dataset that is closely aligned with the domain of application. 3. Evaluate and iterate: Continuously evaluate the model's performance and iterate based on feedback and results to ensure its effectiveness in real-world applications.

By mastering the concepts of language models and transformers, developers can significantly enhance the capabilities of their AI agents, enabling them to understand and generate human-like text in a wide array of applications.

Sentiment Analysis

After gaining a grasp of language models and transformers, the next crucial step in enhancing the NLP capabilities of AI agents is understanding and implementing sentiment analysis. Sentiment analysis, also known as opinion mining, is a technique used to determine the attitude or emotion of the writer or speaker towards a particular topic. It is widely used in customer service to analyze feedback, in social media monitoring, and in market research.

Understanding Sentiment Analysis

Sentiment analysis involves classifying a piece of text as positive, negative, or neutral. Advanced systems can also identify specific emotions such as happiness, anger, or disappointment. This process can be approached in several ways, including rule-based systems that use predefined lexicons of sentimental words, machine learning models that learn from labeled datasets, and hybrid approaches.

Practical Implementation

A simple sentiment analysis can be performed using Python and libraries such as NLTK or more advanced frameworks like TensorFlow or PyTorch for deep learning approaches. Here's a basic example using the TextBlob library, which provides a simple API for common NLP tasks:

```
from textblob import TextBlob text = "I love this
phone. The battery life is amazing!" blob =
TextBlob(text) print(blob.sentiment)
```

This code snippet will output a sentiment polarity and subjectivity score, indicating the sentiment of the text. Polarity ranges from -1 (very negative) to 1 (very positive), and subjectivity ranges from 0 (very objective) to 1 (very subjective).

> **Note:** While libraries like TextBlob are great for simple tasks, more complex sentiment analysis might require training custom models on large datasets using deep learning techniques.

Best Practices and Challenges

Implementing sentiment analysis in AI agents involves several best practices and challenges:

- Data Quality: The accuracy of sentiment analysis is heavily dependent on the quality and quantity of the training data. Ensuring that your data is well-labeled and representative of the use case is crucial.

- Context Understanding: Sentiment can be highly context-dependent. Words that are positive in one context might be negative in another. Advanced models capable of understanding context can significantly improve accuracy.

- Sarcasm and Irony: Detecting sarcasm and irony remains a significant challenge for sentiment analysis models, as they can invert the sentiment of the text. Training models on datasets that include such examples can help.

- Language Support: While sentiment analysis tools and models are widely available for English, support for other languages may be limited. Multilingual models or custom solutions may be necessary for non-English text.

Conversation Handling

With the ability to process text and understand sentiment, AI agents can engage in more meaningful conversations with users. Conversation handling involves managing dialogue flow, maintaining context, and generating appropriate responses.

Dialogue Management

Dialogue management is crucial for maintaining a coherent conversation. It involves interpreting the user's intent, deciding on the next action, and keeping track of the conversation state. State management can be particularly challenging, as it requires the AI to remember past interactions and use them to inform future responses.

Implementing Conversation Handling

Many tools and frameworks can assist in building conversational AI, including Dialogflow, Microsoft Bot Framework, and Rasa. These tools provide functionalities like intent recognition, entity extraction, and dialogue management, simplifying the process of creating sophisticated conversational agents.

For example, using Rasa, you can define intents and entities in a domain file and write stories that describe possible conversation paths. Rasa's machine learning models use these stories to learn how to manage dialogue flow.

Challenges in Conversation Handling

- Maintaining Context: Keeping track of the conversation's context over multiple turns can be complex, especially in open-ended dialogues.
- Understanding Nuance: Interpreting the nuances of human language, including humor, sarcasm, and indirect requests, requires advanced NLP techniques.
- User Satisfaction: Ensuring that conversations are not only technically successful but also satisfying and engaging for users is an ongoing challenge.

Implementing effective sentiment analysis and conversation handling capabilities in AI agents requires a deep understanding of both the technical challenges and the nuances of human communication. By addressing these aspects, developers can create AI agents that offer valuable, engaging interactions for users.

Chapter 7: Computer Vision for AI Agents

Understanding Computer Vision

Computer Vision is a field of Artificial Intelligence (AI) that enables machines to interpret and understand the visual world. Using digital images from cameras and videos, computer vision algorithms can accurately identify and classify objects, and then react to what they "see."

The Basics of Image Processing

Before diving into complex computer vision tasks, it's crucial to understand the fundamentals of image processing. At its core, image processing involves modifying images to enhance their features or extract useful information. This can include tasks such as resizing, filtering, and color adjustment. Image processing serves as the foundation for more advanced computer vision techniques.

Image Representation

Digital images are represented as a grid of pixels, each with a specific intensity value (for grayscale images) or color values (for color images). These values are typically stored in a matrix, which computer vision algorithms can manipulate.

```
# Example of accessing pixel values using Python and
OpenCV import cv2 image =
cv2.imread('path/to/your/image.jpg') # Accessing the
pixel value at row 10, column 15 pixel_value =
```

```
image[10, 15] print(pixel_value)
```

Basic Image Manipulations

Common image manipulations include resizing, cropping, and rotating. These operations help prepare images for further analysis or improve the performance of computer vision models.

```
# Example of resizing an image using Python and
OpenCV import cv2 image =
cv2.imread('path/to/your/image.jpg') resized_image =
cv2.resize(image, (100, 100)) # Resize to 100x100
pixels cv2.imshow("Resized Image", resized_image)
cv2.waitKey(0)
```

Note: It's important to consider aspect ratio and interpolation methods when resizing images to avoid distortion.

Object Detection

Object detection is a crucial aspect of computer vision, allowing AI agents to identify and locate objects within an image or video frame. This capability is fundamental to numerous applications, including autonomous vehicles, security surveillance, and inventory management.

Techniques for Object Detection

There are several approaches to object detection, ranging from traditional methods like Haar cascades to modern deep learning-based techniques such as Convolutional Neural Networks (CNNs) and frameworks like YOLO (You Only Look Once) and SSD (Single Shot MultiBox Detector).

```
# Example of using a pre-trained model in OpenCV for
object detection import cv2 # Load a pre-trained
model and its weights (e.g., YOLO) net =
cv2.dnn.readNet('path/to/yolov3.weights',
'path/to/yolov3.cfg') # Load image image =
cv2.imread('path/to/your/image.jpg') # Convert image
to blob blob = cv2.dnn.blobFromImage(image,
scalefactor=0.00392, size=(416, 416), mean=(0, 0,
0), swapRB=True, crop=False) net.setInput(blob) #
Perform detection outputs =
net.forward(net.getUnconnectedOutLayersNames())
```

Facial Recognition

Facial recognition is a specialized application of computer vision that involves identifying or verifying a person's identity based on their facial features. This technology has significant implications for security systems, authentication processes, and personalized customer experiences.

Implementing Facial Recognition

Facial recognition systems typically involve two main stages: face detection, to locate faces in an image, and face identification, to match detected faces against a database of known individuals.

```
# Example of facial recognition using
face_recognition library in Python import
face_recognition # Load an image with an unknown
face unknown_image = face_recognition.load_image_fil
e("path/to/unknown.jpg") # Find all face encodings
in the unknown image unknown_face_encodings =
face_recognition.face_encodings(unknown_image)
```

Scene Understanding

Beyond identifying individual objects or faces, scene understanding involves interpreting the context of a visual scene, including the relationships between objects and the overall activity. This advanced aspect of computer vision enables AI agents to make sense of complex environments, facilitating applications in robotics, augmented reality, and more.

Techniques for Scene Understanding

Scene understanding can leverage a combination of object detection, semantic segmentation (labeling parts of images with categories), and scene classification (identifying the overall scene type) to provide a comprehensive interpretation of a visual scene.

```
# Example of semantic segmentation using OpenCV and
a pre-trained deep learning model import cv2 # Load
a pre-trained model for semantic segmentation net =
cv2.dnn.readNet('path/to/model.weights',
'path/to/model.cfg') # Load image image =
cv2.imread('path/to/your/image.jpg') # Prepare the
image for the model blob =
cv2.dnn.blobFromImage(image, scalefactor=1.0,
size=(320, 320), mean=(104.00698793, 116.66876762,
122.67891434), swapRB=True, crop=False)
net.setInput(blob) # Perform semantic segmentation
output = net.forward()
```

Best Practices and Tips

When implementing computer vision in AI agents, consider the following best practices:

- Always preprocess images to improve model accuracy. This can include normalization, resizing, and augmentation.

- Choose the right algorithm or model based on the specific requirements of your application. No single approach is best for all scenarios.

- Pay attention to the computational requirements of computer vision models, especially for applications requiring real-time processing.

- Ensure privacy and ethical considerations are addressed, particularly when dealing with facial recognition or other personal data.

Common Challenges and Solutions

Dealing with Varied Lighting Conditions

Varied lighting can significantly impact the performance of computer vision models. Using techniques such as histogram equalization or adaptive thresholding can help mitigate these issues by improving the contrast and visibility of features in images.

Handling Occlusions

Objects or faces partially blocked by other objects pose a challenge for detection and recognition. Training models on a diverse dataset that includes examples of occlusions can improve their robustness.

Real-Time Processing Requirements

Achieving real-time performance is crucial for applications like autonomous driving. Optimizing models for speed, using efficient algorithms, and leveraging hardware accelerations (e.g., GPUs) are key strategies to meet these demands.

By understanding these foundational concepts and techniques in computer vision, readers can start to explore the vast potential of integrating visual perception capabilities into AI agents. The next part of this chapter will delve deeper into advanced topics and explore cutting-edge research in the field.

Object Detection

Object detection is a critical component in the field of computer vision, allowing AI agents to identify and locate objects within an image or video. This capability is fundamental for tasks such as autonomous driving, where the AI must recognize vehicles, pedestrians, and traffic signs, and in retail, for inventory management through product identification.

How Object Detection Works

Object detection algorithms typically involve two main steps: identifying objects within an image and then classifying those objects. These algorithms use features like edges, shapes, and textures to distinguish objects. One of the widely used algorithms for object detection is Convolutional Neural Networks (CNNs).

```
import cv2 import numpy as np # Load a pre-trained
model net = cv2.dnn.readNet('model_path',
'config_path') # Load an image image =
cv2.imread('image_path') blob =
cv2.dnn.blobFromImage(image, scalefactor=1.0,
size=(300, 300), mean=(104, 117, 123)) # Input the
```

```
blob into the network net.setInput(blob) # Perform
object detection detections = net.forward() for i in
range(detections.shape[2]): confidence =
detections[0, 0, i, 2] if confidence > 0.5: #
Confidence threshold box = detections[0, 0, i, 3:7]
* np.array([w, h, w, h]) (startX, startY, endX,
endY) = box.astype("int") # Draw a rectangle around
the detected object cv2.rectangle(image, (startX,
startY), (endX, endY), (255, 0, 0), 2)
```

Note: Replace 'model_path', 'config_path', and 'image_path' with the actual paths to your model configuration, model weights, and input image respectively.

Best Practices and Tips

- Data augmentation: To improve the robustness of your object detection model, use data augmentation techniques such as flipping, rotation, and scaling on your training dataset.

- Choose the right model: Depending on your application's requirements, choose between speed and accuracy. Models like YOLO (You Only Look Once) are faster but might be less accurate compared to others like Faster R-CNN.

Facial Recognition

Facial recognition technology enables AI agents to identify or verify a person from a digital image or video frame. This technology is widely used in security systems, mobile phone authentication, and photo tagging applications.

Understanding Facial Recognition Process

Facial recognition algorithms typically extract features from an individual's face, such as the distance between the eyes, the shape of the nose, and the contour of the lips and cheeks. These features are then compared to a database of known faces to find a match.

```
import face_recognition # Load the known images
image_of_person_1 =
face_recognition.load_image_file("person_1.jpg")
image_of_person_2 =
face_recognition.load_image_file("person_2.jpg") #
Get the face encoding of each person
person_1_face_encoding = face_recognition.face_encod
ings(image_of_person_1)[0] person_2_face_encoding =
face_recognition.face_encodings(image_of_person_2)[0
] known_face_encodings = [ person_1_face_encoding,
person_2_face_encoding ] # Load a new image to check
unknown_image =
face_recognition.load_image_file("unknown.jpg")
unknown_face_encoding =
face_recognition.face_encodings(unknown_image)[0] #
Compare the faces results =
face_recognition.compare_faces(known_face_encodings,
unknown_face_encoding) print(results)
```

This code will output a list of `True` or `False` values indicating which known face(s) match the unknown face.

Challenges and Solutions

- Lighting conditions: Poor lighting can significantly impact the accuracy of facial recognition. Using infrared cameras can mitigate this issue by capturing clear images regardless of the lighting conditions.

- Facial expressions and aging: Over time, facial expressions and aging can alter a person's appearance. Continuous learning and updating the database with recent images can enhance recognition accuracy.

Scene Understanding

Scene understanding extends beyond detecting individual objects or faces. It involves interpreting the context of a scene, including the relationships between objects and the overall setting. This is crucial for AI agents meant to interact dynamically with their environment, such as robots performing complex tasks in varying settings.

Techniques for Scene Understanding

- Semantic segmentation: This involves labeling each pixel in an image with a category label, thereby understanding the scene at a pixel level.
- Depth estimation: Using techniques such as stereo vision or structured light, AI agents can estimate the distance of objects from the camera, helping in understanding the scene's 3D structure.

Implementing Scene Understanding

Implementing scene understanding requires combining multiple computer vision techniques and possibly integrating sensor data beyond just visual inputs. For instance, combining object detection with depth estimation can allow an AI agent to not only recognize objects but also navigate around them.

Best Practices

- Leverage existing datasets: Many public datasets are available for training models on scene understanding tasks. Utilizing these can save time and provide a diverse range of training examples.
- Multi-modal data fusion: Consider integrating data from other sensors, such as LIDAR, to enrich the AI agent's understanding of its environment.

In conclusion, equipping AI agents with the capability to understand and interact with their visual environment is a complex task that requires combining various computer vision techniques. From basic object detection to advanced scene understanding, each component plays a crucial role in creating intelligent systems capable of navigating and interpreting the world around them.

Facial Recognition

Facial recognition technology enables AI agents to identify and verify individuals based on their facial features. This technology has widespread applications, including security systems, user authentication, and personalized customer experiences.

Understanding Facial Recognition

Facial recognition systems analyze the characteristics of a person's face images input through an algorithm to produce a facial signature, a unique numerical representation of the face's features. This signature is then compared to a database of known faces to find a match.

Key Components:

- Face Detection: The first step is detecting the presence of faces in an image or video frame.

- Feature Extraction: Identifying unique features of the face, such as the distance between the eyes, shape of the jawline, and the location of key facial landmarks.

- Face Comparison: Comparing extracted features with a database to find a match.

Implementing Facial Recognition

To implement a basic facial recognition system, one could use pre-trained models available in libraries such as OpenCV or frameworks like TensorFlow. Here's a simple example using OpenCV in Python:

```
import cv2 import face_recognition # Load the jpg
files into numpy arrays known_image =
face_recognition.load_image_file("known_person.jpg")
unknown_image = face_recognition.load_image_file("un
known_person.jpg") # Get the face encodings for each
face in each image file # Since there could be more
than one face in each image, it returns a list of
encodings. # But since we know each image only has
one face, we can grab the first encoding in each
image, hence [0]. known_face_encoding =
face_recognition.face_encodings(known_image)[0]
unknown_face_encoding =
face_recognition.face_encodings(unknown_image)[0] #
Compare faces results = face_recognition.compare_fac
es([known_face_encoding], unknown_face_encoding) if
results[0]: print("This is a known person.") else:
print("This is NOT a known person.")
```

Note: Ensure you have the necessary libraries installed and images stored in your working directory for the above code to function correctly.

Real-World Use Cases

- Security and Surveillance: Enhancing security systems in airports, commercial buildings, and public events by identifying individuals of interest.
- Authentication: Replacing traditional passwords and PINs for device unlocking or account access.
- Personalization: Tailoring digital signage and advertisements in retail environments to match the demographics or even the identity of the viewer.

Challenges and Best Practices

Facial recognition technology, while powerful, faces several challenges such as variations in lighting, facial expressions, and occlusions. Additionally, ethical considerations and privacy concerns are paramount, given the sensitive nature of biometric data.

Best Practices:

- Data Privacy: Implement stringent data protection measures and obtain explicit consent from individuals whose facial data is being captured and analyzed.
- Diverse Dataset: Use a diverse dataset for training to improve the model's accuracy across different ethnicities, ages, and genders.
- Regular Updates: Continuously update the system to adapt to changes in facial appearances over time, such as aging or changes in facial hair.

Scene Understanding

Scene understanding extends beyond detecting individual objects or faces to comprehending the entire context of a scene. It involves recognizing the relationships between objects, the actions taking place, and the overall setting.

Components of Scene Understanding

- Object Detection and Recognition: Identifying and categorizing each object within the scene.
- Scene Categorization: Determining the type of scene (e.g., urban, rural, indoors, outdoors).
- Spatial Relationships: Understanding the positioning and interaction of objects within the scene.
- Action Recognition: Identifying actions or activities being performed.

Implementing Scene Understanding

Implementing scene understanding in AI agents involves integrating multiple computer vision techniques and possibly utilizing deep learning models trained on extensive datasets of annotated images.

Example Frameworks and Libraries:

- TensorFlow and PyTorch: For building and training custom deep learning models.
- OpenCV: For preliminary image processing and feature extraction tasks.

Applications and Challenges

Applications range from autonomous vehicles navigating environments to content recommendation systems that understand user contexts. Challenges include the complexity of integrating multiple perception tasks and the need for large, diverse datasets for training.

Best Practices

- Modular Approach: Decompose the task into smaller, manageable components such as object detection, action recognition, etc.
- Continuous Learning: Employ models capable of online learning to adapt to new scenes and contexts over time.
- Ethical Considerations: Be mindful of privacy and bias, especially when scene understanding is applied in public or sensitive contexts.

In summary, facial recognition and scene understanding are critical components of computer vision that enable AI agents to interpret and interact with the world in sophisticated ways. By mastering these technologies, developers can create more intelligent, responsive, and personalized AI agents.

Scene Understanding

Building upon the fundamentals of image processing and the specialized capabilities of object detection and facial recognition, scene understanding represents the culmination of computer vision's application within AI agents. This capability enables AI agents to interpret complex scenes in real time, identifying not just individual objects or faces but understanding the context and relationships between elements within a visual scene.

What is Scene Understanding?

Scene understanding is the process by which an AI agent can observe a scene and comprehend its contents in a manner similar to how humans perceive their environment. This involves not only recognizing objects and people but also understanding their attributes, the actions being performed, and the overall context of the scene. It's a step beyond basic recognition tasks, integrating various components of computer vision to achieve a holistic interpretation of visual data.

Implementing Scene Understanding

Implementing scene understanding involves several key technologies and methodologies, including but not limited to deep learning, semantic segmentation, and context-aware algorithms. Below are the foundational steps and considerations for enabling scene understanding in AI agents.

Deep Learning Models

Deep learning models, particularly Convolutional Neural Networks (CNNs), are at the heart of effective scene understanding. These models can be trained on vast datasets containing labeled images of various scenes, learning to identify patterns, objects, and their relationships within these images.

```
import tensorflow as tf from
tensorflow.keras.applications import ResNet50 from
tensorflow.keras.preprocessing import image from
tensorflow.keras.applications.resnet50 import
preprocess_input, decode_predictions # Load
Pre-trained ResNet50 model model =
ResNet50(weights='imagenet') # Load an image file to
test, resizing it to 224x224 pixels (required input
size for ResNet50) img_path =
'path/to/your/image.jpg' img =
image.load_img(img_path, target_size=(224, 224)) #
Convert the image to a numpy array and add an
```

```
additional dimension x = image.img_to_array(img) x =
np.expand_dims(x, axis=0) x = preprocess_input(x) #
Make a prediction predictions = model.predict(x)
print('Predicted:', decode_predictions(predictions,
top=3)[0])
```

This code snippet demonstrates the use of a pre-trained ResNet50 model, a type of CNN, for classifying images. For scene understanding, the model's predictions can be further analyzed to extract relationships and context, for example, by identifying objects in conjunction with action recognition models.

Semantic Segmentation

Semantic segmentation involves the process of labeling each pixel in an image with a class corresponding to what the pixel represents. This technique is crucial for understanding the layout and geometry of a scene.

```
# Pseudo-code for semantic segmentation # Assume
'model' is a pre-trained semantic segmentation model
segmented_image = model.predict(scene_image)
```

In practice, this would involve processing the `scene_image` through a segmentation model to produce a `segmented_image`, where each pixel's color corresponds to a class label, such as "person," "car," "tree," etc.

Context-Aware Algorithms

To fully understand a scene, AI agents must also consider the context. This includes recognizing the setting (e.g., a kitchen, a street, a park) and understanding the interactions between objects and people. Context-aware algorithms leverage the outputs of object detection, facial recognition, and semantic segmentation, applying rules or machine learning models to infer the scene's context.

Note: Achieving accurate scene understanding requires large, diverse datasets for training models and significant computational resources for processing images in real time.

Real-World Use Cases

Scene understanding powers numerous applications, from autonomous vehicles navigating roads to surveillance systems monitoring for suspicious activities. In smart homes, AI agents can adjust the environment based on the scene, such as dimming lights when a movie is playing.

Challenges and Best Practices

- Data Diversity: Ensure the training data for scene understanding models is diverse and representative of the real-world scenarios the AI agent will encounter.

- Computation Efficiency: Optimize models for efficiency, enabling real-time processing without sacrificing accuracy.

- Integration: Seamlessly integrate scene understanding with other AI agent capabilities, such as decision-making and action execution, for a cohesive application.

Scene understanding is a complex but incredibly powerful capability for AI agents, enabling a deeper comprehension of visual data that mirrors human perception. By leveraging advanced deep learning models and techniques like semantic segmentation, developers can equip AI agents with the ability to interpret and interact with the world around them in sophisticated and meaningful ways.

Chapter 8: Decision Making and Planning

Decision Trees

Understanding Decision Trees

Decision Trees are a fundamental component of decision-making processes for AI agents. They provide a structured method for an agent to make decisions based on various conditions. Essentially, a decision tree is a flowchart-like tree structure where each internal node represents a "test" on an attribute, each branch represents the outcome of the test, and each leaf node represents a decision or outcome.

Building a Basic Decision Tree

To construct a decision tree, one must start by identifying the attributes or features relevant to the decision-making process. For example, if an AI agent is designed to decide whether to go outside, attributes might include weather conditions, temperature, and time of day.

```
class Node: def __init__(self, attribute):
self.attribute = attribute self.children = [] class
DecisionTree: def __init__(self, root): self.root =
root def add_node(self, attribute, parent): new_node
= Node(attribute) parent.children.append(new_node)
return new_node
```

This simple code snippet outlines the basic structure for building a decision tree. Each node represents a decision based on an attribute, and you can expand the tree by adding more nodes.

Practical Example: Decision Tree for Weather-Based Decision

Consider an AI agent that decides whether to go outside based on the weather. The decision tree might start with a root node testing whether it's raining. If `No`, the next node checks if it's sunny, leading to a decision to go outside. If `Yes` to rain, the next question might be whether the agent has an umbrella, leading to different outcomes.

Best Practices and Common Pitfalls

- Overfitting: Ensure your decision tree doesn't become too complex, as it might overfit to your training data, making it less effective in real-world scenarios. Pruning techniques can help reduce tree complexity.
- Data Preprocessing: Clean and preprocess your data to improve decision tree accuracy. Handle missing values and consider feature selection techniques to identify the most relevant attributes.

Reinforcement Learning

Introduction to Reinforcement Learning

Reinforcement Learning (RL) is a type of machine learning where an agent learns to make decisions by taking actions in an environment to achieve some goal. The agent learns from the consequences of its actions, rather than from being told explicitly what to do, through a system of rewards and punishments.

Key Concepts in Reinforcement Learning

- Agent: The learner or decision-maker.
- Environment: The world through which the agent moves.
- Action: All possible moves the agent can make.
- Reward: Feedback from the environment to assess the action's efficacy.

Implementing a Simple Reinforcement Learning Model

A basic RL model involves defining the state space, action space, and reward mechanism. Here's a simplified example in Python, using a grid system where an agent learns to navigate to a goal.

```python
import numpy as np # Define the environment
grid_size = 4 reward = np.zeros((grid_size,
grid_size)) reward[3, 3] = 1 # Goal position with
reward # Define possible actions actions = ['up',
'down', 'left', 'right'] def move_agent(position,
action): if action == 'up' and position[0] > 0:
position[0] -= 1 elif action == 'down' and
position[0] < grid_size - 1: position[0] += 1 elif
action == 'left' and position[1] > 0: position[1] -=
1 elif action == 'right' and position[1] < grid_size
- 1: position[1] += 1 return position # Reward
function def get_reward(position): return
reward[position[0], position[1]]
```

This code outlines a basic framework for an RL agent navigating a grid. The `move_agent` function updates the agent's position based on the action taken, and the `get_reward` function returns the reward for the new position.

Best Practices in Reinforcement Learning

- Reward Design: Carefully design your reward system. Inconsistent or misleading rewards can lead to suboptimal learning.
- Exploration vs. Exploitation: Balance between exploring new actions to find better solutions (exploration) and using known actions that yield the highest reward (exploitation).
- Simulation Environment: Use a well-designed simulation environment that closely mimics the problem space for training your agents.

Planning Algorithms

Introduction to Planning Algorithms

Planning algorithms allow AI agents to plan a series of actions to achieve a specific goal. Unlike decision trees and reinforcement learning, planning algorithms focus on finding a sequence of actions that leads from an initial state to a goal state.

Types of Planning Algorithms

- Classical Planning: Involves deterministic environments where the outcome of each action is predictable.

- Partial Observable Planning: Used in environments where the agent doesn't have complete information about the state of the world.

Implementing a Basic Planning Algorithm

One of the simplest forms of planning algorithms is the Breadth-First Search (BFS), which explores the state space by expanding the shallowest nodes first.

```
from collections import deque def bfs(initial_state,
goal_state, actions): frontier =
deque([initial_state]) # States yet to be explored
explored = set() # States that have been explored
while frontier: current_state = frontier.popleft()
explored.add(current_state) if current_state ==
goal_state: return True # Goal found for action in
actions: new_state = apply_action(current_state,
action) if new_state not in explored and new_state
not in frontier: frontier.append(new_state) return
False # Goal not found
```

This function searches for a path from an `initial_state` to a `goal_state` by exploring actions that lead to new states. It returns `True` if a path exists and `False` otherwise.

Best Practices and Tips

- State Space Representation: Choose an efficient representation for your state space to optimize the performance of your planning algorithm.

- Goal Definition: Clearly define your goal state. Ambiguous goals can lead to inefficient planning and execution.

Goal-Oriented Behavior

Implementing Goal-Oriented Behavior in AI Agents

Goal-oriented behavior is crucial for creating AI agents capable of making decisions and planning actions based on desired outcomes. This involves defining clear goals and equipping the agent with the ability to evaluate its environment and actions in the context of those goals.

Example: Pathfinding for Delivery Robots

Consider a delivery robot navigating a warehouse. Its goal is to deliver a package to a specific location with the shortest path possible while avoiding obstacles.

1. Define the Goal: The specific location where the package needs to be delivered. 2. Assess the Environment: The layout of the warehouse, including obstacles and paths. 3. Plan the Action: Using planning algorithms like BFS or A* search to find the shortest path. 4. Execute and Adapt: The robot moves along the planned path, adapting to any unexpected obstacles.

Decision trees, reinforcement learning, planning algorithms, and goal-oriented behavior are foundational elements in teaching AI agents to make decisions and plan actions. By understanding and implementing these components, developers can create sophisticated AI agents capable of navigating complex environments and achieving specific goals.

Reinforcement Learning

Reinforcement Learning (RL) is a critical area of study within artificial intelligence that focuses on how agents can learn to make decisions by interacting with their environment. It differs from the decision tree approach by not requiring a model of the environment beforehand. Instead, agents learn optimal behavior through trial and error, receiving rewards or penalties for actions taken.

Understanding Reinforcement Learning

At the heart of RL is the concept of the agent-environment interaction. An agent takes actions in an environment, which in turn responds to these actions and presents new situations to the agent. The environment also provides rewards, numerical values that the agent tries to maximize over time. This setup can be formally described as a Markov Decision Process (MDP), encompassing a set of states, a set of actions, rewards, and the transition probabilities between states.

Key Components of RL

- Agent: The learner or decision-maker.
- Environment: Everything the agent interacts with.
- State: A situation or configuration that the environment can be in.
- Action: A set of all possible moves the agent can make.
- Reward: Feedback from the environment used to guide learning.

The RL Process

1. The agent observes the current state of the environment. 2. Based on this observation, the agent selects and performs an action. 3. The environment transitions to a new state and provides feedback in the form of a reward. 4. The agent updates its knowledge with the new state and reward, typically using this information to improve its action-selection strategy.

Example: Teaching an AI to Play a Game

Consider an AI learning to play a simple video game where the goal is to avoid obstacles. Initially, the AI moves randomly. It receives a positive reward for every frame it survives without hitting an obstacle and a negative reward (or penalty) for colliding with an obstacle. Over time, the AI learns the optimal actions to take in various situations to maximize its score.

```
# Psuedocode for a simple reinforcement learning
loop while not game_over: current_state =
observe_environment() action =
select_action_based_on_current_state() reward,
new_state = take_action(action)
update_knowledge(current_state, action, reward,
new_state)
```

Note: Real-world RL problems are often more complex, involving continuous states and actions, as well as the need to balance exploration (trying new actions) with exploitation (using known strategies).

Challenges in Reinforcement Learning

- Exploration vs. Exploitation: Deciding whether to try new actions to discover more about the environment or to use known actions that give high rewards.

- Sparse Rewards: In some environments, rewards are infrequent or delayed, making it harder for the agent to learn which actions are beneficial.

- Dimensionality: Real-world problems often have a high number of states and actions, making the learning process computationally expensive.

Planning Algorithms

Planning is a critical aspect of AI that involves generating a sequence of actions to achieve a specific goal. Unlike reinforcement learning, planning algorithms typically assume a model of the environment is available or can be constructed.

Understanding Planning

Planning involves taking the current state of the world, the desired end state (goal), and producing a plan that, when executed, transitions the world from the current state to the goal state. This process often involves searching through a space of possible actions and states.

Types of Planning Algorithms

- Classical Planning: Assumes a perfect, deterministic model of the world. Actions have predictable results, and the challenge is to find a sequence of actions that leads to the goal.

- Contingency Planning: Takes into account uncertainty in the environment. Plans include actions to take under various possible contingencies.

- Hierarchical Task Network (HTN) Planning: Involves decomposing the goal into smaller, more manageable tasks.

Example: Pathfinding with A* Algorithm

A* is a popular search algorithm used for pathfinding and graph traversal. It's efficient and guarantees the shortest path under certain conditions. It combines features of Dijkstra's Algorithm (favoring vertices that are close to the starting point) and Greedy Best-First-Search (favoring vertices that are close to the goal).

```
# Pseudocode snippet for A* algorithm open_set =
set([start]) came_from = {} g_score = {vertex:
float('infinity') for vertex in graph}
g_score[start] = 0 f_score = {vertex:
float('infinity') for vertex in graph}
f_score[start] = heuristic_cost_estimate(start,
goal) while open_set: current =
vertex_in_open_set_with_lowest_f_score(open_set,
f_score) if current == goal: return
reconstruct_path(came_from, current)
open_set.remove(current) for neighbor in
neighbors_of(current): tentative_g_score =
g_score[current] + dist_between(current, neighbor)
if tentative_g_score < g_score[neighbor]:
came_from[neighbor] = current g_score[neighbor] =
tentative_g_score f_score[neighbor] =
g_score[neighbor] +
heuristic_cost_estimate(neighbor, goal) if neighbor
not in open_set: open_set.add(neighbor)
```

Note: The `heuristic_cost_estimate` is a heuristic function, often Euclidean distance, used to estimate the cost to reach the goal from a given vertex.

Best Practices and Tips

- Understand the Environment: Whether using RL or planning algorithms, a deep understanding of the environment can significantly impact the choice of algorithm and its configuration.

- Start Simple: Begin with simple models and algorithms. Complexity can always be added later as needed.

- Iterative Improvement: AI agent performance can often be improved iteratively. Start with a baseline and incrementally add features or complexity.

Challenges in Planning

- Computational Complexity: Planning can become computationally expensive as the number of states and actions increases.

- Dynamic Environments: In environments that change unpredictably, maintaining an accurate model for planning can be challenging.

In summary, decision making and planning are central to the development of intelligent AI agents. By understanding and implementing techniques in reinforcement learning and planning algorithms, developers can create agents capable of solving complex, real-world problems autonomously.

Planning Algorithms

After exploring the dynamic and adaptive learning process of Reinforcement Learning (RL), we delve into the structured approach of planning algorithms. Planning is a critical aspect of AI that involves generating a sequence of actions to achieve a specific goal. Unlike RL, which learns from interaction with the environment, planning algorithms require a model of the environment to predict the outcome of actions.

Understanding Planning Algorithms

Planning algorithms can be broadly classified into two types: deterministic and non-deterministic algorithms. Deterministic algorithms assume a predictable environment where every action has a guaranteed outcome. Non-deterministic algorithms, on the other hand, account for uncertainty in the environment, where an action may lead to multiple possible outcomes.

Example: Pathfinding with A*

A (A-star) is a popular deterministic planning algorithm used in pathfinding and graph traversal. The core idea behind A is to find the most efficient path from a start node to a goal node in a weighted graph. It does this by maintaining a priority queue of paths based on a cost function, which is a combination of the path's length and an estimate of the distance to the goal.

```
def a_star(start, goal, graph): open_set =
set([start]) came_from = {} g_score = {node:
float('inf') for node in graph} g_score[start] = 0
f_score = {node: float('inf') for node in graph}
f_score[start] = heuristic(start, goal) while
open_set: current = min(open_set, key=lambda node:
f_score[node]) if current == goal: return
reconstruct_path(came_from, current)
open_set.remove(current) for neighbor in
graph[current]: tentative_g_score = g_score[current]
+ graph[current][neighbor] if tentative_g_score <
g_score[neighbor]: came_from[neighbor] = current
g_score[neighbor] = tentative_g_score
f_score[neighbor] = g_score[neighbor] +
heuristic(neighbor, goal) if neighbor not in
open_set: open_set.add(neighbor) return False
```

Note: The `heuristic` function is problem-specific and estimates the cost from the current node to the goal. A common choice for grid-based pathfinding is the Manhattan distance or Euclidean distance.

Non-deterministic Planning: Dealing with Uncertainty

In real-world applications, the environment often contains elements of uncertainty. Non-deterministic planning algorithms, such as Partially Observable Markov Decision Processes (POMDPs), are designed to handle this uncertainty. POMDPs extend the Markov Decision Process (MDP) framework used in RL to situations where the agent cannot fully observe the state of the environment.

Implementing a POMDP involves defining states, actions, rewards, and a transition model that includes observation probabilities. The goal is to find a policy that maximizes the expected reward, even with incomplete information about the environment's state.

Best Practices and Tips

- Model the Environment Accurately: The effectiveness of planning algorithms heavily depends on the accuracy of the environmental model. Take time to understand and model the environment correctly.

- Choose the Right Algorithm: Determine whether the environment is deterministic or non-deterministic and choose an algorithm that best fits the problem at hand.

- Optimize Performance: Planning algorithms, especially in complex environments, can be computationally intensive. Use heuristic functions and optimization techniques to improve performance.

- Consider Hybrid Approaches: In some cases, combining planning algorithms with learning methods like RL can yield better results, especially in dynamic or partially observable environments.

Challenges and Solutions

One of the main challenges in implementing planning algorithms is computational complexity, especially in large or complex environments. To mitigate this, one can employ heuristic functions to guide the search process, reducing the exploration space.

Another challenge is dealing with dynamic environments where the conditions can change unpredictably. In such cases, adaptive planning methods that can update their plans based on new information are crucial.

Planning algorithms play an essential role in AI agents' ability to make decisions and execute planned actions towards a goal. By understanding and implementing these algorithms, developers can equip their AI agents with the capability to navigate and interact with their environment effectively. Whether dealing with deterministic or non-deterministic environments, the choice and implementation of the right planning algorithm can significantly impact the success of AI applications.

Practical Implementation of Planning Algorithms

Implementing planning algorithms in AI agents requires a systematic approach, from understanding the environment model to selecting the appropriate algorithm for the task. This section will guide you through the key steps and considerations for effectively applying planning algorithms in real-world scenarios.

Environment Modeling

Before an AI agent can plan, it needs an accurate model of its environment. This model should include all possible states the environment can be in, the actions that can be taken, and the expected outcomes of these actions.

- Define States: Start by defining a comprehensive set of states your agent might encounter. For example, in a robotic vacuum cleaner, states could include the location of the robot, the battery level, and whether the dustbin is full.
- List Actions: For each state, list all possible actions the agent can take. Continuing with our vacuum cleaner example, actions might include moving in a direction, starting the cleaning process, or returning to the charging dock.
- Predict Outcomes: Establish the transition model by predicting the outcome of each action in every state. This involves determining the next state given a current state and action.

Choosing a Planning Algorithm

Several planning algorithms exist, each with its strengths and weaknesses. The choice of algorithm depends on the complexity of your task, the environment's dynamics, and the computational resources available.

- Classical Planning: Best for deterministic environments with a small number of states. It involves generating a sequence of actions that leads from the initial state to the goal state.
- Partial Order Planning: Useful in environments where actions can be performed in parallel, reducing the total plan length.

- Hierarchical Task Network (HTN) Planning: Ideal for complex tasks that can be broken down into simpler subtasks. This method plans at different levels of abstraction, making it efficient for large, complex environments.

Implementing a Simple Planner

Let's consider a simple path-finding scenario where an AI agent must navigate a grid to reach a goal location. We'll use a basic search algorithm for our planner.

```
def simple_planner(grid, start, goal): # Initialize
the frontier with the starting position frontier =
[start] came_from = {} came_from[start] = None #
Loop until the frontier is empty while frontier:
current = frontier.pop(0) # Check if the goal has
been reached if current == goal: break # Check all
four directions for next in [(0, 1), (1, 0), (0,
-1), (-1, 0)]: # Calculate the next cell's position
next = (current[0] + next[0], current[1] + next[1])
if next in grid and next not in came_from:
frontier.append(next) came_from[next] = current #
Reconstruct path from start to goal current = goal
path = [] while current != start:
path.append(current) current = came_from[current]
path.append(start) path.reverse() return path
```

In this example, `simple_planner` takes a grid, start, and goal locations as inputs and returns the path from start to goal. It uses a simple breadth-first search algorithm, which is sufficient for uncomplicated environments but might not be optimal for more complex scenarios.

Best Practices and Tips

- Preprocessing: For large or complex environments, consider preprocessing the environment to identify key waypoints or areas of interest. This can reduce the computational workload during planning.

- Adaptivity: Be prepared to adapt your planning strategy based on the agent's performance. In dynamic environments, periodically re-evaluating the plan can help the agent adjust to changes.

- Debugging: Planning algorithms can be complex, making bugs challenging to track down. Visualizing the agent's planned path and state transitions can be incredibly helpful for debugging.

Planning algorithms are a powerful tool in the AI developer's toolkit, enabling agents to make informed decisions and act towards achieving their goals. By carefully modeling the environment, choosing the right algorithm, and following best practices, you can implement effective planning mechanisms in your AI agents.

In the next section, we'll explore goal-oriented behavior in AI agents, building on the foundation of decision-making and planning discussed here.

Chapter 9: Memory and Learning Systems

Memory and Learning Systems in AI Agents

To build intelligent AI agents capable of navigating and interacting within their environments, it's crucial to incorporate mechanisms for memory and learning. These components allow agents to recall past experiences, learn from them, and adapt their behaviors over time. This section delves into the fundamentals of implementing memory and learning systems in AI agents, covering both theoretical concepts and practical applications.

Short-term and Long-term Memory

Understanding Memory Types

Memory in AI agents can broadly be classified into two types: short-term memory (STM) and long-term memory (LTM). Short-term memory is transient, holding information temporarily for immediate processing and decision-making. Long-term memory, on the other hand, stores information over extended periods, allowing the agent to recall past experiences and learned behaviors.

```
# Example of a basic memory structure in Python
class AIAgentMemory: def __init__(self):
self.short_term_memory = [] self.long_term_memory =
{} def remember_short_term(self, information): #
Assuming a simple FIFO mechanism for STM if
```

```
len(self.short_term_memory) >= 5: # Limit STM
capacity self.short_term_memory.pop(0) # Remove the
oldest entry
self.short_term_memory.append(information) def
remember_long_term(self, key, information): # Store
information in LTM with a unique key
self.long_term_memory[key] = information def
recall_long_term(self, key): # Retrieve information
from LTM return self.long_term_memory.get(key, "Not
Found")
```

Note: The above code is a simplistic representation. In practice, memory mechanisms in AI agents are more complex and require efficient data structures and algorithms for management and retrieval.

Practical Considerations

- Capacity: STM is typically limited in capacity, necessitating efficient management to prioritize relevant information. LTM, while generally larger, still requires organization to facilitate quick retrieval.

- Decay: Information in STM may need to decay or be replaced as new information becomes available, while LTM should maintain stability over time.

- Encoding: Effective mechanisms are needed to encode experiences into a format suitable for storage, particularly for LTM.

Learning from Experience

Learning mechanisms enable AI agents to adapt their behaviors based on experiences. This section explores foundational learning strategies that can be employed.

Reinforcement Learning

Reinforcement Learning (RL) is a powerful method where agents learn to make decisions by receiving rewards or penalties for their actions. This trial-and-error approach allows agents to discover strategies that maximize their cumulative reward.

```
# Simplified Reinforcement Learning example
agent_state = "initial_state" action =
choose_action(agent_state) reward =
perform_action(action) update_knowledge(agent_state,
action, reward)
```

In practice, RL involves complex algorithms like Q-learning or Deep Q-Networks (DQN) for managing the relationships between states, actions, and rewards.

Supervised and Unsupervised Learning

- Supervised Learning: The agent learns from a dataset containing input-output pairs, learning to map inputs to the correct outputs.

- Unsupervised Learning: Here, the agent learns patterns and structures from unlabelled data, useful for clustering or anomaly detection tasks.

Adaptation Strategies

Dynamic Environment Handling

AI agents often operate in dynamic environments where conditions can change unpredictably. Adaptation strategies involve the agent adjusting its behavior in response to environmental changes, ensuring continued effectiveness.

- Online Learning: Agents continuously update their knowledge base and decision-making strategies based on new information, without the need for retraining from scratch.

- Evolutionary Algorithms: These algorithms simulate natural selection by generating a population of solutions, iteratively selecting and breeding the most successful ones to adapt to changing environments.

Knowledge Representation

The way knowledge is represented within an AI agent significantly influences its ability to learn and recall information. Common approaches include:

Semantic Networks

Semantic networks are graphical representations of knowledge where nodes represent concepts, and edges represent the relationships between them. This structure allows agents to efficiently navigate and infer relationships between concepts.

Decision Trees

Decision trees are hierarchical structures that model decision pathways. Each node represents a decision point, and each path from root to leaf represents a decision sequence, culminating in an outcome or action.

```
class DecisionNode: def __init__(self, question,
true_branch, false_branch): self.question = question
self.true_branch = true_branch self.false_branch =
false_branch # Example of a decision tree node
is_sunny = DecisionNode("Is it sunny?", "Go to the
beach", "Stay indoors")
```

Warning: While powerful, decision trees can become overly complex and prone to overfitting, especially with large or noisy datasets.

Best Practices and Tips

- Incremental Learning: Start with simple models and incrementally increase complexity as the agent's performance improves.

- Data Management: Efficiently manage and preprocess data for learning, ensuring that the agent focuses on relevant information.

- Experimentation: Experiment with different memory structures, learning algorithms, and knowledge representation methods to find the best fit for your AI agent.

Common Challenges

- Scalability: Ensuring that memory and learning systems scale with the complexity of tasks and environments.

- Generalization: Balancing the agent's ability to perform well in seen scenarios while also adapting to novel situations.

- Resource Management: Managing computational resources effectively, especially for agents with extensive memory or complex learning algorithms.

Actionable Steps

1. Define the Memory Structure: Start by defining a simple memory structure for your AI agent, considering the balance between STM and LTM. 2. Select a Learning Algorithm: Choose a learning algorithm that suits your agent's needs, starting with something simple like Q-learning. 3. Implement Knowledge Representation: Decide on a method for representing knowledge within your agent, such as semantic networks or decision trees. 4. Iterate and Refine: Continuously test, evaluate, and refine your agent's memory and learning capabilities, using real-world scenarios as benchmarks.

By understanding and implementing memory and learning systems, AI agents can significantly improve their performance and adaptability, paving the way for more intelligent and autonomous systems.

Learning from Experience

Learning from experience is a cornerstone of artificial intelligence that enables AI agents to improve their performance and adapt to new situations over time. This section explores the mechanisms and strategies AI agents use to learn from their interactions with the environment.

Reinforcement Learning

Reinforcement learning (RL) is a type of machine learning where an agent learns to make decisions by taking actions in an environment to achieve some goal. The agent receives feedback in the form of rewards or penalties, guiding it towards the most beneficial actions.

Key Concepts of Reinforcement Learning

- Agent: The AI entity that learns from its experiences.
- Environment: The world in which the agent operates and learns.
- Action: A set of operations that the agent can perform.
- Reward: Feedback from the environment that evaluates the agent's actions.
- Policy: A strategy that the agent follows to decide its actions.

Example: Implementing a Simple Q-Learning Agent

Q-Learning is a popular RL technique used to learn the value of an action in a particular state.

```
import numpy as np # Initialize Q-table with zeros
Q_table = np.zeros([state_space, action_space]) #
Hyperparameters alpha = 0.1 # Learning rate gamma =
0.99 # Discount factor for episode in
range(total_episodes): state = environment.reset()
while True: action = np.argmax(Q_table[state]) #
Choose the action with the highest value next_state,
reward, done, info = environment.step(action) # Take
action # Update Q-table Q_table[state, action] =
Q_table[state, action] + alpha * (reward + gamma *
np.max(Q_table[next_state]) - Q_table[state,
action]) state = next_state if done: break
```

Note: The Q-table represents the value of performing a certain action in a specific state, guiding the agent's decision-making process.

Learning from Interaction and Feedback

Apart from reinforcement learning, AI agents can learn from direct interactions and feedback within their environment. This can be seen in scenarios where agents learn from humans or other agents by receiving corrections or instructions.

Implementing Feedback-Based Learning

Consider an AI agent designed to learn from user feedback in a conversational interface. When the user highlights incorrect responses, the agent adjusts its future responses accordingly.

```
def adjust_response_based_on_feedback(response,
feedback): if feedback == 'incorrect': # Modify the
agent's response mechanism modify_response(response)
else: reinforce_response(response)
```

This simplistic function illustrates how feedback can directly influence the learning mechanism of an AI agent, promoting more accurate responses over time.

Adaptation Strategies

The ability to adapt is crucial for AI agents operating in dynamic environments. Adaptation involves modifying behaviors based on new information or changes within the environment.

Dynamic Learning

Dynamic learning enables AI agents to update their knowledge base continuously without needing to be retrained from scratch. This approach is vital for agents in rapidly changing environments.

Techniques for Dynamic Learning

- Online Learning: The agent learns from new data as it becomes available, adjusting its model in real-time.

- Transfer Learning: Leveraging knowledge gained from one task to improve performance on a related task.

- Evolutionary Algorithms: Using mechanisms inspired by biological evolution, such as mutation and selection, to evolve the agent's strategies over time.

Real-World Application: Autonomous Vehicles

Autonomous vehicles are a prime example of AI agents that must continually adapt to changing conditions. These vehicles use a combination of sensors and learning algorithms to navigate roads, avoid obstacles, and respond to dynamic elements like traffic and weather.

```
while vehicle.is_operating(): sensor_data =
vehicle.get_sensor_data() decision =
learning_algorithm.decide(sensor_data)
vehicle.execute(decision)
```

In this simplified example, the `learning_algorithm` continuously updates its decision-making process based on real-time sensor data, exemplifying dynamic adaptation.

Knowledge Representation

For AI agents to learn and adapt, they must have a mechanism for representing knowledge. Knowledge representation involves structuring information in a form that the agent can understand and utilize.

Types of Knowledge Representation

- Semantic Networks: Graph structures representing objects and their interrelationships.
- Rule-Based Systems: Sets of rules defining actions to be taken under specific conditions.
- Ontologies: Formal representations of knowledge within a domain, including concepts and relationships.

Implementing a Rule-Based System

Rule-based systems are widely used in AI for representing procedural knowledge.

```
rules = { 'if temperature is cold then action is
wear_coat', 'if raining then action is
carry_umbrella' } def
apply_rules(environment_conditions): actions = []
for rule in rules: if evaluate_condition(rule,
environment_conditions):
actions.append(extract_action(rule)) return actions
```

This example demonstrates how rules can guide the behavior of an AI agent, allowing it to react appropriately to different environmental conditions.

Incorporating memory and learning systems into AI agents enables them to remember past experiences, learn from interactions, and adapt to new situations. Techniques such as reinforcement learning, dynamic learning, and knowledge representation are central to developing intelligent, autonomous agents capable of operating in complex, real-world environments. By understanding and implementing these strategies, developers can create AI agents that not only perform tasks but also improve and evolve over time.

Adaptation Strategies

Adapting to new challenges and environments is crucial for AI agents to remain effective over time. This section delves into the strategies AI agents use to adapt their behavior based on their experiences and the changes in their operating environment.

Exploration vs. Exploitation

One of the fundamental challenges in machine learning, especially in reinforcement learning, is balancing exploration and exploitation. Exploration involves the AI agent trying new actions to discover their effects, which is crucial for learning about unknown environments. Exploitation, on the other hand, involves using the knowledge the agent has already acquired to make the best decision.

```
# Example of an epsilon-greedy strategy for
balancing exploration and exploitation import numpy
as np epsilon = 0.1 # Probability of exploring if
np.random.rand() < epsilon: action =
np.random.choice(all_possible_actions) # Explore
else: action = best_known_action # Exploit
```

Note: The value of `epsilon` can be adjusted over time, typically decreasing as the agent learns more about the environment, to shift the balance from exploration to exploitation.

Transfer Learning

Transfer learning is a strategy where knowledge gained while solving one problem is applied to a different but related problem. For AI agents, this means leveraging previous experiences to adapt to new environments or tasks more quickly.

For instance, an AI agent trained to play one type of video game might transfer some of its learned behaviors to a different game with similar mechanics, thus reducing the learning time required for the new game.

Online Learning

Online learning refers to the ability of an AI agent to continuously update its knowledge base from ongoing experiences. This is in contrast to batch learning, where the agent is trained on a fixed dataset. Online learning is particularly useful for environments that change over time, allowing the AI agent to adapt to new patterns and information.

```
# Simplified online learning update def
update_model(model, new_data, learning_rate=0.01): #
Update the model incrementally with the new data
model.adjust_weights(new_data, learning_rate) return
model
```

Knowledge Representation

For AI agents to learn and adapt, they need to store and manage knowledge effectively. This section focuses on how AI agents represent and utilize knowledge.

Semantic Networks

Semantic networks are a form of knowledge representation that organizes information in networks of nodes and edges, where nodes represent concepts or entities, and edges represent the relationships between them. This structure is particularly useful for representing complex relationships in a way that's understandable for both the AI agent and human developers.

```
# Example structure of a semantic network
semantic_network = { "Cat": {"is_a": "Animal",
"has": ["Whiskers", "Tail"]}, "Dog": {"is_a":
"Animal", "has": ["Tail"]}, }
```

Ontologies

Ontologies are a step beyond semantic networks, providing a formal representation of knowledge within a domain. They define the types, properties, and interrelationships of the entities that exist for a particular domain. Ontologies are powerful tools for AI agents, enabling them to reason about the entities and their relationships within their environment.

```
# Basic example of ontology concepts ontology = {
"Animal": {"properties": ["hasHeart"], "instances":
["Cat", "Dog"]}, "hasHeart": {"type": "Property",
"domain": "Animal", "range": "Boolean"}, }
```

Best Practices and Tips

- Balance exploration and exploitation carefully to ensure effective learning without getting stuck in suboptimal behaviors.

- Utilize transfer learning to leverage existing knowledge, reducing the time and resources needed for learning new tasks.

- Implement online learning for environments that change over time, allowing your AI agents to continuously adapt.

- Use semantic networks and ontologies for complex knowledge representation, facilitating better decision-making and reasoning by AI agents.

Common Challenges

- Balancing exploration and exploitation can be difficult, as too much exploration can lead to inefficiency, and too much exploitation can prevent the discovery of better strategies.

- Transfer learning requires careful consideration of the similarities between tasks. Misapplied, it can lead to negative transfer, where knowledge from one task hinders performance on another.

- Online learning involves challenges in ensuring the agent does not forget previous knowledge (catastrophic forgetting) while integrating new information.

Practical Exercise

Create a simple semantic network for a domain of your choice (e.g., a hobby or interest). Define at least five entities and their relationships. Implement this network in Python and write functions to add new entities and relationships, demonstrating the dynamic nature of knowledge representation in AI agents.

Knowledge Representation

Representing knowledge accurately and efficiently is essential for AI agents to learn and make decisions. Knowledge representation in AI involves the way information is stored, organized, and interpreted by an AI system. This section explores the different methods and structures used to represent knowledge, how they impact learning and memory, and offers examples of their implementation.

Symbolic vs. Sub-symbolic Representation

Knowledge can be represented in two main forms: symbolic and sub-symbolic. Symbolic representation uses discrete symbols to represent objects, concepts, and relationships within a domain. Logic rules and semantic networks are common examples of symbolic representation. In contrast, sub-symbolic representation relies on continuous values and distributed representations, such as those found in neural networks.

Symbolic Representation Example

```
# A simple example of a symbolic representation
knowledge_base = { "apple": {"type": "fruit",
"color": "red"}, "banana": {"type": "fruit",
"color": "yellow"} } # Accessing knowledge
print(knowledge_base["apple"]["color"]) # Output:
red
```

This example demonstrates how an AI agent might store and access symbolic knowledge about objects.

Sub-symbolic Representation Example

Sub-symbolic representations are less intuitive to humans but are powerful for handling complex, nuanced data. Neural networks, a form of sub-symbolic representation, can learn and represent information through the adjustment of weights between interconnected nodes.

```
# Pseudocode for a neural network representation
class NeuralNetwork: def __init__(self):
self.weights = [...] # Complex structure of weights
def forward_pass(self, input_data): # Process
input_data through network layers return output_data
# Neural networks abstract and encode knowledge in
the network's weights
```

Ontologies and Taxonomies

Ontologies and taxonomies provide structured ways to represent knowledge hierarchically, defining the types of things that exist in a domain and their interrelations. Ontologies are crucial for semantic web applications, natural language processing, and any AI system that needs to understand and reason about various entities and their relationships.

Implementing a Basic Ontology

Creating an ontology involves defining classes (general concepts), instances (individual examples of classes), and the relationships between them. Tools like Protégé can be used for building ontologies in formats like OWL (Web Ontology Language).

This snippet outlines a basic hierarchy where `Apple` and `Banana` are subclasses of `Fruit`, establishing a clear relationship between these concepts.

> **Note:** While symbolic methods like ontologies offer clear, structured knowledge representation, they often require more manual effort to create and maintain. Sub-symbolic methods, such as those used in machine learning, can automatically learn and adapt representations from data.

Challenges and Best Practices

Implementing effective knowledge representation in AI agents faces several challenges, including the complexity of the domain, the dynamism of the environment, and the scalability of the representation method. Best practices involve:

- Choosing the right representation method based on the problem domain and requirements.

- Ensuring the scalability of the knowledge representation to accommodate new knowledge.

- Balancing the trade-offs between the interpretability of symbolic representations and the flexibility of sub-symbolic representations.

Practical Exercise

As a practical exercise, try implementing a simple symbolic knowledge base for a domain of your choice. Define at least ten concepts and their relationships, and write code to query this knowledge base.

Knowledge representation is a foundational aspect of creating intelligent AI agents capable of learning and making decisions. By understanding and applying the right representation strategies, developers can enhance the capabilities of their AI systems to interpret and interact with the world more effectively.

Chapter 10: Multi-Agent Systems

Introduction to Multi-Agent Systems

Multi-Agent Systems (MAS) represent a significant branch of artificial intelligence where multiple autonomous entities, known as agents, interact within an environment to achieve individual or collective goals. These agents can communicate, cooperate, coordinate, or negotiate with each other, leading to complex but efficient problem-solving strategies that are difficult or impossible for an individual agent to achieve. This system's strength lies in its flexibility and scalability, making it applicable in various fields such as robotics, distributed computing, and even online marketplaces.

Understanding Agents in MAS

An agent in a MAS context is an entity with the capability to autonomously perform actions in an environment to achieve specified objectives. Each agent possesses its own set of characteristics:

- Autonomy: Operates without the direct intervention of humans or others and has control over its actions and internal state.

- Social ability: Communicates and cooperates with other agents and humans.

- Reactivity: Perceives and responds to changes in the environment in a timely fashion.

- Proactiveness: Exhibits goal-directed behavior by taking initiative.

Key Concepts in MAS

- Agent Communication: Agents in a MAS need a method to communicate, which can range from simple signal systems to complex languages designed for agent interaction.

- Coordination Strategies: To work efficiently towards a common goal, agents must have strategies for planning and dividing tasks among themselves.

- Distributed Systems: MAS often operate in distributed systems, where each agent runs on different hardware and collaborates over a network.

- Swarm Intelligence: This is an emergent behavior where simple agents following simple rules lead to complex and intelligent global behavior, inspired by natural systems like ant colonies or bird flocks.

Agent Communication

Effective communication is crucial in MAS for coordinating tasks, sharing knowledge, and making decisions. There are two primary forms of communication in MAS:

Direct Communication

Agents exchange messages directly with one another using a predefined protocol. This method is akin to human conversation and can be implemented using message passing techniques.

```
# Example of direct communication in Python using a
simple message structure class Agent: def
send_message(self, recipient, message):
recipient.receive_message(message) def
receive_message(self, message): print(f"Received
```

```
message: {message}") # Usage agent1 = Agent() agent2
= Agent() agent1.send_message(agent2, "Hello, Agent
2!")
```

Indirect Communication

Also known as stigmergy, this method involves agents communicating through the environment, for example, by leaving markers or signals that other agents can perceive and interpret.

```
# Example of indirect communication via the
environment environment = {} def
leave_marker(agent_id, location, marker):
environment[location] = (agent_id, marker) def
check_marker(location): return
environment.get(location, None) # Agent 1 leaves a
marker leave_marker('agent1', 'A1', 'Resource
found') # Agent 2 checks for markers marker_info =
check_marker('A1') if marker_info: print(f"Marker
found by {marker_info[0]}: {marker_info[1]}")
```

Challenges in Agent Communication

- Interoperability: Ensuring that agents developed by different teams or using different technologies can understand each other.

- Scalability: Maintaining effective communication as the number of agents grows.

- Security: Protecting the communication from malicious agents or external threats.

Coordination Strategies

Coordination among agents is essential for dividing tasks, avoiding conflicts, and ensuring that the MAS operates efficiently. Some strategies include:

Task Allocation

Distributing tasks among agents based on their capabilities, current workload, or other criteria to optimize overall system performance.

```
# Example of a simple task allocation strategy def
allocate_tasks(agents, tasks): allocation = {} for
task in tasks: best_agent = min(agents, key=lambda
agent: agent.estimate_effort(task))
allocation[best_agent] = task return allocation
```

Negotiation

Agents can negotiate task responsibilities, resources, or other aspects through protocols such as the Contract Net Protocol (CNP).

Synchronization

Ensuring that agents working on interdependent tasks coordinate their actions so that the system operates smoothly.

Distributed Systems and MAS

MAS are inherently distributed, with agents potentially running on different machines. This setup presents unique challenges and opportunities:

Challenges

- Latency: Communication delays can affect the system's responsiveness and efficiency.
- Fault Tolerance: The system must continue to operate despite individual agent failures.
- Consistency: Ensuring that all agents have a consistent view of the system state can be difficult.

Opportunities

- Scalability: Distributed systems can easily scale up by adding more agents and resources.
- Robustness: The system can be more resilient to failures, as tasks can be reassigned to operational agents.

Swarm Intelligence

Swarm intelligence is a form of artificial intelligence inspired by the collective behavior of social colonies in nature, such as ants, bees, and birds. It is characterized by the emergence of complex, intelligent behaviors from simple agents following simple rules, without a centralized control structure.

Examples of Swarm Intelligence

- Ant Colony Optimization (ACO): Used for solving optimization problems by mimicking the pheromone trail-laying and following behavior of ants.

- Particle Swarm Optimization (PSO): Inspired by the social behavior of bird flocking or fish schooling, used for numerical optimization.

```
# Pseudocode for a basic Particle Swarm Optimization
for each particle in swarm: initialize particle
repeat until convergence: for each particle in
swarm: calculate fitness value if current fitness >
best fitness: update best fitness and position
update velocity and position based on personal and
global best
```

Benefits of Swarm Intelligence in MAS

- Flexibility: Easily adapts to changes in the environment.

- Scalability: Can efficiently operate with a large number of agents.

- Robustness: The system can continue to function even if several agents fail.

Multi-Agent Systems represent a powerful paradigm in artificial intelligence, enabling the development of complex, distributed, and adaptive systems. Through effective communication, coordination, and leveraging principles like swarm intelligence, MAS can solve problems that are intractable for individual agents. As we continue to explore the capabilities and applications of MAS, the potential for innovation in areas such as robotics, logistics, and environmental monitoring is immense. Understanding the foundational concepts and strategies discussed in this chapter is essential for anyone looking to develop or work with MAS.

Agent Communication

Effective communication is the backbone of multi-agent systems (MAS), enabling agents to share knowledge, negotiate tasks, and synchronize actions. Understanding the protocols and methods for agent communication is crucial for building robust MAS.

Communication Protocols

Communication protocols define the rules that agents follow when exchanging messages. Two widely used protocols in MAS are the Agent Communication Language (ACL) and the Foundation for Intelligent Physical Agents (FIPA).

- Agent Communication Language (ACL): ACL is a high-level protocol that provides a standardized framework for agent messages. It includes a set of performatives (action words) that specify the intent of each message, such as `request`, `inform`, or `refuse`.

```
Example Message: Performative: REQUEST Sender:
AgentA Receiver: AgentB Content: "Please provide
current weather data."
```

- Foundation for Intelligent Physical Agents (FIPA): FIPA defines a comprehensive architecture and set of interaction protocols for heterogeneous and interoperable MAS. It covers various aspects of agent communication, including message structure, interaction protocols, and agent management services.

Message Encoding

For agents to understand each other, the content of their messages must be encoded in a mutually understandable format. Two common formats are:

- XML: Extensible Markup Language (XML) is a flexible text format that can be used to encode messages in a structured way.

```
inform AgentA AgentB Current temperature is 22°C.
```

- JSON: JavaScript Object Notation (JSON) is a lightweight data-interchange format that is easy for humans to read and write and easy for machines to parse and generate.

```
{ "performative": "inform", "sender": "AgentA",
"receiver": "AgentB", "content": "Current
temperature is 22°C." }
```

> **Note:** When designing MAS, it's essential to choose a message encoding format that all agents can support and process efficiently.

Coordination Strategies

Coordination among agents is necessary to ensure that the system achieves its goals efficiently and effectively. There are several strategies for coordinating the actions of multiple agents:

Task Allocation

Task allocation involves assigning tasks to agents based on their capabilities, availability, and current workload. A common approach is the Contract Net Protocol (CNP), where an agent seeking assistance (the manager) sends a call for proposal (CFP) to other agents (the bidders). The bidders then submit proposals, and the manager selects the best offer.

Shared Goals and Plans

Agents can be designed to work towards shared goals, requiring them to develop and execute coordinated plans. This often involves planning algorithms that take into account the actions and plans of other agents to avoid conflicts and redundancies.

Synchronization

Synchronizing actions among agents is crucial, especially in time-sensitive applications. This can be achieved through explicit synchronization points in their plans or by using clocks and time-based protocols to ensure actions are carried out at the right moments.

Distributed Systems

MAS are often implemented as distributed systems, where agents operate on different processors or across networked computers. This setup enhances the system's scalability and fault tolerance but introduces challenges in terms of communication latency, data consistency, and system management.

Architectures for Distributed MAS

- Peer-to-Peer (P2P): In a P2P architecture, agents communicate directly with each other without a central coordinator. This can improve system resilience and scalability but may require more sophisticated discovery and routing mechanisms.

- Client-Server: In this architecture, agents (clients) communicate with one or more central servers that manage tasks, data, or coordination. This can simplify some aspects of system design but may create bottlenecks or single points of failure.

Handling Failures

In distributed systems, failures can occur at any time. MAS should be designed to handle agent failures gracefully, using strategies such as redundancy, where critical tasks are assigned to multiple agents, or recovery protocols that enable agents to take over tasks from failed counterparts.

Swarm Intelligence

Swarm intelligence is inspired by the behavior of natural systems, such as ant colonies or bird flocks, where simple agents follow simple rules but collectively exhibit complex, intelligent behavior.

Principles of Swarm Intelligence

- Decentralization: There is no central control; agents operate based on local information and simple rules.

- Scalability: The system can easily adapt to the addition or removal of agents.

- Robustness: The system can continue to operate even if individual agents fail.

Applications

Swarm intelligence principles are applied in various domains, including optimization problems (using algorithms like Ant Colony Optimization), robotics (swarm robotics for exploration or search and rescue missions), and network management.

By leveraging the principles of agent communication, coordination strategies, distributed systems, and swarm intelligence, developers can create sophisticated multi-agent systems capable of solving complex, real-world problems. The key to success lies in carefully designing the agents' abilities to interact and cooperate towards achieving their goals, ensuring the system is scalable, robust, and adaptable to changing environments.

Coordination Strategies

Achieving coherent behavior among agents in a multi-agent system (MAS) requires effective coordination strategies. Coordination ensures that agents work together towards common or complementary goals without conflict or redundancy, thereby improving the efficiency and effectiveness of the system as a whole.

Task Allocation

Task allocation involves distributing tasks among agents based on their capabilities, availability, and the overall goal of the system. A common approach is to use auction-based mechanisms, where tasks are bid on by agents, and the "winning" agent is assigned the task based on specific criteria such as lowest cost or shortest completion time.

```
# Simple Auction-Based Task Allocation Example tasks
= ['task1', 'task2', 'task3'] agents = {'agent1':
{'cost': 10, 'time': 2}, 'agent2': {'cost': 12,
'time': 1}, 'agent3': {'cost': 8, 'time': 3}} def
allocate_tasks(tasks, agents): allocation = {} for
task in tasks: best_agent, best_cost = None,
float('inf') for agent, details in agents.items():
if details['cost'] < best_cost: best_agent,
best_cost = agent, details['cost'] allocation[task]
= best_agent print(f'Task {task} allocated to
{best_agent}') return allocation
allocate_tasks(tasks, agents)
```

Note: Real-world task allocation in MAS is often complex and may require more sophisticated approaches, such as multi-round auctions or negotiation-based mechanisms, to deal with dynamic environments and incomplete information.

Synchronization

Synchronization is crucial for ensuring that tasks requiring concurrent actions from multiple agents are executed smoothly. For example, in a warehouse robot system, synchronization ensures that robots do not collide and that goods are transported efficiently.

A practical approach to synchronization is the use of shared schedules or clocks, where agents coordinate their actions based on a common time reference. Another method involves explicit synchronization messages that signal readiness or completion of tasks.

Conflict Resolution

Conflicts in MAS can arise from resource contention, inconsistent goals, or overlapping tasks. Effective conflict resolution strategies are necessary to prevent deadlock and ensure the system's goals are met.

One common approach is the use of negotiation protocols, where agents iteratively propose solutions until a consensus is reached. Another strategy is the establishment of priority rules, where conflicts are resolved based on predefined criteria, such as agent role or task urgency.

```
# Simple Priority-Based Conflict Resolution Example
conflicts = [('agent1', 'agent2'), ('agent2',
'agent3')] priorities = {'agent1': 1, 'agent2': 2,
'agent3': 3} # Lower number indicates higher
priority def resolve_conflicts(conflicts,
priorities): resolutions = [] for conflict in
conflicts: # The agent with higher priority wins
winner = sorted(conflict, key=lambda x:
priorities[x])[0] resolutions.append(f'{winner}
resolves conflict between {conflict}') return
resolutions print(resolve_conflicts(conflicts,
priorities))
```

Best Practices and Tips

- Understand the System's Goals: Clearly defining the system's objectives is crucial for selecting the appropriate coordination strategies.

- Scalability: Consider how coordination mechanisms will scale with the number of agents and the complexity of tasks.

- Flexibility: Implement coordination strategies that can adapt to changing conditions and unexpected events.

- Efficiency: Aim for coordination mechanisms that minimize communication overhead and computational complexity.

Common Challenges

Implementing effective coordination in MAS can be challenging due to issues such as:

- Scalability: As the number of agents and tasks increases, coordination becomes more complex and resource-intensive.
- Dynamic Environments: Changing conditions can render pre-established plans obsolete, requiring dynamic adjustment of coordination strategies.
- Incomplete Information: Agents may not have full knowledge of the system or other agents, leading to suboptimal decision-making.

Addressing Challenges

To overcome these challenges, developers can:

- Use Decentralized Approaches: Instead of central coordination, allow agents to make local decisions based on shared protocols and conventions.
- Implement Learning Mechanisms: Enable agents to learn from interactions and adapt their coordination strategies over time.
- Employ Robust Communication: Ensure reliable and efficient communication mechanisms to support coordination even in dynamic or uncertain environments.

By understanding and addressing these challenges, developers can create MAS that are both effective and resilient, capable of achieving complex goals through coordinated effort.

Distributed Systems

When discussing multi-agent systems (MAS), it's crucial to understand the role of distributed systems as a foundational technology. Distributed systems allow agents to operate on separate hardware while still communicating and coordinating their actions, essentially enabling the scalability and flexibility needed for complex MAS applications.

Understanding Distributed Systems

A distributed system is a network of autonomous computers that communicate with each other in order to achieve a common goal. This architecture is essential for multi-agent systems where agents might be spread across different locations, each performing tasks concurrently.

```
Key Characteristics: - Concurrency of components -
Independent failure modes - No global clock
```

These characteristics pose unique challenges in terms of data consistency, fault tolerance, and synchronization. However, they also allow for systems that are more robust, scalable, and flexible.

Implementation Challenges

Implementing a distributed MAS involves addressing several challenges:

- Communication: Agents must be able to exchange information reliably and efficiently, even in the presence of network failures or delays.

- Coordination: With no global clock, ensuring that agents work together in a coherent manner requires sophisticated synchronization mechanisms.

- Consistency: Maintaining a consistent view of the system's state across different agents can be complex, especially when data changes frequently.

- Fault Tolerance: The system must be capable of continuing operation even when individual agents or network components fail.

Practical Example: Distributed Task Allocation

Consider a scenario where multiple robots (agents) are deployed in a warehouse to pick and place items. These robots need to communicate with each other to avoid collisions and ensure that items are picked and placed efficiently.

```
# Simplified example of a message passing mechanism
between agents def send_message(receiver_id,
message): # Code to send a message to another agent
pass def receive_message(): # Code to receive
messages from other agents pass def
coordinate_pickup(robot_id, item_location): #
Example function to coordinate picking up an item if
is_nearby(robot_id, item_location):
send_message(robot_id, "Pick up item at " +
str(item_location)) else: # Find another robot
closer to the location other_robot_id =
find_nearest_robot(item_location)
send_message(other_robot_id, "Pick up item at " +
str(item_location)) def is_nearby(robot_id,
location): # Determine if a robot is near a specific
location pass def find_nearest_robot(location): #
Find the robot nearest to the specified location
pass
```

This example illustrates basic communication and coordination among distributed agents in a multi-agent system. Each robot agent communicates with others to ensure tasks are assigned efficiently based on proximity.

Best Practices for Distributed MAS

- Design for failure: Assume that components will fail and design the system to handle failures gracefully.
- Use standardized communication protocols: This ensures interoperability and simplifies the development of agent communication mechanisms.
- Implement scalable synchronization mechanisms: As the number of agents grows, synchronization becomes more challenging but is critical for system coherence.
- Prioritize security: In distributed systems, security issues like unauthorized access and data tampering are more prevalent. Secure communication channels and data validation are essential.

Troubleshooting Common Issues

- Network Delays and Failures: Implement retry mechanisms and timeouts for critical communications.
- Inconsistent Data: Use consensus algorithms or distributed ledgers to maintain data consistency across agents.
- Complex Debugging: Enhance logging and monitoring capabilities to trace issues across distributed components.

Distributed systems offer a powerful foundation for building scalable and flexible multi-agent systems. By understanding and addressing the inherent challenges, developers can create robust MAS that leverage the full potential of distributed computing.

Swarm Intelligence

Swarm intelligence stands as a compelling paradigm within the realm of multi-agent systems (MAS), drawing inspiration from the natural world's social organisms. This approach leverages the collective behaviors of simple agents, which, despite their individual simplicity, can accomplish complex tasks through interaction. Such systems are particularly noted for their robustness, scalability, and flexibility.

Fundamental Principles of Swarm Intelligence

Swarm intelligence is rooted in several key principles: decentralization of control, lack of a global model, simple rules followed by agents, and high levels of interaction. These principles enable the system to adapt dynamically to changing environments and to solve complex problems without a central command structure.

Example: Ant Colony Optimization

One of the most celebrated examples of swarm intelligence in action is Ant Colony Optimization (ACO). This algorithm mimics the behavior of ants searching for food. Each ant explores random paths, leaving behind a pheromone trail. Subsequent ants are likely to follow stronger pheromone trails, reinforcing the path to the food source. Over time, the most efficient route becomes the most traveled one, effectively solving optimization problems.

```
# Pseudocode for a simple Ant Colony Optimization
initialize pheromone levels while not converged: for
each ant: select path based on pheromone strength
update pheromone trail based on quality of solution
evaporate some pheromone to avoid convergence on
```

> **Note:** The efficiency of ACO and other swarm-based algorithms hinges on the balance between exploration (finding new paths) and exploitation (using known good paths).

Applications of Swarm Intelligence

Swarm intelligence is not just a theoretical concept but has practical applications across various domains. Among these, the most prominent include:

- Optimization Problems: From routing vehicles to scheduling tasks, swarm algorithms like ACO or Particle Swarm Optimization (PSO) offer powerful solutions.
- Robotics: Swarm robotics utilize the principles of swarm intelligence to coordinate the behavior of multiple robots, enabling them to perform tasks like area mapping or search and rescue operations without direct human intervention.
- Networks: In telecommunications, swarm techniques can optimize network routing and bandwidth allocation.

Challenges and Best Practices

Implementing swarm intelligence comes with its set of challenges. The initial setup of parameters (such as pheromone evaporation rate in ACO) can significantly affect the system's performance. Moreover, while decentralization is a strength, it can also lead to difficulties in controlling the swarm's overall direction.

To mitigate these challenges, it is advisable to:

- Start with simple models and gradually introduce complexity.

- Carefully analyze the problem domain to align with the strengths of swarm intelligence.

- Conduct extensive simulations to fine-tune parameters before deployment.

Swarm intelligence offers a unique and effective approach to designing multi-agent systems capable of solving complex problems through simple agent interactions. By understanding and applying the principles of swarm intelligence, developers can harness the power of collective behavior to create robust, adaptive, and efficient systems.

As we delve further into multi-agent systems, the next section will explore the integration of learning mechanisms within these systems, paving the way for even more dynamic and intelligent behaviors.

Chapter 11: AI Agents in Healthcare

Introduction to AI Agents in Healthcare

The healthcare sector has seen a significant transformation with the advent of artificial intelligence (AI). AI agents, in particular, are revolutionizing the way care is delivered, making processes more efficient and improving patient outcomes. These intelligent systems can analyze vast amounts of data, learn from it, and make decisions or recommendations based on their learning. This chapter delves into the practical applications of AI agents in healthcare settings, focusing on medical diagnosis assistance, patient monitoring, drug interaction analysis, and healthcare workflow automation.

Medical Diagnosis Assistance

The Role of AI Agents

AI agents in medical diagnosis work by processing and analyzing medical data, such as patient records, imaging scans, and genetic information. They use machine learning algorithms to identify patterns and anomalies that may suggest a particular diagnosis. This not only aids doctors in making more accurate diagnoses but also in detecting diseases at earlier stages.

Example: Deep Learning for Cancer Detection

One of the most notable examples is the use of deep learning models to detect cancerous tumors in imaging scans. These AI agents are trained on thousands of images to recognize the subtle signs of cancer, often with a higher degree of accuracy than human radiologists.

```
import keras from keras.models import Sequential
from keras.layers import Conv2D, MaxPooling2D,
Flatten, Dense # Example of a simple CNN model for
image classification def build_model(): model =
Sequential([ Conv2D(32, (3, 3), activation='relu',
input_shape=(64, 64, 3)), MaxPooling2D(pool_size=(2,
2)), Flatten(), Dense(128, activation='relu'),
Dense(1, activation='sigmoid') ]) return model model
= build_model() model.compile(optimizer='adam',
loss='binary_crossentropy', metrics=['accuracy']) #
Note: This code snippet is for illustration
purposes. Training and data preprocessing steps are
required.
```

Note: The success of these models depends heavily on the quality and diversity of the training data. Models trained on limited or biased datasets may not perform well across different populations.

Challenges and Solutions

One challenge in deploying AI for medical diagnosis is the lack of transparency in how these models make their decisions. This "black box" problem can be mitigated through techniques like model interpretability, which help explain the model's reasoning.

Another challenge is ensuring the privacy and security of sensitive medical data. Implementing robust data protection measures and using encrypted data for training AI models are essential steps to address these concerns.

Patient Monitoring

Continuous Health Monitoring

AI agents are increasingly used for continuous health monitoring, leveraging wearable devices and sensors that collect data on vital signs, physical activity, and other health metrics in real-time. These agents analyze the data to detect anomalies that may indicate a health issue or a deterioration in the patient's condition.

Example: Heart Rate Monitoring for Arrhythmia Detection

AI-powered devices can monitor heart rate data to detect arrhythmias, sending alerts to both patients and healthcare providers if irregular patterns are detected. This facilitates early intervention and can be life-saving in critical situations.

```
# Example of a simple anomaly detection algorithm
for heart rate monitoring def
detect_arrhythmia(heart_rate_data): # Assuming
heart_rate_data is a list of heart rate measurements
normal_range = (60, 100) # Normal resting heart rate
range in beats per minute anomalies = [hr for hr in
heart_rate_data if hr < normal_range[0] or hr >
normal_range[1]] return anomalies # Note: This is a
simplified example. Real-world applications use more
complex algorithms and consider more variables.
```

Challenges and Solutions

Ensuring the accuracy and reliability of the sensors and the AI algorithms is crucial in patient monitoring. Regular calibration of sensors and ongoing validation of AI models against clinical outcomes are necessary to maintain trust in these systems.

Privacy is another significant concern, especially when dealing with continuous monitoring. Transparent data handling policies and secure data transmission protocols are vital to protect patient privacy.

Drug Interaction Analysis

Predicting Adverse Drug Reactions

AI agents can analyze medical records and databases to predict potential adverse drug reactions (ADRs) by understanding the complex interactions between different medications, patient histories, and genetic factors. This capability is crucial in preventing harmful side effects and ensuring patient safety.

Example: Machine Learning for Identifying Drug Interactions

By training on historical data of known drug interactions and patient outcomes, AI models can predict how new or combination drugs might interact. This helps in making informed prescribing decisions.

```
import numpy as np from sklearn.ensemble import
RandomForestClassifier # Example of using a
RandomForestClassifier to predict drug interactions
def train_model(X_train, y_train): model =
RandomForestClassifier() model.fit(X_train, y_train)
return model # X_train represents features extracted
from the drug and patient data # y_train represents
labels indicating the presence or absence of adverse
reactions # Note: Actual implementation would
require a detailed dataset and feature engineering.
```

> **Warning:** While AI can significantly enhance drug interaction analysis, it cannot replace the clinical judgment of healthcare professionals. It should be used as a tool to support, not substitute, professional decision-making.

Challenges and Solutions

Data quality and completeness are major challenges in this area. Building comprehensive databases that include detailed drug information, patient histories, and genetic data is essential for effective AI analysis.

Another challenge is the dynamic nature of drug data, with new medications and findings emerging regularly. Continuous learning mechanisms for AI models are necessary to keep up with the latest information.

Healthcare Workflow Automation

Streamlining Operations

AI agents can automate routine tasks in healthcare settings, such as scheduling appointments, managing patient records, and processing insurance claims. This not only increases efficiency but also allows healthcare professionals to focus more on patient care.

Example: Natural Language Processing for Documentation

Natural Language Processing (NLP) AI agents can transcribe and analyze voice notes from doctors, automatically updating patient records with relevant information. This reduces the administrative burden on medical staff.

```
from transformers import pipeline # Example of using
a Hugging Face pipeline for transcription nlp =
pipeline("automatic-speech-recognition") # Assuming
audio_clip is an audio file of a doctor's voice
notes transcription = nlp(audio_clip) # The
transcription can then be processed and integrated
into the patient's record
```

Challenges and Solutions

The integration of AI into existing healthcare systems poses significant challenges, including technical compatibility issues and resistance from staff accustomed to traditional workflows. Providing adequate training and demonstrating the benefits of AI can help mitigate these challenges.

Ensuring the accuracy of AI-powered tools, especially in critical tasks like patient record management, is paramount. Rigorous testing and validation processes, along with clear protocols for human oversight, are essential for safe and effective implementation.

AI agents hold tremendous potential to improve efficiency, accuracy, and outcomes in healthcare. From assisting with medical diagnoses to automating administrative tasks, these intelligent systems can support healthcare professionals and patients in myriad ways. However, challenges such as data privacy, model transparency, and integration into existing systems must be carefully managed. With ongoing advancements in AI technology and increasing adoption in the healthcare sector, the future of AI agents in healthcare looks promising.

Practical Applications of AI Agents in Healthcare

In the realm of healthcare, AI agents are pioneering advancements that not only enhance the efficiency of medical professionals but also improve patient care. This section delves into the key practical applications of AI agents, providing insights into their operation and the benefits they offer.

Medical Diagnosis Assistance

AI agents have made significant strides in assisting with medical diagnoses. These intelligent systems are trained on vast datasets of medical records and images, enabling them to recognize patterns and anomalies that may elude human observers.

Example: Deep Learning for Cancer Detection

One notable application is in cancer detection, where deep learning models, a subset of AI, analyze medical images such as X-rays, MRIs, or CT scans to identify malignant tumors with high accuracy. For instance, a deep learning model developed for detecting skin cancer surpassed the diagnostic accuracy of dermatologists in a head-to-head comparison.

```
# Example of a simple deep learning model for image
classification from keras.models import Sequential
from keras.layers import Conv2D, MaxPooling2D,
Flatten, Dense model = Sequential([ Conv2D(32, (3,
3), activation='relu', input_shape=(64, 64, 3)),
MaxPooling2D(pool_size=(2, 2)), Flatten(),
Dense(128, activation='relu'), Dense(1,
activation='sigmoid') ])
model.compile(optimizer='adam',
loss='binary_crossentropy', metrics=['accuracy'])
```

Patient Monitoring

AI agents are also revolutionizing patient monitoring, particularly for those with chronic conditions or in critical care. By continuously analyzing data from wearable devices or bedside monitors, AI can predict adverse events before they occur, allowing for preemptive care interventions.

Real-World Use Case: Predictive Analytics in Heart Failure

An AI system designed for heart failure patients can analyze data from wearable devices, such as heart rate and activity level, to predict the risk of an imminent heart failure exacerbation. This enables healthcare providers to adjust treatment plans proactively, potentially saving lives.

Drug Interaction Analysis

With the growing number of medications prescribed to patients, the risk of adverse drug interactions increases. AI agents are adept at analyzing the potential interactions between thousands of drugs, identifying risks that may not be immediately apparent to healthcare providers.

Implementing AI for Drug Safety

AI models can process extensive pharmacological databases to predict interactions based on the chemical properties of drugs, their mechanisms of action, and patient-specific factors. This analysis can be integrated into prescribing systems, alerting physicians to potential problems before they occur.

Healthcare Workflow Automation

AI agents contribute to the automation of routine tasks in healthcare settings, freeing up medical staff to focus on more complex and patient-centered activities. This includes everything from scheduling appointments to managing patient records.

Case Study: Automated Patient Scheduling

An AI-powered system can analyze appointment requests, prioritize them based on urgency, and automatically schedule them in an optimal manner, considering the availability of medical staff and resources. This not only improves efficiency but also enhances patient satisfaction by reducing wait times.

Best Practices and Tips

To maximize the benefits of AI agents in healthcare, it is essential to adhere to best practices and understand the common challenges.

Data Privacy and Security

When implementing AI in healthcare, maintaining the confidentiality and security of patient data is paramount. It's crucial to comply with regulations such as the Health Insurance Portability and Accountability Act (HIPAA) in the U.S. and the General Data Protection Regulation (GDPR) in the EU.

Continuous Learning and Adaptation

AI models should be continuously updated with new data to improve their accuracy and relevance. This requires a feedback loop where outcomes are monitored, and the AI is refined based on real-world performance.

Interdisciplinary Collaboration

The development and integration of AI agents in healthcare require close collaboration between clinicians, data scientists, and IT professionals. This ensures that the solutions are not only technically sound but also clinically relevant and user-friendly.

Practical Exercise: Implement an AI Agent for Patient Triage

As a hands-on exercise, consider developing a simple AI agent that can triage patient inquiries submitted via an online portal. The agent should classify inquiries based on urgency and direct them to the appropriate department.

1. Collect and label a dataset of inquiry texts with categories (e.g., urgent, non-urgent, billing, appointment requests). 2. Train a natural language processing (NLP) model to classify the inquiries based on the text. 3. Integrate the model with the patient portal to automatically triage incoming inquiries.

This exercise not only reinforces the understanding of AI agent development but also highlights the potential for AI to streamline and improve healthcare processes.

In conclusion, AI agents hold immense potential to transform healthcare, making it more efficient, effective, and patient-centered. By carefully implementing and integrating these technologies, healthcare providers can significantly enhance the quality of care they deliver.

Patient Monitoring

AI agents have revolutionized patient monitoring by providing real-time, continuous surveillance of patient health metrics. These systems leverage a combination of wearable devices, embedded sensors, and machine learning algorithms to offer unprecedented insights into patient health, enabling early detection of potential health issues before they become critical.

Real-Time Health Data Analysis

AI agents analyze data from various sources, including wearables like smartwatches and medical devices like ECG or blood pressure monitors. They continuously assess health metrics, such as heart rate, blood pressure, glucose levels, and oxygen saturation, to identify abnormalities or trends that may indicate a deterioration in the patient's health.

```
# Example of a simple AI agent algorithm for
monitoring heart rate def
analyze_heart_rate(heart_rates): """Simple analysis
to identify abnormal heart rates.""" abnormal_rates
= [rate for rate in heart_rates if rate < 60 or rate
> 100] if abnormal_rates: return "Potential issue
detected" return "Heart rate within normal limits" #
Sample data heart_rates = [75, 77, 72, 110, 69, 85]
analysis_result = analyze_heart_rate(heart_rates)
print(analysis_result)
```

Predictive Health Insights

Beyond real-time analysis, AI agents employ predictive models to forecast potential health issues based on historical and current data. These models can predict the likelihood of future events, such as heart attacks or diabetic episodes, allowing for preemptive medical intervention.

> **Note:** The effectiveness of predictive insights depends significantly on the quality and quantity of data collected, highlighting the importance of comprehensive data integration.

Drug Interaction Analysis

One of the more complex challenges in healthcare is managing patient medications, especially considering potential adverse drug interactions. AI agents are increasingly used to automate the analysis of drug interactions, improving patient safety and treatment outcomes.

Automated Medication Management

AI agents can process vast databases of pharmaceutical compounds and their interactions. By analyzing a patient's current medications, these systems can identify possible adverse reactions and suggest alternatives or dosage adjustments.

```
# Example pseudo-code for drug interaction analysis
def check_drug_interactions(patient_medications):
```

```
"""Checks for potential drug interactions."""
interactions = [] for drug in patient_medications:
for other_drug in patient_medications: if
drug_interacts_with(drug, other_drug):
interactions.append((drug, other_drug)) return
interactions # Sample medication list
patient_medications = ["DrugA", "DrugB", "DrugC"]
potential_interactions =
check_drug_interactions(patient_medications) if
potential_interactions: print("Potential drug
interactions detected:", potential_interactions)
else: print("No drug interactions detected.")
```

Personalized Medicine

By integrating patient-specific data, such as genetic information and past medical history, AI agents can further refine their analysis, leading to highly personalized medication plans. This approach not only reduces the risk of adverse reactions but also enhances the effectiveness of treatments.

Healthcare Workflow Automation

AI agents are instrumental in streamlining healthcare workflows, from patient intake and scheduling to billing and claims processing. By automating routine tasks, these systems free up medical staff to focus on patient care, improving operational efficiency and reducing administrative burden.

Streamlined Patient Intake

AI-powered chatbots and virtual assistants can automate the initial stages of patient intake, gathering preliminary information and triaging patients based on urgency and medical need. This reduces wait times and ensures that patients receive timely care.

Efficient Scheduling and Resource Allocation

AI algorithms can optimize scheduling by analyzing patient appointments, healthcare provider availability, and resource requirements to minimize downtime and improve the utilization of medical facilities.

Automated Billing and Claims Processing

AI agents can also automate the billing and claims process, reducing errors and expediting reimbursements. By analyzing treatment codes and insurance policies, these systems ensure that claims are accurate and compliant, minimizing the risk of denial or delay.

The integration of AI agents in healthcare represents a significant leap forward in patient care and operational efficiency. From real-time patient monitoring to automated drug interaction analysis and workflow optimization, these intelligent systems are reshaping the healthcare landscape. As technology continues to evolve, the potential for AI agents in healthcare will only expand, promising a future where medical care is more personalized, proactive, and accessible.

Drug Interaction Analysis

The complexity and sheer one pre data one in understanding how different drugs so with each one pose significant challenges in more. AI one, per with the ability to process and analyze end datasets, their become per tools in their potential per interactions, enhancing patient safety, their optimizing one outcomes.

St Drug Interactions

AT interactions can alter the way pre medication works, potentially causing serious side effects end diminishing the my effect of one ar more dis. AI agents can sift through databases of drug information, patient records, and current medical research to predict and identify harmful drug interactions before they occur.

Example: AI-Powered Drug Interaction Checker

Consider an AI system designed to assist healthcare professionals by providing instant drug interaction checks. This system could be integrated into electronic health record (EHR) systems, automatically analyzing prescribed medications against a comprehensive database of known drug interactions.

```
def check_drug_interaction(drug_list): # This
function simulates checking for drug interactions #
In a real-world application, this would involve
querying a comprehensive drug interaction database
interactions = find_interactions(drug_list) if
interactions: return {"status": "Interactions
Found", "details": interactions} else: return
{"status": "No Interactions Found"} def
find_interactions(drug_list): # Placeholder for
interaction finding logic # In practice, this could
involve complex algorithms and data analysis return
"Possible interaction between Drug A and Drug B" #
Example usage prescribed_drugs = ["Drug A", "Drug
B", "Drug C"] result =
check_drug_interaction(prescribed_drugs)
print(result)
```

Note: The above code is a simplified example. In practice, the function `find_interactions` would involve sophisticated algorithms capable of analyzing interactions based on chemical properties, patient history, and other relevant factors.

Best Practices for Implementing AI in Drug Interaction Analysis

- Data Privacy and Security: Ensure that all patient data and drug information are handled in compliance with HIPAA and other relevant data protection regulations.

- Continuous Update and Validation: Drug databases and interaction algorithms should be regularly updated with the latest research findings and validated for accuracy.

- Integration with Healthcare Systems: Seamless integration with existing EHR and pharmacy management systems is crucial for the practical utility of AI-driven drug interaction analysis tools.

- User Training: Healthcare professionals should receive adequate training on how to interpret and act on the insights provided by AI systems.

Healthcare Workflow Automation

Streamlining administrative tasks and clinical workflows through AI agents not only increases efficiency but also allows healthcare providers to devote more time to patient care. Automation of routine tasks, such as scheduling, billing, and clinical documentation, is a key area where AI can make a significant impact.

Automated Patient Scheduling

AI-powered scheduling systems can optimize appointment bookings by analyzing patterns in no-show rates, appointment type durations, and patient preferences. This results in improved access to care, maximized resource utilization, and enhanced patient satisfaction.

Real-World Implementation Example

An AI scheduling assistant could automatically send appointment reminders, reschedule missed appointments, and adjust schedules in real-time based on cancellations or emergency cases. By integrating with the healthcare provider's calendar system, the AI assistant ensures optimal scheduling without manual intervention.

```
// Example of an AI scheduling assistant feature
function sendAppointmentReminders(appointments) {
appointments.forEach(appointment => { if
(shouldSendReminder(appointment.date)) { // Logic to
send reminder via preferred communication method
console.log(`Sending reminder for appointment on
${appointment.date}`); } }); } function
shouldSendReminder(appointmentDate) { // Determine
if a reminder should be sent based on current date
and appointment date const reminderThreshold = 2; //
days before appointment const daysUntilAppointment =
getDaysUntil(appointmentDate); return
daysUntilAppointment <= reminderThreshold; }
```

Warning: While automating scheduling can significantly enhance efficiency, it's essential to maintain a human-in-the-loop system for handling complex cases and exceptions that the AI might not be equipped to manage.

Challenges and Considerations

- Customization and Flexibility: The AI system must be customizable to adapt to the specific workflows and preferences of different healthcare facilities.

- Interoperability: Ensuring that AI systems can seamlessly communicate with various healthcare IT systems is crucial for effective workflow automation.

- User Acceptance: Encouraging adoption among healthcare staff requires demonstrating the tangible benefits of AI automation, addressing concerns, and providing adequate training.

By addressing these challenges, AI agents can revolutionize healthcare workflows, making them more efficient, accurate, and focused on patient care.

Chapter 12: AI Agents in Finance

AI Agents in Finance

The financial sector has experienced a significant transformation with the integration of Artificial Intelligence (AI). From automating stock trading to assessing risks and detecting fraud, AI agents are reshaping how financial institutions operate. This chapter delves into the various applications of AI agents in finance, offering practical examples and guidance on building and implementing these technologies.

Trading Algorithms

Trading algorithms are at the forefront of financial technology, leveraging AI to buy and sell stocks with minimal human intervention. These algorithms analyze vast amounts of market data, identify trading opportunities, and execute trades at speeds and volumes unattainable by human traders.

Understanding Algorithmic Trading

Algorithmic trading involves the use of complex AI models to make trading decisions based on market data analysis. These models can process historical and real-time data to forecast market movements and execute trades accordingly.

Example: Moving Average Crossover

A simple yet effective trading strategy is the Moving Average Crossover. It involves two moving averages of a stock's price: a short-term average and a long-term average. When the short-term average crosses above the long-term average, it's a signal to buy. Conversely, when it crosses below, it's a signal to sell.

```
import numpy as np import pandas as pd # Example
using pandas to calculate moving averages def
moving_average_crossover(data, short_window,
long_window): signals =
pd.DataFrame(index=data.index) signals['signal'] =
0.0 # Short moving average signals['short_mavg'] =
data['Close'].rolling(window=short_window,
min_periods=1, center=False).mean() # Long moving
average signals['long_mavg'] =
data['Close'].rolling(window=long_window,
min_periods=1, center=False).mean() # Create signals
signals['signal'][short_window:] =
np.where(signals['short_mavg'][short_window:] >
signals['long_mavg'][short_window:], 1.0, 0.0) #
Generate trading orders signals['positions'] =
signals['signal'].diff() return signals
```

Note: This code snippet is a simplified representation. In practice, trading algorithms are much more complex and need to account for various factors, including transaction costs and slippage.

Best Practices and Challenges

- Data Quality: Ensure the data fed into the algorithm is accurate and clean. Erroneous data can lead to misleading analysis and poor trading decisions.

- Backtesting: Always backtest your strategy on historical data before going live. This step helps identify potential issues and refine the algorithm.

- Risk Management: Implement strict risk management rules to protect against significant losses. This includes setting stop-loss orders and limiting the amount of capital allocated to any single trade.

Risk Assessment

AI agents also play a crucial role in risk assessment, helping financial institutions identify and mitigate potential risks. By analyzing historical data, AI models can predict the likelihood of default on loans, detect anomalies in investment portfolios, and more.

Credit Scoring Models

One common application is the development of credit scoring models. These models assess the creditworthiness of borrowers by analyzing their financial history, transaction behaviors, and other relevant data.

Example: Logistic Regression for Credit Scoring

```
from sklearn.model_selection import train_test_split
from sklearn.linear_model import LogisticRegression
from sklearn.metrics import classification_report,
confusion_matrix # Sample data preparation X =
data.drop('default', axis=1) # Features y =
data['default'] # Target variable # Splitting data
into training and test sets X_train, X_test,
y_train, y_test = train_test_split(X, y,
test_size=0.2, random_state=42) # Model training
model = LogisticRegression() model.fit(X_train,
y_train) # Predictions and evaluation predictions =
model.predict(X_test)
print(classification_report(y_test, predictions))
```

Warning: Credit scoring models must comply with legal standards and ethical considerations. It's crucial to ensure that these models do not discriminate based on race, gender, or other protected characteristics.

Fraud Detection

Fraud detection is another critical area where AI agents are making a significant impact. By analyzing transaction patterns and behaviors, AI models can identify suspicious activities and flag them for review.

Anomaly Detection Techniques

Anomaly detection techniques are widely used in fraud detection. These techniques identify outliers in data that deviate significantly from the norm, which could indicate fraudulent activity.

Example: Isolation Forest for Anomaly Detection

```
from sklearn.ensemble import IsolationForest #
Example dataset X = data # Assuming data is a
DataFrame with transaction features # Isolation
Forest model model =
IsolationForest(n_estimators=100,
contamination='auto') model.fit(X) # Detect
anomalies scores = model.decision_function(X)
outliers = model.predict(X) data['score'] = scores
data['outlier'] = outliers
```

Tip: Regularly update your fraud detection models to adapt to new fraud patterns and techniques. Fraudsters are constantly evolving their strategies, so staying ahead is key.

Financial Planning

AI agents assist individuals and organizations in financial planning, offering personalized advice based on financial goals, risk tolerance, and market conditions. They can automate budgeting, investment planning, and even tax optimization, providing a comprehensive financial planning service.

Robo-Advisors

Robo-advisors are AI-powered platforms that provide automated, algorithm-driven financial planning services with minimal human supervision. They make investment decisions based on the user's financial situation and goals.

Implementing a Basic Robo-Advisor

While building a fully functional robo-advisor requires complex algorithms and regulatory compliance, the concept can be illustrated through a simplified example.

```
def simple_robo_advisor(income, savings_goal,
risk_tolerance): # Simplified decision-making
process if risk_tolerance == 'high': investment =
'stocks' elif risk_tolerance == 'medium': investment
= 'mixed funds' else: investment = 'bonds'
savings_plan = savings_goal / 12 # Monthly savings
goal advice = f"To meet your savings goal, consider
investing in {investment} and saving {savings_plan}
monthly." return advice
```

> **Note**: Real-world robo-advisors use sophisticated models to evaluate thousands of investment options, adjusting recommendations based on market performance and the user's changing financial situation.

AI agents are revolutionizing the finance sector, offering unprecedented efficiencies in trading, risk assessment, fraud detection, and financial planning. By understanding and implementing these technologies, businesses and individuals can make more informed decisions, mitigate risks, and optimize financial outcomes. The practical examples and guidelines provided in this chapter serve as a foundation for exploring the vast potential of AI in finance.

Risk Assessment

Risk assessment is a crucial aspect of the financial sector, where AI agents can significantly contribute by evaluating the potential risks associated with investments, lending, and insurance policies. These agents utilize a variety of data sources, including market trends, historical data, and real-time events, to predict and quantify risk levels accurately.

Understanding Risk Assessment with AI

AI agents in risk assessment leverage machine learning models to analyze and interpret complex datasets. By training these models on historical data, AI agents can identify patterns and correlations that humans might overlook. This capability allows for a more nuanced understanding of risk, leading to better decision-making.

Example: Credit Scoring

One practical application of AI in risk assessment is in credit scoring. Traditional credit scoring methods rely on a set of predefined criteria, which may not always capture the nuanced financial behavior of individuals. AI agents, however, can analyze an individual's transaction history, spending patterns, and even social media activity to generate a more accurate credit score.

```
# Example Python snippet for a simple credit scoring
model from sklearn.ensemble import
RandomForestClassifier from sklearn.model_selection
import train_test_split import pandas as pd # Load
dataset data = pd.read_csv('credit_data.csv') #
Preprocess data # Assume 'data' has been
preprocessed X = data.drop('default', axis=1) y =
data['default'] # Split data into training and test
sets X_train, X_test, y_train, y_test =
train_test_split(X, y, test_size=0.2,
```

```
random_state=42) # Initialize and train model model
= RandomForestClassifier(n_estimators=100)
model.fit(X_train, y_train) # Evaluate model
accuracy = model.score(X_test, y_test) print(f'Model
Accuracy: {accuracy*100:.2f}%')
```

Note: The above code is a simplified example. In practice, the model would need extensive tuning and validation to ensure its reliability and accuracy.

Best Practices in AI Risk Assessment

1. Data Quality: Ensure the data used for training the AI models is of high quality, diverse, and representative of the scenarios the model will encounter. 2. Model Transparency: Use models that are explainable, allowing stakeholders to understand how risk assessments are made. 3. Continuous Learning: Implement systems for models to learn from new data and real-world outcomes to adapt to changing market dynamics.

Fraud Detection

Fraud detection is another area where AI agents bring substantial value to the financial sector. By identifying potentially fraudulent transactions in real-time, AI agents can significantly reduce financial losses and improve customer trust.

Techniques in AI Fraud Detection

AI agents in fraud detection often employ a combination of machine learning techniques, including anomaly detection, pattern recognition, and natural language processing, to identify suspicious activities.

Anomaly Detection

Anomaly detection involves identifying data points or behaviors that deviate significantly from the norm. AI agents can monitor transactions in real-time, flagging those that appear unusual based on learned patterns.

```
# Example Python snippet for anomaly detection from
sklearn.svm import OneClassSVM import numpy as np #
Simulated transaction data (amounts only for
simplicity) transactions = np.array([[10], [20],
[15], [5000]]) # Notice the outlier # Train anomaly
detection model model =
OneClassSVM(gamma='auto').fit(transactions) #
Predict anomalies preds =
model.predict(transactions) print(preds) # Output: [
1 1 1 -1] where -1 indicates an anomaly
```

Implementing Effective Fraud Detection Systems

1. Real-time Processing: Implement systems capable of processing and analyzing transactions in real-time to catch fraud as it happens. 2. Balancing False Positives: Tune detection models to minimize false positives, ensuring legitimate transactions are not unnecessarily flagged. 3. Adaptive Models: Continuously update models with new data to adapt to evolving fraud techniques.

Financial Planning

AI agents also offer innovative solutions in financial planning, helping individuals and businesses optimize their financial decisions based on predictive analytics and personalized recommendations.

Personalized Financial Advice

Through machine learning and data analysis, AI agents can provide personalized financial advice, considering an individual's financial goals, risk tolerance, and historical financial behavior.

Example: Investment Portfolio Optimization

AI agents can analyze market data, financial news, and an individual's financial history to recommend an optimized investment portfolio tailored to the individual's preferences and goals.

```
# Pseudo-code for portfolio optimization def
optimize_portfolio(historical_data,
user_preferences): # Analyze historical market data
# Factor in user preferences and risk tolerance #
Use optimization algorithms to suggest the best
portfolio return optimized_portfolio
```

Tip: Incorporation of user feedback loops can enhance the personalization and effectiveness of financial planning AI agents.

Challenges and Solutions

- Data Privacy: Ensuring user data is handled securely and in compliance with regulations is paramount.

- Complex Financial Products: Dealing with complex financial products requires sophisticated models that can understand and analyze a wide range of financial instruments.

- Adapting to Market Changes: Continuous learning mechanisms are necessary to adapt AI models to rapid market changes and new financial regulations.

By addressing these challenges, AI agents can significantly enhance risk assessment, fraud detection, and financial planning processes, making financial services more efficient, secure, and personalized.

Fraud Detection

Fraud detection represents a critical application of AI agents within the financial sector, aimed at identifying and preventing unauthorized financial activities. By leveraging advanced algorithms and machine learning techniques, these agents can analyze transactional data in real time to detect patterns indicative of fraudulent behavior.

How AI Agents Conduct Fraud Detection

AI agents in fraud detection employ a range of machine learning models, including decision trees, neural networks, and anomaly detection algorithms, to analyze transactions. These models are trained on vast datasets comprising both fraudulent and legitimate transactions to learn the distinguishing patterns.

For instance, a neural network might analyze factors such as transaction amount, location, frequency, and timing to determine the likelihood of fraud. An anomaly detection algorithm, on the other hand, focuses on identifying transactions that deviate significantly from a user's typical behavior, flagging these as potential fraud.

```
from sklearn.ensemble import IsolationForest import
numpy as np # Sample transaction data (amount,
location code, time since last transaction) X =
np.array([[200, 1, 5], [5000, 2, 0.5], [150, 1, 24],
...]) # Initialize the anomaly detection model clf =
IsolationForest(random_state=42) clf.fit(X) #
Predict anomalies (potential fraud) predictions =
clf.predict(X)
```

Important Note: It's crucial to continuously update the models with new data to adapt to evolving fraudulent strategies.

Real-World Use Cases

A notable example of AI in fraud detection is its implementation in credit card transactions. AI agents continuously monitor transactions, comparing each against established patterns of legitimate behavior and previously identified fraudulent transactions. When a suspicious transaction is detected, the agent can automatically flag it for review or even block the transaction, pending further investigation.

Another use case involves insurance claims, where AI agents analyze claims to identify patterns or anomalies that suggest fraud. This not only helps in preventing financial losses but also streamlines the claims process for legitimate cases.

Best Practices and Tips

- Data Privacy and Security: Given the sensitivity of financial data, it's essential to ensure that AI systems adhere to data protection regulations and employ robust security measures to prevent data breaches.

- Model Transparency: Financial institutions should strive for a level of transparency in their AI models to build trust among users and regulators. Explainable AI (XAI) techniques can help in this regard, making the decision-making process of AI agents understandable to humans.

- Continuous Learning: Fraudulent strategies are constantly evolving. It's important for AI agents to continuously learn from new data, adapting their detection algorithms accordingly.

Common Challenges

- False Positives: One of the major challenges in fraud detection is minimizing false positives, where legitimate transactions are incorrectly flagged as fraudulent. This requires a delicate balance in the sensitivity of the detection algorithms.

- Data Skewness: Fraudulent transactions are relatively rare compared to legitimate ones, leading to imbalanced datasets. Techniques such as oversampling the minority class or using anomaly detection algorithms can help mitigate this issue.

- Evolving Fraud Techniques: As detection methods improve, so do the strategies employed by fraudsters. Keeping the detection models up to date with the latest fraud trends is essential.

Actionable Steps

1. Data Collection and Preparation: Gather and preprocess transactional data, ensuring it's clean and formatted correctly

for model training. 2. Model Selection and Training: Choose appropriate machine learning models based on the specifics of the fraud detection task. Train the models using historical transaction data. 3. Evaluation and Deployment: Evaluate the models' performance using metrics like accuracy, precision, recall, and F1-score. Deploy the most effective models for real-time fraud detection. 4. Monitoring and Updating: Continuously monitor the performance of deployed models, and regularly update them with new data to maintain their effectiveness.

Implementing AI agents for fraud detection can significantly enhance the ability of financial institutions to prevent unauthorized transactions, protect customer data, and reduce financial losses. By following best practices and addressing common challenges, developers can build robust AI systems that effectively combat fraud in the dynamic landscape of the financial industry.

Financial Planning

Financial planning, an essential aspect of fiscal health for both individuals and organizations, benefits significantly from the application of AI agents. These agents can analyze vast amounts of financial data to provide personalized advice, automate budgeting, and enhance investment strategies.

The Role of AI in Financial Planning

AI agents in financial planning leverage machine learning algorithms and data analysis to offer insights and forecasts that were previously impossible or highly labor-intensive. They can process complex financial scenarios in real-time, considering an array of factors such as market trends, historical data, and personal financial goals.

Example: Personalized Investment Advice

Consider an AI agent designed to provide personalized investment advice. This agent uses historical market data, analyzes the user's financial goals, risk tolerance, and investment preferences to recommend a tailored investment portfolio.

```
# Pseudo-code example for a simple investment advice
AI agent def recommend_portfolio(user_profile,
historical_data): # Analyze user profile for risk
tolerance and investment goals risk_tolerance =
analyze_risk_tolerance(user_profile)
investment_goals =
analyze_investment_goals(user_profile) # Analyze
historical market data market_analysis =
analyze_market_data(historical_data) # Generate
personalized investment recommendations
portfolio_recommendations =
generate_recommendations( risk_tolerance,
investment_goals, market_analysis ) return
portfolio_recommendations
```

Note: The actual implementation would require a more complex algorithm, incorporating various machine learning models to analyze data and predict future market trends.

Best Practices in AI-based Financial Planning

Implementing AI in financial planning requires adherence to best practices to ensure accuracy, reliability, and user trust:

- Data Privacy and Security: Given the sensitive nature of financial data, it's crucial to implement robust data encryption and anonymization techniques to protect user information.

- Transparency: Users should be informed about how their data is used and how recommendations are generated, fostering trust.

- Continuous Learning: AI models should be regularly updated with new data to refine their predictions and adapt to changing market conditions.

Common Challenges and Solutions

- Data Quality: High-quality, accurate data is fundamental for reliable predictions. Regular data audits and cleaning processes can mitigate issues related to data quality.

- Model Complexity: Complex models may offer better accuracy but at the cost of interpretability. Balancing complexity with the ability to explain recommendations is essential.

- Regulatory Compliance: Financial services are heavily regulated. Ensuring that AI agents comply with relevant laws and regulations is paramount.

Practical Exercise: Building a Budgeting AI Agent

1. Data Collection: Gather historical financial data, including income, expenses, and savings. 2. Model Selection: Choose a machine learning model suitable for pattern recognition and prediction. Decision trees or linear regression models could be a good start. 3. Feature Engineering: Identify key features that affect budgeting, such as monthly income, regular expenses, and unexpected costs. 4. Training and Testing: Train your model with historical data and test its accuracy in predicting future expenses and savings. 5. Implementation: Develop a simple interface where users can input their financial data, receive budgeting advice, and track their spending against the AI-generated budget.

Implementing AI agents in financial planning offers the opportunity to revolutionize how individuals and organizations approach their financial health. By leveraging the power of machine learning and data analysis, these agents can provide personalized advice, enhance decision-making, and ultimately, contribute to more effective and strategic financial planning.

AI Agents for Fraud Detection

In the realm of finance, one of the most critical applications of AI agents is in fraud detection. With the increasing volume of online transactions, the potential for fraudulent activities has risen exponentially. AI agents, equipped with machine learning algorithms, play a pivotal role in identifying and mitigating these risks in real-time.

Understanding Fraud Detection with AI

Fraud detection involves identifying irregular patterns or anomalies that deviate from the norm in financial transactions. AI agents are trained on vast datasets of genuine and fraudulent transactions to learn these patterns. The use of deep learning, a subset of machine learning, has proven particularly effective in recognizing complex patterns that are indicative of fraudulent activity.

Example: Transaction Monitoring

Consider an AI agent designed for transaction monitoring. It continuously scans transactions, looking for anomalies such as unusually large amounts, transactions from a new location, or a sudden spike in activity. Here's a simplified example of how this might be coded:

```
def detect_fraud(transaction): if transaction.amount
> threshold_amount: return "High-risk transaction
detected." elif transaction.location not in
user_known_locations: return "Unusual location
detected." elif transaction.frequency >
user_average_frequency: return "Unusually frequent
transactions detected." else: return "No fraud
detected."
```

Note: This example is oversimplified for illustrative
purposes. Real-world AI fraud detection systems use
complex algorithms and consider numerous variables.

Best Practices in AI-Driven Fraud Detection

1. Data Quality: Ensure the data used to train the AI agent is
comprehensive, accurate, and relevant. Poor data quality can
lead to false positives or negatives in fraud detection. 2.
Continuous Learning: Fraud patterns evolve, so it's essential for
AI agents to continuously learn from new transactions and
feedback to stay effective. 3. Transparency and Explainability:
It's crucial for financial institutions to understand how AI
decisions are made, especially in sensitive areas like fraud
detection. This aids in compliance and trust-building.

Real-World Use Case: Credit Card Fraud Detection

A prominent application of AI in fraud detection is in
monitoring credit card transactions. AI agents analyze each
transaction in real-time, comparing it against learned patterns of
fraud. Suspicious transactions are flagged for further
investigation or blocked outright, significantly reducing the
incidence of fraud.

Challenges and Solutions

- False Positives: One challenge is the high rate of false positives, where legitimate transactions are flagged as fraudulent. To mitigate this, AI systems can be fine-tuned to be more accurate and incorporate feedback loops where human analysts review and correct the AI's decisions.

- Evolving Fraud Techniques: As fraud techniques evolve, AI models must adapt. Implementing adaptive learning, where the AI agent updates its models based on new fraud patterns, is crucial.

AI agents have revolutionized fraud detection in finance, offering a powerful tool to identify and prevent fraudulent activities. By understanding the principles of AI-driven fraud detection, implementing best practices, and overcoming common challenges, financial institutions can protect themselves and their customers from the ever-present threat of fraud.

Chapter 13: AI Agents in Education

Introduction to AI Agents in Education

The realm of education stands on the brink of a transformative shift, thanks to the advent and integration of Artificial Intelligence (AI) agents. These autonomous AI systems are not just revolutionizing the way educational content is delivered but are also personalizing the learning experience for students across the globe. This section delves into the foundational aspects of AI agents in education, exploring their potential to act as tutors, content generators, personalized learning facilitators, and automated assessment tools.

Personalized Learning with AI Agents

One of the most significant contributions of AI agents in education is their ability to tailor learning experiences to the individual needs of students. Unlike traditional educational models that adopt a one-size-fits-all approach, AI-powered systems analyze the learning habits, strengths, and weaknesses of each student to deliver customized content and assessments.

How AI Agents Personalize Learning

AI agents employ machine learning algorithms to process data on students' performance and learning styles. This data, gathered from quizzes, assignments, and interactive activities, enables the AI to identify patterns and preferences unique to each learner.

```
# Example Python code for a simple machine learning
model to personalize content from sklearn.cluster
import KMeans import numpy as np # Sample dataset:
student scores in quizzes (out of 10) student_scores
= np.array([[8, 7], [4, 5], [9, 9], [5, 3], [7, 8],
[6, 4]]) # Applying KMeans clustering to group
students based on performance kmeans =
KMeans(n_clusters=2,
random_state=0).fit(student_scores) # Predicting
clusters (learning groups) predicted_groups =
kmeans.predict([[9, 8], [3, 4]])
print(predicted_groups)
```

Note: This example uses KMeans clustering from the Scikit-learn library to group students based on their quiz scores, illustrating a basic form of personalization.

Challenges and Solutions

While the promise of personalized learning is vast, implementing it is not without challenges. Data privacy concerns, the complexity of accurately modeling student learning, and the need for extensive and diverse data sets to train algorithms are significant hurdles. Addressing these challenges requires robust data protection measures, interdisciplinary collaboration to develop sophisticated models, and ongoing efforts to ensure the diversity and inclusivity of data sets.

AI Tutoring Systems

AI tutoring systems represent another groundbreaking application of AI agents in education. These systems can guide students through learning materials at their own pace, provide immediate feedback, and offer explanations for complex concepts, functioning much like a human tutor but with unlimited patience and scalability.

Implementing AI Tutoring Systems

The development of an AI tutoring system involves the creation of a domain-specific knowledge base, a student model that adapts to individual learning progress, and a pedagogical model that dictates the teaching strategy.

```
// Pseudocode for a simple AI tutoring system
decision-making process IF student_answer is correct
THEN provide positive feedback move to next concept
ELSE identify mistake provide targeted explanation
offer similar problem for practice END IF
```

Warning: AI tutoring systems require careful design to avoid reinforcing misconceptions. The feedback loop should be designed to ensure that incorrect responses lead to constructive learning opportunities.

Real-World Example: Duolingo

Duolingo, a popular language learning app, leverages AI to offer personalized tutoring. It adapts the difficulty of exercises based on the learner's performance, ensuring that the pace and content are suitable for their skill level. This adaptive learning approach makes education more effective and engaging.

Content Generation by AI

AI agents are not only changing how we teach but also what we teach. Through content generation, AI can create educational materials, such as reading passages, problems, and even entire courses, tailored to specific subjects, difficulty levels, and learning objectives.

Techniques in AI-Generated Content

Natural Language Processing (NLP) and Generative Pre-trained Transformers (GPT) are at the heart of AI's ability to generate readable, coherent, and relevant educational content. These technologies enable AI to understand context, generate new content, and even interact with users in natural language.

```python
# Example Python code snippet using GPT-3 for
generating a math problem import openai
openai.api_key = 'your_api_key_here' response =
openai.Completion.create( engine="davinci",
prompt="Create a word problem involving linear
equations for a 9th-grade student.",
temperature=0.5, max_tokens=100, top_p=1.0,
frequency_penalty=0.0, presence_penalty=0.0 )
print(response.choices[0].text.strip())
```

Note: The example above uses OpenAI's GPT-3 to generate a math problem suitable for a 9th-grade student. This illustrates the potential of AI in creating customized educational content.

Ethical Considerations

The use of AI for content generation in education raises important ethical questions, particularly regarding accuracy and bias. Ensuring that the generated content is factually correct and free from biases is crucial. Regular oversight by educational professionals and continuous training of AI on diverse and accurate datasets are essential measures.

Assessment Automation

Automated assessments, powered by AI, are transforming the evaluation process in education by providing timely, objective, and personalized feedback to students. This automation extends to grading assignments, quizzes, and even essays, freeing up valuable time for educators to focus on teaching.

How It Works

AI systems use machine learning models to evaluate responses based on a set of criteria. For objective assessments, such as multiple-choice questions, the process is straightforward. However, assessing subjective responses, like essays, requires advanced NLP techniques to analyze content quality, coherence, grammar, and relevance.

```python
# Example Python code for automated multiple-choice
question grading def grade_mcq(answer_key,
student_answers): score = 0 for answer,
student_answer in zip(answer_key, student_answers):
if answer == student_answer: score += 1 return score
answer_key = ['A', 'B', 'C', 'D'] student_answers =
['A', 'B', 'D', 'D'] print(f"Student score:
{grade_mcq(answer_key, student_answers)}/4")
```

Warning: While automated assessments can significantly enhance efficiency, they should not entirely replace human evaluation, especially for complex and nuanced assignments. The human touch remains essential for providing context-specific feedback and addressing unique student needs.

The integration of AI agents into the educational sector holds the promise of making learning more accessible, personalized, and efficient. From personalized learning environments and AI tutoring systems to content generation and assessment automation, AI has the potential to significantly enhance both teaching and learning experiences. However, realizing this potential requires careful consideration of the challenges, including ethical concerns, data privacy, and the need for human oversight. As we continue to explore and expand the capabilities of AI in education, it is crucial to maintain a balanced approach that leverages technology to complement and augment human efforts rather than replace them.

Personalized Learning

The concept of personalized learning through AI agents involves tailoring educational content and learning paths to meet the unique needs and abilities of each student. Unlike traditional one-size-fits-all approaches, AI-driven personalized learning systems assess individual student performance, learning styles, and preferences to create a custom learning experience.

Implementing AI for Personalized Learning

To implement an AI-driven personalized learning system, educators and developers can follow these steps:

1. Data Collection: Gather data on students' learning styles, historical performance, and preferences. This can include quiz results, reading habits, and interaction data with previous learning material.

2. Machine Learning Model Training: Use the collected data to train a machine learning model. The model should be capable of identifying patterns and making predictions about the most effective learning strategies for each student.

```
from sklearn.model_selection import train_test_split
from sklearn.ensemble import RandomForestClassifier
# Example: Training a simple model for personalized
learning recommendations X_train, X_test, y_train,
y_test = train_test_split(student_features,
learning_outcomes, test_size=0.2) model =
RandomForestClassifier() model.fit(X_train, y_train)
```

3. Adaptive Content Delivery: Based on the model's recommendations, the learning platform dynamically adjusts the content, pacing, and learning methods to suit each student's needs.

Note: It's crucial to regularly update the model with new data to refine and improve the learning experience over time.

Benefits and Challenges

Benefits:

- Increased Engagement: Students are more likely to engage with content tailored to their interests and learning pace.
- Improved Outcomes: Personalized paths can address individual weaknesses, leading to better academic performance.
- Efficient Learning: Time is not wasted on material the student already understands, making learning more efficient.

Challenges:

- Data Privacy: Collecting and using data for personalized learning raises concerns about student privacy and data security.
- Bias in AI Models: If not carefully managed, AI models can inherit biases from their training data, potentially disadvantaging certain groups of students.

Tutoring Systems

AI-driven tutoring systems represent a significant leap forward in educational technology, offering students 24/7 access to personalized instruction and feedback.

Building an AI Tutor

An AI tutor system typically involves the following components:

- Natural Language Processing (NLP): Allows the AI to understand and interact with students in natural language.
- Content Knowledge Base: A comprehensive database of subject matter that the AI can draw upon to teach and answer questions.
- Adaptive Learning Algorithms: Adjust the difficulty and topics of questions based on the student's performance and progress.

```python
import nltk # Example: Using NLP for simple language
understanding in an AI tutor from nltk.chat.util
import Chat, reflections pairs = [ (r"Hi|Hello|Hey",
["Hello!", "Hey there!", "Hi there!"]), (r"How do
you work?", ["I analyze your questions and provide
the best possible answers based on my knowledge
base."]), ] chatbot = Chat(pairs, reflections)
chatbot.converse()
```

Real-World Use Cases

Duolingo: A popular language-learning platform that uses AI to personalize lessons and provide immediate feedback on exercises.

Khan Academy: Uses AI algorithms to offer practice exercises and instructional videos that adapt to the learner's pace.

Best Practices and Tips

- Continuous Feedback Loop: Implement mechanisms for students to provide feedback on the AI's responses and explanations, allowing for continuous improvement.

- Multimodal Learning: Incorporate visual, auditory, and interactive elements to cater to different learning styles.

- Ethical Considerations: Ensure the AI tutor promotes fairness, respects privacy, and avoids reinforcing stereotypes.

Content Generation

AI agents can also play a pivotal role in generating educational content, from creating personalized learning materials to generating new questions and exercises.

Techniques and Tools

- GPT (Generative Pre-trained Transformer): This AI model can generate coherent and contextually relevant text based on a given prompt, making it ideal for creating educational content.

```
from transformers import GPT2LMHeadModel,
GPT2Tokenizer tokenizer =
GPT2Tokenizer.from_pretrained('gpt2') model =
GPT2LMHeadModel.from_pretrained('gpt2') inputs =
tokenizer.encode("The fundamentals of quantum
mechanics are", return_tensors='pt') outputs =
model.generate(inputs, max_length=100,
num_return_sequences=5) for i, output in
enumerate(outputs): print(f"Generated Text {i+1}:
{tokenizer.decode(output,
```

```
skip_special_tokens=True)}")
```

- Automated Question Generation (AQG): Techniques for automatically generating quiz questions and answers from educational content, enhancing the breadth of learning materials.

Advantages and Limitations

Advantages:

- Scalability: Enables the rapid creation of a wide variety of learning materials.

- Customization: Can generate content tailored to the curriculum and individual learning needs.

Limitations:

- Quality Control: Automatically generated content may require human review to ensure accuracy and appropriateness.

- Complexity of Topics: AI may struggle with generating content for highly complex or nuanced subjects.

Assessment Automation

Automating the assessment process using AI can significantly reduce the workload on educators, provide immediate feedback to students, and personalize future learning experiences based on assessment outcomes.

Implementing Automated Assessments

- Designing AI-Graded Assignments: Create assignments that can be effectively graded by AI, such as multiple-choice questions, fill-in-the-blanks, or even short answer questions using NLP.

- Feedback Mechanisms: Develop systems that not only grade but also provide constructive feedback to help students learn from their mistakes.

```
# Example: Simple NLP for grading short answer
questions from sklearn.feature_extraction.text
import TfidfVectorizer from sklearn.metrics.pairwise
import cosine_similarity student_answer = "The
capital of France is Paris." correct_answer = "Paris
is the capital of France." vect =
TfidfVectorizer().fit([student_answer,
correct_answer]) vectorized =
vect.transform([student_answer, correct_answer])
similarity_score =
cosine_similarity(vectorized[0:1], vectorized)[0][1]
print(f"Similarity Score: {similarity_score}")
```

Challenges and Considerations

- Fairness and Bias: Ensure the AI grading system is fair and does not disadvantage any student group.

- Transparency: Students should understand how their work is graded and be able to contest grades they believe to be inaccurate.

AI agents offer a multitude of opportunities to enhance the learning experience, from personalized learning paths and 24/7 tutoring systems to content generation and automated assessments. While these technologies promise to revolutionize education, it's essential to approach their implementation with care, addressing challenges such as data privacy, bias, and ensuring quality. With ongoing advancements in AI and machine learning, the future of education looks increasingly personalized, accessible, and engaging.

Tutoring Systems

AI-powered tutoring systems represent a significant leap forward in educational technology, offering students personalized assistance similar to what they might receive from a human tutor but with the scalability and accessibility that digital platforms provide. These systems utilize natural language processing (NLP), machine learning (ML), and often speech recognition to interact with students, assess their understanding, and provide feedback or further explanation.

Key Components of AI Tutoring Systems

AI tutoring systems are built around several core technologies:

- Natural Language Processing (NLP): Enables the AI to understand and respond to student queries in natural language, making the interaction intuitive.

- Machine Learning Algorithms: These algorithms analyze student responses to tailor subsequent questions and material, ensuring that the difficulty level is appropriate and that students are challenged but not overwhelmed.

- Speech Recognition: For voice-enabled tutoring systems, speech recognition allows students to communicate verbally with the AI, making the learning experience more accessible and varied.

Building an AI Tutoring System

To build a basic AI tutoring system, you would start with defining the subject matter and scope. For instance, a math tutoring system might cover algebraic concepts. You would then gather or create a dataset of questions, answers, and explanations in this area.

1. Choose a Programming Language: Python is a popular choice due to its extensive libraries for AI, NLP (like NLTK, spaCy), and ML (like TensorFlow, PyTorch). 2. Develop a Knowledge Base: This involves creating a structured set of subject matter content, including questions, answers, hints, and explanations. 3. Implement NLP Capabilities: Use NLP libraries to process and understand student inputs. 4. Incorporate ML Algorithms: These algorithms will analyze student responses to adapt the difficulty and focus of questions and explanations. 5. Integrate Speech Recognition (Optional): If creating a voice-activated system, integrate speech recognition capabilities.

```
# Example: Simple NLP implementation for
understanding student queries import spacy nlp =
spacy.load("en_core_web_sm") # Load the English
tokenizer, tagger, parser, NER, and word vectors def
understand_query(query): doc = nlp(query) # Process
the query here (e.g., looking for specific keywords
or intents) return "processed query" # This is a
simplistic example. In practice, you would have a
more complex function to analyze and respond to the
query.
```

Note: Building an effective AI tutoring system requires a substantial dataset and significant tuning of the ML models to accurately interpret and respond to a wide range of student inputs.

Challenges and Solutions

• Understanding Natural Language: NLP is not perfect and can struggle with ambiguity or nuanced language. Enhancing the dataset and using context-aware NLP models can help.

- Adapting to Each Student: It's challenging to perfectly adapt to every student's learning style. Implementing a feedback loop where students can indicate if an explanation was helpful can refine the system's responses.

- Keeping Content Up-to-Date: Curriculums change, and educational content needs regular updates. Automating part of this process and involving educators in content review can mitigate this issue.

Content Generation

Another promising application of AI in education is automatic content generation. AI can create personalized learning materials, generate practice questions, or even produce entire educational courses.

Techniques for AI-Generated Content

- Natural Language Generation (NLG): AI systems use NLG to convert data into readable text, enabling the automatic creation of summaries, explanations, and content.

- Adaptive Learning Materials: AI algorithms analyze student performance to generate or recommend customized learning materials that address the student's weaknesses or gaps in knowledge.

Implementing AI for Content Generation

To implement AI-driven content generation, one would typically:

1. Define Content Parameters: What type of content needs to be generated? (e.g., practice questions, summaries, etc.) 2.

Select an AI Model: Choose an AI model suited for NLG tasks. GPT-3, for example, is a powerful model capable of generating high-quality text. 3. Train the Model: If necessary, train the model on domain-specific data to improve relevance and accuracy. 4. Integrate with Learning Management Systems (LMS): For seamless delivery, integrate the content generation system with existing LMS platforms.

```
# Example: Generating a summary with a pre-trained
model from transformers import pipeline summarizer =
pipeline("summarization") text = """Your long
educational text goes here.""" summary =
summarizer(text, max_length=50, min_length=25,
do_sample=False) print(summary[0]['summary_text'])
```

Warning: AI-generated content should be reviewed for accuracy and appropriateness before being used in educational settings.

Best Practices and Tips

- Quality Control: Regularly review and update the AI model to maintain high-quality output.

- Ethical Considerations: Be mindful of bias in AI-generated content and strive for inclusivity and fairness.

- User Feedback: Incorporate user feedback mechanisms to refine and improve the content generation process.

By harnessing AI for tutoring systems and content generation, educators can provide more personalized, engaging, and effective learning experiences. However, it's crucial to navigate the challenges thoughtfully and ensure that these technologies complement traditional teaching methods rather than replace them.

Content Generation

With the advancement of AI technologies, content generation has become an increasingly viable tool for educational purposes. AI agents can now create educational content, including quizzes, textbooks, and even interactive learning modules, tailored to fit the curriculum and the individual needs of students. This section explores how AI agents facilitate content generation and the impact this has on education.

Automated Quiz Creation

AI agents can generate quizzes based on the material covered in textbooks or lectures, making the process of assessing students' understanding more efficient. For example, an AI agent can analyze a chapter of a textbook and formulate multiple-choice questions, true/false statements, or short-answer questions.

```
# Example of a simple AI-based quiz generator from
text_analysis_tools import analyze_text,
generate_questions text = """The water cycle, also
known as the hydrological cycle, is the process by
which water circulates between the earth's oceans,
atmosphere, and land, involving precipitation as
rain and snow, drainage in streams and rivers, and
return to the atmosphere by evaporation and
transpiration.""" # Analyze the text to identify key
concepts key_concepts = analyze_text(text) #
Generate quiz questions based on key concepts
questions = generate_questions(key_concepts) for
question in questions: print(question)
```

Note: The above code is a simplified illustration. Real-world applications would require more sophisticated NLP and ML models to accurately generate relevant and challenging questions.

Customized Textbook Generation

AI agents can compile and customize textbooks to match the syllabus of a course or the learning pace and style of individual students. By analyzing existing educational resources, AI can recommend or create chapters that cover all necessary topics in a manner that is most suitable for the student's learning.

Interactive Learning Modules

Interactive learning modules created by AI agents offer an engaging alternative to traditional learning methods. These modules can include simulations, virtual lab experiments, and interactive scenarios that adapt based on the student's responses and progress. Such an approach not only makes learning more engaging but also enhances understanding by allowing students to experiment and observe outcomes in a controlled, virtual environment.

Assessment Automation

Assessment automation is another crucial area where AI agents are making significant inroads. By automating the grading process and providing instant feedback to students, AI agents can significantly reduce the workload on educators and allow them to focus more on teaching and less on administrative tasks.

Automated Grading

AI agents equipped with NLP capabilities can grade open-ended responses as well as structured assignments like quizzes and multiple-choice tests. These agents can understand the context of the answer, compare it with the expected response, and even provide constructive feedback.

```
# Example of AI-based automated grading from
grading_agent import GradeEssay essay_text = "Here
is an essay submitted by a student."
expected_keywords = ["hydrological cycle",
"evaporation", "precipitation"] grade, feedback =
GradeEssay(essay_text, expected_keywords)
print(f"Grade: {grade}, Feedback: {feedback}")
```

Instant Feedback

Providing instant feedback is crucial for the learning process, as it allows students to understand their mistakes and learn from them immediately. AI agents can offer personalized feedback on a wide range of assignments, enabling students to improve their skills more efficiently.

Challenges and Best Practices

While AI agents offer numerous benefits in the education sector, there are challenges to consider, such as ensuring content accuracy, maintaining privacy and security, and avoiding bias in automated assessments. Best practices include continuous monitoring and updating of AI models, incorporating feedback from educators and students, and adhering to ethical guidelines in AI development and deployment.

By addressing these challenges and following best practices, AI agents can significantly enhance the educational experience, offering personalized, efficient, and engaging learning opportunities to students worldwide.

Chapter 14: AI Agents in Customer Service

Introduction to AI Agents in Customer Service

Customer service is a critical component of any business, directly impacting customer satisfaction, retention, and the overall success of the company. With the advent of artificial intelligence (AI), businesses now have the opportunity to enhance their customer service operations by deploying AI agents. These agents, often referred to as chatbots, are programmed to interact with customers, answer inquiries, and solve problems, mimicking human-like interactions. This section delves into the fundamentals of using AI agents in customer service, covering their development, integration, and the benefits they offer to both businesses and customers.

Building Chatbots for Customer Service

Chatbots are at the forefront of AI application in customer service, providing an immediate, 24/7 response mechanism to customer inquiries. The development of a chatbot involves several key steps, beginning with defining its purpose and scope.

Defining Chatbot Objectives

Before diving into the technicalities of chatbot development, it's crucial to identify the chatbot's primary objectives. These objectives might include answering frequently asked questions (FAQs), guiding customers through troubleshooting processes, or even making product recommendations. Having clear objectives helps in designing the chatbot's conversation flow and determining the necessary AI technologies, such as natural language processing (NLP) and machine learning (ML).

Implementing NLP and ML

NLP and ML are the backbone technologies that enable chatbots to understand and generate human-like responses. Here's a basic example of implementing NLP in a chatbot:

```
from nltk.chat.util import Chat, reflections pairs =
[ (r'hi|hello', ['Hello! How can I assist you
today?']), (r'(.*) issue with (.*)', ['I understand
you have an issue with %2, could you provide more
details?']), (r'bye|thank you', ['You're welcome!
Have a great day.']) ] chatbot = Chat(pairs,
reflections) chatbot.converse()
```

This simple example uses the Natural Language Toolkit (NLTK) in Python, showcasing how a chatbot can be programmed to respond to basic customer inputs. For more sophisticated interactions, developers can leverage advanced ML models to enable the chatbot to learn from interactions and improve its responses over time.

User Experience and Interface Design

The effectiveness of a chatbot significantly depends on its user experience (UX) and interface design. Chatbots should be designed to facilitate easy and natural conversations. This involves using conversational prompts, providing clear responses, and incorporating fallback strategies for when the chatbot fails to understand a query.

> **Note:** Always design chatbots with escalation paths to human agents for complex issues that the AI cannot resolve. This ensures that customer inquiries are not left unanswered.

Integrating Chatbots into Customer Service Platforms

Once the chatbot is developed, the next step is its integration into existing customer service platforms. This could include websites, mobile apps, or social media platforms. Integration involves:

- API Connections: Establishing API connections between the chatbot and the business's customer relationship management (CRM) system allows for seamless data exchange and personalization of customer interactions.

- Omnichannel Support: For businesses present on multiple platforms, creating an omnichannel support system ensures that customers receive consistent service across all channels.

- Testing and Feedback: Before full deployment, it's critical to test the chatbot across various scenarios and gather feedback to make necessary adjustments.

Ticket Management with AI

Beyond chatbots, AI agents can significantly enhance ticket management in customer service. AI can automatically categorize, prioritize, and assign tickets based on their content and urgency. This automation speeds up response times and frees human agents to focus on more complex issues.

Implementing AI in ticket management requires training models on historical ticket data, enabling the AI to learn and make informed decisions. Integration with the CRM system is also essential for a holistic view of customer interactions.

Analyzing Customer Interactions for Service Improvement

AI agents can do more than just interact with customers; they can also analyze these interactions to identify trends, customer sentiment, and areas for improvement. Using AI for customer interaction analysis involves:

- Sentiment Analysis: Determining the customer's sentiment (positive, negative, neutral) towards the service or product.

- Trend Identification: Identifying common issues or questions, which can inform FAQs or product improvements.

- Personalization: Tailoring responses and recommendations based on the customer's history and preferences.

Best Practices and Tips

- Privacy and Transparency: Always inform customers when they are interacting with AI and ensure data privacy and security practices are in place.

- Continuous Learning: Regularly update and train your AI models with new data to improve accuracy and effectiveness.

- Human-in-the-loop (HITL): Even with advanced AI, having a human-in-the-loop approach ensures that complex issues are handled appropriately, and AI decisions are monitored for accuracy.

Challenges and Solutions

Implementing AI in customer service is not without its challenges, including data privacy concerns, the potential for misinterpretation by AI, and the need for continuous model training. To mitigate these challenges:

- Data Privacy: Implement stringent data handling and privacy policies, and use anonymization techniques where possible.

- AI Misinterpretation: Incorporate multiple layers of validation and escalation paths to human agents to catch and correct misinterpretations.

- Continuous Training: Establish a routine for periodically training the AI models on new data, incorporating feedback from both customers and human agents.

Integrating AI agents into customer service can significantly enhance the efficiency and quality of customer interactions. By building and deploying chatbots, automating ticket management, and analyzing customer interactions, businesses can provide a more personalized and responsive service. However, it's essential to approach implementation with a focus on privacy, transparency, and continuous improvement to overcome the potential challenges and maximize the benefits of AI in customer service.

Building Effective Chatbots

Chatbots are at the forefront of enhancing customer service through AI. Creating a chatbot that is both effective and user-friendly requires careful planning, development, and continuous improvement. Here, we delve into the essentials of building chatbots that genuinely enhance the customer service experience.

Understanding User Needs

The first step in developing a chatbot is understanding the specific needs of your users. This involves analyzing customer queries, identifying common issues, and determining the types of interactions that can be automated. For instance, if a significant portion of customer queries involves tracking orders, your chatbot should be designed to handle such requests efficiently.

```
# Example: Intent recognition for order tracking
from intent_recognition_module import
IntentRecognizer recognizer = IntentRecognizer()
intent = recognizer.recognize("Where is my order?")
if intent == "order_tracking": # Proceed with order
tracking logic
```

Designing Conversational Flows

Once you've identified the key functionalities, the next step is designing conversational flows. This involves mapping out how the chatbot will interact with users, from greeting messages to handling various types of inquiries. It's crucial to design these flows to be as intuitive and natural as possible.

```
# Example: Conversational flow for order tracking
conversational_flow = { "greeting": "Hello! How can
I help you today?", "order_tracking": { "query":
"Please provide your order number.", "response":
"Your order is on its way and should arrive by
[date]." }, "fallback": "I'm sorry, I didn't
understand that. Can you rephrase?" }
```

Implementing Natural Language Processing (NLP)

To process and understand user queries effectively,
chatbots must leverage Natural Language Processing (NLP).
NLP allows chatbots to parse human language, identify
intentions, and respond in a way that mimics human
conversation. Many frameworks and libraries, such as NLTK,
spaCy, and TensorFlow, offer robust NLP capabilities.

```
# Example: Basic NLP with spaCy import spacy nlp =
spacy.load("en_core_web_sm") doc = nlp("I'd like to
know the status of my order.") for token in doc:
print(token.text, token.lemma_, token.pos_)
```

Continuous Learning and Improvement

A key aspect of maintaining an effective chatbot is the
ability to learn from interactions and improve over time. This
can be achieved through machine learning techniques, where
the chatbot is trained on a dataset of customer interactions and
continuously updated based on new data.

```
# Example: Updating chatbot model with new data from
chatbot_model import ChatbotModel model =
ChatbotModel() new_data = [("How can I return an
item?", "returns_policy")] model.update(new_data)
```

Ticket Management with AI

Beyond chatbots, AI agents can significantly enhance ticket management systems. By automating ticket categorization, prioritization, and routing, businesses can improve response times and resolution rates.

Automating Ticket Categorization

Using AI to automatically categorize tickets as they come in can save valuable time and ensure that issues are directed to the appropriate teams. This can be achieved through keyword analysis or more sophisticated NLP techniques.

```
# Example: Ticket categorization with keyword
matching def categorize_ticket(description):
keywords = { "refund": "billing", "broken":
"technical support", "delivery": "logistics" } for
keyword, category in keywords.items(): if keyword in
description.lower(): return category return "general
inquiries"
```

Prioritizing Tickets

AI can also assess the urgency of tickets, prioritizing them based on predefined criteria, such as the severity of the issue or the customer's status. This ensures that critical issues are addressed promptly.

```
# Example: Ticket prioritization based on severity
def prioritize_ticket(category, description): if
"urgent" in description.lower() or category ==
"technical support": return "high" else: return
"low"
```

Routing Tickets to the Right Team

Finally, AI can facilitate the routing of tickets to the appropriate team or individual, based on the issue category, team availability, or expertise required. This streamlines the resolution process, leading to higher customer satisfaction.

```
# Example: Routing tickets based on expertise def
route_ticket(category): team_expertise = {
"billing": "Finance Team", "technical support":
"Tech Support Team", "logistics": "Logistics Team" }
return team_expertise.get(category, "Customer
Service Team")
```

Best Practices and Tips

When implementing AI in customer service, there are several best practices to follow:

- Start small and scale gradually: Begin with simple automations and gradually introduce more complex AI functionalities based on feedback and performance.

- Focus on user experience: Ensure that interactions with AI agents are seamless, intuitive, and as human-like as possible.

- Monitor and iterate: Regularly review the performance of AI agents, gather user feedback, and make necessary adjustments to improve effectiveness and accuracy.

- Ensure privacy and security: Be transparent about the use of AI in customer interactions and ensure that all data is handled securely in compliance with relevant regulations.

By following these guidelines and continuously improving based on real-world feedback, businesses can leverage AI to significantly enhance their customer service operations, leading to increased customer satisfaction and loyalty.

Implementing Ticket Management Systems

Ticket management is a critical component of customer service that can be significantly enhanced through the use of AI agents. By automating the ticketing process, businesses can streamline operations, reduce response times, and improve overall customer satisfaction.

Basics of Ticket Management

At its core, a ticket management system is designed to track and handle customer service requests efficiently. This system collects customer issues, categorizes them for easy triage, and assigns them to the appropriate service representative. Implementing AI into this system can automate these processes, making them more efficient and effective.

```
# Example of a simple ticket categorization using
Python import re def
categorize_ticket(ticket_description): if
re.search(r'\b(error|issue|bug)\b',
ticket_description, re.I): return 'Technical
```

```
Support' elif
re.search(r'\b(refund|return|exchange)\b',
ticket_description, re.I): return 'Sales Support'
else: return 'General Inquiry' # Sample ticket
description ticket_description = "I'm having an
issue with my recent purchase and would like to
request a refund." category =
categorize_ticket(ticket_description) print(f"Ticket
Category: {category}")
```

This example uses basic Python code with regular expressions to categorize tickets based on keywords found in the ticket description. While simple, it demonstrates the foundational logic behind more complex AI-driven categorization systems.

Automating Response Generation

AI can not only categorize tickets but also generate initial responses to common queries. This can significantly reduce the workload on customer service representatives, allowing them to focus on more complex issues.

```
# Example of automated response generation def
generate_response(category): responses = {
'Technical Support': "Thank you for reaching out.
Can you provide more details about the issue you're
facing?", 'Sales Support': "We're sorry to hear
about your experience. Could you provide your order
number?", 'General Inquiry': "Thank you for your
inquiry. How can we assist you today?" } return
responses.get(category, "Thank you for contacting
us. We will get back to you shortly.") # Using the
previously determined category response =
generate_response(category) print(f"Automated
Response: {response}")
```

Best Practices and Challenges

Implementing AI in ticket management requires careful consideration of several best practices and potential challenges:

- Data Privacy and Security: Ensure that the AI system complies with data protection regulations and safeguards customer information.

- Continuous Learning: AI models should be continuously trained on new data to improve their accuracy and effectiveness over time.

- User Feedback Integration: Incorporate user feedback into the AI model's training process to refine its responses and categorizations.

Note: One common challenge is maintaining the balance between automation and human touch. It's crucial to determine which cases should be escalated to human agents to preserve the quality of customer service.

Analyzing Customer Interactions

Beyond handling individual tickets, AI agents can analyze overall customer interaction patterns to identify trends, pain points, and opportunities for service improvement.

Sentiment Analysis

Sentiment analysis involves evaluating customer feedback, reviews, and interactions to gauge overall sentiment towards the company or product. This can help businesses identify areas that require attention or improvement.

```
# Example of sentiment analysis using Python from
textblob import TextBlob feedback = "I love this
product! It has made my life so much easier." blob =
TextBlob(feedback) sentiment =
blob.sentiment.polarity # Ranges from -1 (negative)
to 1 (positive) print(f"Sentiment Score:
{sentiment}")
```

Trend Analysis

AI can also be used to identify trends in customer service requests, such as an increase in technical issues after a product update. This information can guide businesses in proactively addressing potential problems.

Implementing Service Automation

Service automation, powered by AI, can transform the customer experience by providing faster resolutions, personalized interactions, and 24/7 support availability. It's important to integrate these systems seamlessly with existing customer service processes to enhance, rather than replace, the human element.

> **Warning**: Over-reliance on automation can lead to customer frustration if AI agents are unable to address complex or nuanced issues. Always provide an easy option for customers to escalate their concerns to a human agent.

By leveraging AI in ticket management and customer interaction analysis, businesses can achieve a higher level of service efficiency and customer satisfaction. However, the key to success lies in the thoughtful implementation and continuous improvement of these technologies.

Analyzing Customer Interactions

Analyzing customer interactions is paramount in refining the customer service experience. AI agents can be employed to scrutinize conversations, emails, and feedback, identifying patterns and insights that can lead to improved service strategies.

Understanding Sentiment Analysis

Sentiment analysis is a technique used by AI to interpret and classify emotions within text data. This method allows AI agents to gauge customer satisfaction, detect frustration, and even predict potential churn by analyzing the tone and context of customer communications.

```
from textblob import TextBlob text = "I'm really
disappointed with the service I received." blob =
TextBlob(text) sentiment = blob.sentiment.polarity
print("Sentiment Polarity:", sentiment)
```

This code snippet demonstrates a basic sentiment analysis using TextBlob, a Python library. A sentiment polarity score closer to -1 indicates a negative sentiment, while a score closer to 1 suggests a positive sentiment.

Note: While sentiment analysis can provide valuable insights into customer emotions, it's important to remember its limitations. Sarcasm, slang, and nuanced language can sometimes lead to inaccurate interpretations.

Implementing Chat Analysis

Beyond sentiment analysis, AI agents can dissect chat logs and email threads to identify common issues, track resolution times, and even automate responses to frequently asked questions. This level of analysis can highlight operational inefficiencies and training opportunities for customer service representatives.

Implementing chat analysis involves: 1. Collecting data: Ensure that you have permission to analyze customer interactions. 2. Processing data: Cleanse the data for analysis, removing any irrelevant content or personal information. 3. Analyzing data: Use natural language processing (NLP) tools to examine the content for insights. 4. Acting on insights: Use the analysis to inform decisions on training, process improvements, and AI agent responses.

Real-World Use Case: Telecommunication Company

A leading telecommunication company implemented AI agents to analyze customer service chats. By identifying the most common issues faced by customers, the company was able to create a targeted FAQ section on their website. This move significantly reduced the volume of incoming customer service requests, allowing agents to focus on more complex issues.

Service Automation

Automating aspects of customer service can dramatically improve efficiency and customer satisfaction. AI agents can be programmed to handle routine inquiries, process transactions, and more, freeing human agents to tackle more nuanced and complex problems.

Building an Automated Response System

An effective automated response system can resolve common queries without human intervention. Here are steps to build one:

1. Identify common queries: Use chat analysis to determine the most common customer questions. 2. Script responses: Create clear, concise responses to these common questions. 3. Implement an AI agent: Use an AI framework to develop an agent that can understand customer queries and deliver the scripted responses. 4. Continuous improvement: Regularly update the response scripts and AI agent's understanding based on customer interaction analysis.

```
# Example of a simple automated response system from
simpleai import text_response query = "What are your
opening hours?" response = text_response(query)
print(response)
```

> **Warning:** Always offer an option for customers to escalate their query to a human agent. Automation should enhance, not replace, human interaction.

Best Practices and Tips

• Transparency: Clearly communicate to customers when they are interacting with an AI agent.

- Escalation Path: Ensure there's a smooth transition from AI to human support.

- Monitoring and Feedback: Regularly review the performance of AI systems and incorporate customer feedback for improvements.

Common Challenges

- Language and Dialects: AI agents may struggle with understanding diverse languages and dialects.

- Complex Queries: Some queries are too complex for AI agents and require human intervention.

- Customer Resistance: Some customers may be resistant to interacting with AI agents, preferring human contact.

By leveraging AI for analyzing customer interactions and automating services, businesses can significantly enhance their customer service efficiency and effectiveness. However, it's crucial to balance automation with human touch to cater to diverse customer preferences and needs.

Chapter 15: AI Agents in Smart Homes

Introduction to Smart Home AI Agents

Smart homes, equipped with interconnected devices and sensors, offer a fertile ground for deploying AI agents. These agents can manage, control, and automate various aspects of home life, making it more convenient, efficient, and secure. From adjusting the thermostat to optimizing energy usage, AI agents can learn from your habits and make decisions on your behalf, often in ways that are imperceptible yet profoundly impactful.

What is a Smart Home AI Agent?

A Smart Home AI Agent is a software entity that performs tasks for its user based on its environment, user inputs, and pre-defined objectives. It can control smart devices, manage tasks, and even learn from user interactions to improve over time. Unlike traditional automation systems, AI agents in smart homes are capable of more complex decision-making processes, thanks to advancements in AI and machine learning technologies.

The Role of AI Agents in Home Automation

Home automation involves the control of household appliances, lighting, climate, entertainment systems, and security devices. AI agents elevate home automation by introducing adaptive learning capabilities, allowing the system to recognize patterns in user behavior and adjust controls accordingly.

- Device Control: AI agents can manage a wide array of smart home devices, from thermostats and lights to smart locks and cameras, often through voice commands or mobile apps.

- Energy Management: By analyzing usage patterns and environmental data, AI agents can optimize energy consumption, leading to cost savings and reduced environmental impact.

- Security Systems: Enhanced with AI, home security systems can differentiate between normal activity and potential threats, alerting homeowners and authorities when necessary.

- Personal Assistance: Beyond managing physical devices, AI agents offer personalized assistance, like setting reminders, providing weather updates, and integrating with calendars and emails.

Building a Basic Smart Home AI Agent

Creating a simple AI agent for smart home control involves understanding the basics of AI, programming, and the smart home ecosystem. For our example, we'll focus on a basic agent that can control a smart light bulb based on time and ambient light conditions.

Prerequisites

- Hardware: A smart light bulb compatible with a programmable platform like Raspberry Pi or Arduino.

- Software: Python programming environment with libraries for AI (e.g., TensorFlow, PyTorch) and IoT device control (e.g., MQTT protocol library).

Step-by-Step Implementation

1. Setting Up Your Development Environment:

Ensure Python is installed on your system, along with necessary libraries. For IoT communication, MQTT is a lightweight messaging protocol that's widely supported.

```
pip install paho-mqtt tensorflow numpy
```

2. Connecting to the Smart Light Bulb:

Use the MQTT protocol to establish a connection between your AI agent and the smart bulb. This involves configuring the MQTT broker settings and subscribing to the relevant topics.

```
import paho.mqtt.client as mqtt # MQTT Broker
settings MQTT_BROKER = "mqtt.example.com" MQTT_PORT
= 1883 MQTT_TOPIC = "home/livingroom/light" def
on_connect(client, userdata, flags, rc):
print("Connected with result code "+str(rc))
client.subscribe(MQTT_TOPIC) client = mqtt.Client()
client.on_connect = on_connect
client.connect(MQTT_BROKER, MQTT_PORT, 60)
```

3. Implementing Decision Logic:

For the AI agent to control the light based on ambient light and time, you'll need to implement logic that checks these conditions and sends the appropriate command to the smart bulb.

```
import datetime def
control_light(ambient_light_level): now =
datetime.datetime.now() if now.hour > 18 or now.hour
```

```
< 6 or ambient_light_level < 50:
client.publish(MQTT_TOPIC, "ON") else:
client.publish(MQTT_TOPIC, "OFF")
```

4. Adding Learning Capability:

To incorporate learning, you could implement a simple reinforcement learning algorithm that adjusts the light-on/light-off thresholds based on user feedback, optimizing for energy efficiency and user satisfaction.

```
# Simplified example of reinforcement learning
adjustment def adjust_thresholds(feedback): global
light_on_threshold if feedback == "too dark":
light_on_threshold -= 10 # Decrease the threshold to
turn on the light earlier elif feedback == "too
bright": light_on_threshold += 10 # Increase the
threshold to turn off the light later
```

Challenges and Considerations

- Security: AI agents in smart homes must be secure to protect against unauthorized access and control. Implement robust authentication and encryption mechanisms.

- Privacy: Ensure that user data is handled with care, providing transparency and control over data collection and usage.

- Interoperability: With a myriad of smart home devices available, ensuring your AI agent can communicate across different platforms and standards is crucial.

Real-World Use Cases

Smart Home AI agents are not just theoretical constructs; they're actively transforming homes around the world. Here are a few examples:

- Energy Efficiency: Google Nest learns your heating and cooling preferences and adjusts the temperature to save energy when you're away.
- Elderly Care: Systems like Cherry Home use AI to monitor the well-being of elderly residents, detecting falls and unusual behavior without compromising privacy.
- Personalized Experiences: Amazon Alexa and Google Assistant offer customized information and control over home environments through voice commands, learning from each interaction to improve responses.

The integration of AI agents into smart homes represents a significant leap forward in home automation and management. By harnessing the power of AI, these agents can provide unprecedented levels of convenience, efficiency, and security. However, developers and users alike must remain mindful of the challenges, particularly around security and privacy. As technology advances, the potential for AI in smart homes will continue to expand, opening up new possibilities for innovative applications and services.

> **Note:** The code examples provided are simplified to illustrate the concepts. In a real-world scenario, additional considerations such as error handling, device compatibility, and user interface design would be necessary.

This exploration into the world of Smart Home AI Agents is just the beginning. As the technology evolves, so too will the capabilities and applications of these intelligent systems, promising a future where our homes are not just connected, but truly smart.

Device Control Through AI Agents

Device control stands as a cornerstone in smart home automation, with AI agents playing a pivotal role in managing and orchestrating the myriad devices found in a modern home. These agents can seamlessly control lighting, heating, ventilation, air conditioning (HVAC) systems, and even multimedia devices, ensuring comfort and convenience for the inhabitants.

Understanding Device Control Mechanisms

At the heart of smart home device control is the concept of IoT (Internet of Things), where devices are interconnected and communicate over a network. AI agents leverage this connectivity to send commands and receive status updates from devices. For instance, an AI agent might adjust the thermostat based on the ambient temperature or time of day.

```
# Example: Python pseudocode to adjust a smart
thermostat def adjust_thermostat(target_temp):
current_temp = get_current_temperature() if
current_temp < target_temp: turn_on_heating() elif
current_temp > target_temp: turn_off_heating()
```

Practical Implementation

To implement effective device control, one must first ensure that all devices are connected to a common network and are capable of receiving commands. Many smart home devices offer APIs (Application Programming Interfaces) that allow AI agents to interact with them.

For a practical example, consider automating your home's lighting system. An AI agent could use light sensors to determine when it's getting dark and turn on the lights. Similarly, it can turn off lights in unoccupied rooms to save energy.

```python
# Python pseudocode for automated lighting control
def control_lights(sensor_data, occupancy_status):
if sensor_data['light_level'] < threshold and
occupancy_status['room'] == 'occupied':
turn_on_lights() else: turn_off_lights()
```

Note: Always ensure that the devices you intend to control support remote API interactions and are securely connected to your network to prevent unauthorized access.

Energy Management with AI Agents

Energy efficiency is another critical aspect of smart homes where AI agents can make a significant impact. By monitoring and analyzing energy consumption patterns, AI agents can optimize the use of electrical devices to reduce waste and save on utility bills.

Strategies for Energy Optimization

AI agents can employ several strategies for energy optimization, including:

- Scheduling: Operating devices during off-peak hours to take advantage of lower energy rates.

- Predictive Maintenance: Identifying devices that are consuming more energy than usual, possibly due to malfunction, and alerting homeowners or scheduling maintenance.

- Adaptive Control: Adjusting device settings in real-time based on current energy consumption levels and user preferences.

Implementing Energy Management

To implement energy management, an AI agent needs access to energy consumption data. Smart meters and smart plugs can provide this data, allowing the AI to analyze patterns and make adjustments accordingly.

```
# Python pseudocode for energy management def
optimize_energy_usage(device_usage, energy_rates):
for device, usage in device_usage.items(): if
is_peak_hours() and device not in essential_devices:
turn_off_device(device) elif
can_operate_in_off_peak(device) and not
is_peak_hours(): schedule_device_operation(device)
```

> **Tip:** Integrating weather forecasts can further enhance energy management, allowing AI agents to anticipate changes in heating or cooling needs.

Security Systems Enhanced by AI

Security is a paramount concern for homeowners, and AI agents bring sophisticated capabilities to smart home security systems. By integrating AI, these systems can offer not only intrusion detection but also anomaly detection, facial recognition, and automated emergency responses.

Advanced Security Features

AI-powered security systems can include:

- Anomaly Detection: Learning normal patterns of behavior and identifying deviations that could indicate unauthorized access.
- Facial Recognition: Identifying known individuals and alerting homeowners to strangers.
- Automated Alerts: Sending notifications to homeowners or authorities in case of a security breach.

Deploying AI in Security Systems

Implementing AI in security systems involves integrating cameras and sensors with AI algorithms capable of processing and analyzing video and sensor data in real-time.

```
# Python pseudocode for anomaly detection in
security systems def detect_anomalies(activity_log):
normal_activities = learn_normal_activities() for
activity in activity_log: if activity not in
normal_activities: alert_homeowner(activity)
```

Personal Assistance Through AI Agents

Beyond controlling devices and managing energy or security, AI agents serve as personal assistants, offering reminders, managing schedules, and even providing companionship through conversational interfaces.

Features of AI Personal Assistants

These assistants can:

- Manage Schedules: Keeping track of appointments and reminding homeowners of upcoming events.
- Information Retrieval: Answering questions by searching the internet or accessing connected services.
- Conversational Interaction: Providing a more natural, human-like interface for interaction with technology.

Building a Personal AI Assistant

Creating a personal AI assistant involves programming the AI to understand natural language queries and respond in a helpful manner. This can be achieved using natural language processing (NLP) libraries and APIs.

```
# Python pseudocode for a simple AI personal
assistant def respond_to_query(query): response =
process_query_with_nlp(query) return
generate_natural_language_response(response)
```

> **Best Practice:** Ensure privacy and data security when implementing AI personal assistants, particularly when they handle sensitive information.

As we have seen, AI agents can transform a smart home into a more comfortable, efficient, and secure environment. From device control and energy management to security and personal assistance, the possibilities are vast. By understanding the mechanisms, practical implementations, and potential challenges, developers can create AI agents that significantly enhance the quality of life in smart homes.

Energy Management through AI Agents

Energy management in smart homes is a critical area where AI agents can significantly contribute. By optimizing energy consumption, these agents not only reduce utility bills but also contribute to a more sustainable environment.

The Role of AI in Energy Optimization

AI agents in smart homes collect data from various sources such as temperature sensors, occupancy sensors, and energy consumption patterns. They use this information to make decisions that optimize energy use without compromising the comfort of the inhabitants. For example, an AI agent can learn the household's usual patterns and adjust the heating or cooling system to operate more efficiently based on when the home is typically occupied or empty.

```
# Example: AI Agent Adjusting Thermostat Settings
Based on Occupancy if
occupancy_sensor.detects_presence(): thermostat.set_
temperature(preferred_occupied_temperature) else: th
ermostat.set_temperature(preferred_unoccupied_temper
ature)
```

Important Note: When implementing AI for energy management, ensure that data privacy and security are top priorities. The personal data collected for optimizing energy use must be protected from unauthorized access.

Predictive Energy Management

One of the most advanced features of smart home AI agents is predictive energy management. By analyzing historical energy usage data and combining it with real-time data from sensors,

AI agents can predict future energy needs and adjust systems accordingly. This predictive capability allows for even greater energy savings and efficiency.

For instance, if the AI agent predicts a cold front moving in, it could preemptively adjust the home's heating system to ensure it operates at an optimal level before the occupants feel the change in temperature, avoiding any unnecessary energy use to rapidly heat the home later.

Implementing Renewable Energy Sources

Integrating renewable energy sources, like solar panels, into the smart home ecosystem is another area where AI agents shine. They can manage the storage and usage of renewable energy more effectively. Based on the prediction of energy needs and the availability of solar energy, AI agents can decide whether to store the energy in batteries, use it immediately, or sell it back to the grid.

```
# Example: AI Agent Managing Solar Energy Usage if
solar_energy_available > energy_demand:
battery.store(solar_energy_available -
energy_demand) elif solar_energy_available <
energy_demand and battery.stored_energy() >
energy_needed: battery.supply_energy(energy_needed)
else: grid.supply_deficit()
```

Best Practices and Challenges

When incorporating AI into energy management systems, there are several best practices to follow:

- Data Accuracy: Ensure the data collected from sensors and other sources is accurate and reliable. Incorrect data can lead to suboptimal decisions by the AI agent.

- User Preferences: Always consider the comfort and preferences of the home's inhabitants. The system should learn and adapt to their needs, not the other way around.
- Security Measures: Implement robust security measures to protect against cyber threats. Smart homes are increasingly becoming targets for hackers.

One of the main challenges is the initial setup and integration of AI agents with existing home systems. It requires a significant investment in terms of time and resources. Additionally, maintaining the system to adapt to new devices or changing user preferences can be demanding.

Real-World Use Case: Smart Thermostats

Smart thermostats are a prime example of AI agents in energy management. They learn from the household's habits, adjust heating and cooling systems for optimal comfort, and can be controlled remotely. Users have reported significant savings on their energy bills, showcasing the tangible benefits of integrating AI into home energy management.

AI agents play a pivotal role in optimizing energy management in smart homes. From adjusting thermostat settings based on occupancy to integrating renewable energy sources, these intelligent systems can significantly reduce energy consumption and costs. By following best practices and overcoming implementation challenges, homeowners can enjoy the benefits of a truly smart, energy-efficient home.

Security Systems Enhanced by AI Agents

In the realm of smart homes, security is a paramount concern that benefits greatly from the integration of AI agents.

These agents elevate traditional security systems by introducing advanced features such as real-time threat detection, facial recognition, and anomaly detection, transforming the way homeowners approach their home's security.

Real-Time Threat Detection

AI agents enhance security systems by providing real-time threat detection capabilities. By continuously monitoring security cameras, sensors, and other data sources, they can identify potential threats the moment they occur. For instance, an AI agent can analyze video feeds to detect unusual activities or unauthorized entry into the premises.

```
# Example of pseudo-code for real-time threat
detection def detect_threat(video_feed): # Analyze
the video feed analysis = analyze_video(video_feed)
# Check for any unusual activity if
analysis.detects_unusual_activity():
raise_alert("Potential threat detected")
```

Note: The actual implementation requires integrating machine learning models trained on datasets to recognize various threat patterns.

Facial Recognition for Enhanced Security

Facial recognition is another area where AI agents contribute significantly to smart home security. By learning and recognizing the faces of household members and regular visitors, AI agents can automatically manage access control, thereby enhancing security and convenience.

```
# Example of pseudo-code for facial recognition def
recognize_face(image): # Compare the captured image
with known faces match =
face_recognition_system.compare(image, known_faces)
if match.is_known_face():
grant_access(match.person_name) else: deny_access()
```

Facial recognition technology must be implemented with privacy and ethical considerations in mind, ensuring that data is securely stored and used in compliance with relevant laws and regulations.

Anomaly Detection for Predictive Security

Anomaly detection allows AI agents to identify patterns and activities that deviate from the norm, which could indicate potential security threats or system failures. By analyzing historical data and ongoing activity, AI agents can predict and mitigate issues before they escalate.

```
# Example of pseudo-code for anomaly detection def
check_for_anomalies(activity_log): # Analyze
activity patterns is_anomalous =
anomaly_detection_model.predict(activity_log) if
is_anomalous: raise_alert("Anomalous activity
detected")
```

This capability is particularly useful in preventing burglaries, detecting fire hazards, or identifying system malfunctions early.

Best Practices and Tips

Implementing AI in smart home security systems requires careful consideration of several factors:

- Privacy: Ensure that all data, especially biometric data from facial recognition, is handled with strict privacy measures.

- Accuracy: Continuously train and update the AI models to improve accuracy and reduce false positives and negatives.

- Ethics: Be transparent with household members and visitors about the use of AI and facial recognition technologies.

- Integration: Seamlessly integrate AI agents with existing home automation systems for a unified smart home experience.

Common Challenges and Troubleshooting

- False Alarms: Fine-tune sensitivity settings and update AI models regularly to distinguish between real threats and non-threatening anomalies.

- Data Security: Implement robust encryption and access controls to safeguard sensitive data against unauthorized access.

- System Compatibility: Ensure that AI agents are compatible with existing security hardware and software to avoid integration issues.

By addressing these challenges and following best practices, homeowners can harness the power of AI to create a safer, more secure living environment. AI agents not only enhance security measures but also offer a more personalized and efficient approach to home safety, showcasing the potential of artificial intelligence in transforming everyday life.

Personal Assistance Through AI Agents

In the modern smart home, AI agents are not just about managing security or automating routine tasks; they also serve as personal assistants, offering a level of interaction and convenience previously unattainable. These AI-powered assistants can manage calendars, provide reminders, handle communication, and even assist with daily decision-making.

Managing Calendars and Schedules

AI agents excel in organizing and managing personal calendars and schedules. By integrating with various calendar services, they can help keep track of appointments, meetings, and important events, ensuring you never miss an important date.

```
# Example: Integrating an AI agent with a calendar
API import calendar_api # Initialize AI agent
ai_agent = AIAssistant() # Sync with user's calendar
user_calendar =
ai_agent.sync_calendar(account_details) # Add a new
event event_details = { "title": "Team Meeting",
"start_time": "2023-07-10 10:00", "end_time":
"2023-07-10 11:00", "description": "Monthly team
strategy meeting." }
ai_agent.add_event(user_calendar, event_details)
```

Note: This example assumes the existence of a fictional `calendar_api` and an `AIAssistant` class capable of interacting with it. In a real-world scenario, you would use specific API libraries provided by calendar services like Google Calendar or Microsoft Outlook.

Providing Reminders and Alerts

Apart from managing schedules, AI agents can proactively provide reminders and alerts for upcoming events, deadlines, or even personal tasks like taking medication. These reminders can be delivered through various channels, including smartphone notifications, emails, or smart speakers, ensuring that the information is received in the most convenient way for the user.

Handling Communication

One of the more advanced features of personal assistant AI agents is their ability to handle communication on behalf of the user. This can range from reading and summarizing emails to sending pre-defined responses, or even managing text and voice messages. With natural language processing capabilities, AI agents can understand the context of messages and provide appropriate responses, significantly reducing the time users spend on routine communication tasks.

```
# Example: Handling incoming emails with an AI agent
def handle_incoming_email(email, ai_agent): if
ai_agent.detect_spam(email):
ai_agent.move_to_spam(email) elif
ai_agent.is_urgent(email):
ai_agent.notify_user(email) else:
ai_agent.auto_reply(email, "Thank you for your
message. I'll get back to you as soon as possible.")
```

Assisting with Decision Making

AI agents can also assist with daily decision-making by providing information, recommendations, or even generating reports based on user preferences and historical data. For instance, an AI agent can suggest the best time to leave for an appointment based on current traffic conditions or recommend a movie to watch based on previous viewing habits.

Best Practices and Tips

1. Privacy and Security: Always ensure that the AI agent and connected services adhere to strict privacy and security standards to protect personal data. 2. Customization: Take advantage of customization options to tailor the AI agent's responses and actions according to personal preferences and needs. 3. Regular Updates: Keep the AI agent and its integrations updated to benefit from the latest features and improvements.

Common Challenges

- Integration Complexity: Integrating AI agents with existing services and devices can sometimes be challenging due to compatibility issues or complex setup processes.

- Accuracy of Tasks: Ensuring that AI agents correctly understand and execute tasks requires ongoing training and refinement of their natural language processing capabilities.

By leveraging AI agents as personal assistants, smart home users can enjoy an enhanced level of convenience and efficiency, transforming the way they manage their daily lives.

Chapter 16: Testing and Validation

Introduction to Testing and Validation

Testing and validation form the cornerstone of developing robust and reliable AI agents. As these systems make decisions autonomously, ensuring their correctness and reliability under various conditions is paramount. This part of the chapter delves into the methodologies and practices for effectively testing and validating AI agents, providing a foundation for developing systems that perform as intended and can be trusted in real-world applications.

Testing Methodologies

Unit Testing

Unit testing involves testing the smallest parts of an application in isolation (e.g., functions or methods). For AI agents, this could mean testing individual components like data preprocessing routines, model prediction functions, or decision-making algorithms.

```
def test_preprocessing(): raw_data = "Sample data"
expected_output = "Processed data" assert
preprocess(raw_data) == expected_output
```

This code snippet demonstrates a simple unit test for a hypothetical data preprocessing function. Unit tests like these are essential for catching low-level bugs and ensuring that each component of your AI agent functions correctly.

Integration Testing

Once individual components have been unit tested, integration testing verifies that these components work together as expected. For AI agents, this might involve testing the flow from data ingestion and preprocessing, through to prediction making and action selection.

> **Note:** Integration testing can help identify issues in the interaction between components that were not evident during unit testing.

System Testing

System testing evaluates the AI agent as a whole, ensuring it meets the specified requirements. This is a high-level test to check the agent's end-to-end functionality in an environment that simulates real-world conditions as closely as possible.

Stress Testing

Stress testing involves evaluating how an AI agent performs under extreme conditions, such as high data volumes, rapid input changes, or limited computational resources. This type of testing is crucial for applications where the agent must operate reliably under high-stress circumstances.

Performance Evaluation

Evaluating the performance of AI agents involves more than just correctness; it also includes assessing efficiency, scalability, and adaptability. Performance metrics vary widely depending on the type of AI agent and its application domain, but common metrics include accuracy, response time, and resource utilization.

Accuracy

Accuracy is a measure of how often the AI agent makes correct predictions or decisions. It's a fundamental metric for classification problems but must be balanced with other metrics like precision and recall in more complex scenarios.

Response Time

Response time measures how quickly an AI agent can process input and provide an output. For many applications, particularly those involving real-time decision-making, low response time is crucial.

Resource Utilization

Resource utilization assesses how efficiently an AI agent uses computational resources, such as CPU and memory. Efficient use of resources is essential for deploying AI agents on limited hardware, such as mobile devices or embedded systems.

Error Handling

Robust error handling is critical for ensuring that AI agents can recover gracefully from unexpected situations. This includes handling invalid input data, dealing with unavailable resources, and managing failures in external systems.

Try-Catch Blocks

Try-catch blocks are a fundamental technique for managing runtime errors. They allow your AI agent to attempt an operation that may fail and then catch the error, preventing the entire system from crashing.

```
try: # Attempt to execute a risky operation
risky_operation() except Exception as e: # Handle
the error log_error(e)
```

Validating Input Data

Ensuring that input data is valid before processing it is crucial for preventing many types of errors. Input validation can range from simple checks, like ensuring numeric inputs are within a certain range, to more complex schema validations for structured data.

Quality Assurance

Quality assurance (QA) encompasses all activities designed to ensure that an AI agent meets its specified requirements and user expectations. This includes rigorous testing, code reviews, documentation, and adherence to best practices.

Code Reviews

Code reviews involve systematically examining source code. They are an opportunity to catch bugs, ensure adherence to coding standards, and share knowledge among team members. For AI projects, code reviews can also focus on model architecture, data handling practices, and the use of algorithms.

Documentation

Comprehensive documentation is invaluable for maintaining and scaling AI agents. This includes documenting the design and architecture of the system, the data it uses, and how its components interact. Good documentation ensures that knowledge is preserved and that new team members can quickly become productive.

Testing and validation are critical components of AI agent development, ensuring that these systems perform correctly, efficiently, and reliably. By employing a variety of testing methodologies, carefully evaluating performance, implementing robust error handling, and maintaining high standards of quality assurance, developers can build AI agents that are both powerful and dependable. In the next section, we will explore practical case studies and delve deeper into advanced testing and validation techniques.

By focusing on these foundational aspects of AI agent development, practitioners can significantly reduce the risk of errors and failures in production environments, paving the way for broader adoption and trust in autonomous systems.

Testing Methodologies for AI Agents

AT AI agents one a blend of traditional software testing techniques and specialized approaches tailored more the unique challenges of AI systems. St these so pre who for ensuring the reliability and performance of AI agents in various dis.

Unit Testing

Unit testing dis testing the smallest parts of an application their isolation (e.g., functions ar methods one For AI ar, this

means Y individual components, such as data preprocessing so or model prediction methods, to ensure they work as expected.

```
def test_preprocessing(data): # Example test for a
preprocessing function processed_data =
preprocess_data(data) assert
isinstance(processed_data, ExpectedDataType)
```

Integration Testing

Integration testing focuses on combining individual components and testing them as a group. This step is vital for AI agents, as it ensures that different parts of the system (e g, data processing pipelines, learning algorithms, and decision-making modules) work together seamlessly.

```
def test_agent_integration(): # Example test to
ensure components integrate correctly data =
```

```
collect_data() processed_data =
preprocess_data(data) predictions =
model.predict(processed_data) assert
predictions_meet_certain_criteria(predictions)
```

System Testing

System testing evaluates the AI agent as a whole, ensuring it meets the specified requirements. This includes testing the agent in environments that simulate real-world conditions, which is critical for autonomous agents expected to operate in dynamic and potentially unpredictable settings.

Performance Testing

Performance testing is crucial for AI agents, especially those intended for time-sensitive applications. It involves assessing the response time, resource usage, and scalability of the agent under different workloads.

> **Note:** Performance bottlenecks can significantly impair the functionality of AI agents, making thorough performance testing a necessity.

Performance Evaluation Metrics

Evaluating the performance of AI agents goes beyond traditional software metrics to include aspects unique to AI, such as accuracy, precision, recall, and F1 score for classification tasks, or mean squared error (MSE) and mean absolute error (MAE) for regression tasks.

Accuracy vs. Precision vs. Recall

- Accuracy measures the proportion of true results (both true positives and true negatives) among the total number of cases examined.
- Precision is the ratio of true positives to all positive predictions, highlighting the agent's ability to minimize false positives.
- Recall (or sensitivity) measures the ratio of true positives to all actual positives, assessing the agent's capability to find all relevant cases.

F1 Score

The F1 score combines precision and recall into a single metric by taking their harmonic mean. It provides a balanced view of the model's performance, especially in imbalanced datasets.

```
from sklearn.metrics import f1_score # Assuming
y_true and y_pred are the true labels and the
predictions, respectively score = f1_score(y_true,
y_pred) print(f"F1 Score: {score}")
```

Error Handling and Anomalies

Error handling in AI agents involves not only catching software exceptions but also identifying and addressing anomalies in the agent's performance, such as unexpected predictions or behaviors.

- Logging and Monitoring: Implementing comprehensive logging and monitoring to track the agent's decisions and actions can help in quickly identifying and rectifying issues.

- Anomaly Detection: Integrating anomaly detection mechanisms can alert developers to unusual patterns or errors in the data or the agent's performance.

Quality Assurance Best Practices

Ensuring the quality of AI agents involves adhering to best practices throughout the development and deployment phases.

Continuous Testing and Integration

Adopting a continuous testing and integration approach allows for the early detection of errors and inconsistencies, facilitating smoother development cycles.

Validating with Diverse Datasets

Testing AI agents against diverse and comprehensive datasets ensures robustness and generalizability, reducing the risk of bias and improving the agent's ability to perform in varied conditions.

Peer Reviews and Code Audits

Regular peer reviews and code audits help in maintaining code quality, ensuring adherence to best practices, and identifying potential issues early.

Documentation and Version Control

Maintaining thorough documentation and using version control systems are essential for tracking changes, understanding system evolution, and facilitating collaboration among developers.

Practical Exercise: Implementing a Testing Suite for Your AI Agent

1. Unit Test Implementation: Start by writing unit tests for each component of your AI agent. Focus on critical functions like data preprocessing, model training, and prediction generation.

2. Integration Testing: Develop integration tests that assess the interaction between components. Ensure data flows correctly through the system and that integrated components produce expected outcomes.

3. System Testing: Simulate real-world scenarios to test your AI agent as a whole. Evaluate its performance, reliability, and response to unexpected situations.

4. Performance Evaluation: Use the discussed performance metrics to evaluate your agent. Identify areas of improvement and optimize accordingly.

5. Error Handling Mechanisms: Implement robust error handling and anomaly detection mechanisms. Ensure your agent can gracefully recover from failures and unexpected states.

By following these steps and incorporating the discussed methodologies and best practices, you can ensure that your AI agent is reliable, efficient, and ready for real-world applications.

Performance Evaluation of AI Agents

Performance evaluation is a critical aspect of developing and deploying AI agents. It involves assessing an AI system's efficiency, accuracy, and reliability under various conditions. This section explores key metrics and techniques for evaluating the performance of your AI agents.

Key Performance Indicators (KPIs)

To effectively evaluate an AI agent, it's essential to define clear Key Performance Indicators (KPIs). These metrics will vary depending on the application but typically include:

- Accuracy: Measures the percentage of correct predictions or decisions made by the AI agent compared to the total number of cases evaluated.

- Precision and Recall: Used in classification problems to evaluate the quality of the output. Precision is the ratio of true positive results to all positive predictions, while recall (also known as sensitivity) measures the ratio of true positive results to all actual positives.

- F1 Score: The harmonic mean of precision and recall, providing a single metric to assess the balance between them.

- Latency: The time it takes for the AI agent to make a decision or prediction.

- Throughput: The number of tasks or decisions an AI agent can handle in a given time frame.

For instance, in a chatbot designed for customer service, KPIs might include accuracy of answers, latency in responding to user queries, and throughput during peak usage times.

Evaluation Techniques

Evaluating the performance of AI agents requires a combination of techniques:

- Cross-validation: A method used to evaluate the model's performance on unseen data. It involves dividing the dataset into a certain number of 'folds' or subsets, training the model on all but one subset, and validating it on the remaining subset. This process is repeated multiple times, with each subset used exactly once as the validation data.

- A/B Testing: Comparing two versions of an AI agent (A and B) by dividing the user base or data into two groups and assessing which version performs better according to predefined KPIs.

- Simulation and Synthetic Data: Using simulated environments or synthetic data to test AI agents in controlled conditions that mimic real-world scenarios.

  Note: When using synthetic data or simulations, ensure that the scenarios are realistic and cover a broad range of potential situations the AI agent might encounter in production.

Real-world Use Cases

Consider a self-driving car AI. Performance evaluation might involve simulated urban environments to test navigation and obstacle avoidance capabilities under various conditions (weather, traffic, etc.). Key metrics could include the accuracy of object detection, decision-making latency, and the ability to reach a destination safely and efficiently.

Error Handling and Quality Assurance

AI agents, like any software system, can encounter errors. Error handling and quality assurance are about anticipating, detecting, and resolving these issues to ensure the AI agent functions reliably.

Strategies for Error Handling

- Graceful Degradation: Designing AI agents to handle errors by degrading functionality in a controlled manner, ensuring that the system remains operational albeit with reduced capabilities.

- Failover Mechanisms: Implementing backup systems or components that can take over in case of failure, ensuring continuity of service.

- Monitoring and Alerts: Continuous monitoring of the AI agent's performance to detect anomalies or errors, coupled with an alert system to notify developers or operators of potential issues.

```
# Example: Basic monitoring with logging import
logging try: # AI agent operation
perform_operation() except Exception as e:
logging.error("Error encountered during operation:
%s", str(e)) # Implement failover or graceful
degradation
```

Quality Assurance Best Practices

- Regular Code Reviews: Ensuring that the AI agent's codebase is regularly reviewed by multiple developers to catch potential errors and improve code quality.

- Automated Testing: Implementing automated testing frameworks to continuously test the AI agent as new code is integrated.

- User Feedback Loops: Incorporating feedback mechanisms to gather input from end-users or operators about the AI agent's performance and usability, which can be invaluable for identifying unnoticed issues.

Warning: Avoid overfitting in AI models by ensuring that your testing and validation datasets are separate from the training dataset. Overfitting occurs when a model is too closely tailored to the training data, making it perform poorly on new, unseen data.

Practical Exercise

As a practical exercise, implement a simple monitoring system for your AI agent using the logging example provided. Next, design a test case using cross-validation to evaluate your AI agent's performance on unseen data. This exercise will help reinforce the concepts of performance evaluation and error handling.

By meticulously evaluating performance, handling errors gracefully, and ensuring quality, you can build reliable and efficient AI agents capable of operating in diverse and challenging real world environments.

Error Handling in AI Agents

Error handling is a pivotal aspect of developing resilient and reliable AI agents. Unlike traditional software, AI agents operate in environments filled with uncertainty and unpredictability. This section delves into strategies for identifying, managing, and mitigating errors in AI systems.

Types of Errors in AI Systems

AI systems can encounter a range of errors, broadly classified into systematic errors and random errors. Systematic errors are consistent and predictable faults that occur due to flaws in the system design or data. Random errors, on the other hand, occur unpredictably due to the inherent uncertainty in AI environments.

- Systematic Errors: Often arise from biased data or flawed algorithms. For example, an AI agent trained on non-representative data may consistently misinterpret inputs that were not adequately covered in its training set.
- Random Errors: These are often due to the complex and dynamic nature of AI operational environments. For instance, a voice recognition agent might misinterpret commands in an unexpectedly noisy environment.

Strategies for Error Handling

Effective error handling in AI involves a combination of proactive and reactive strategies. Proactively, developers can implement rigorous validation checks and design systems with fault tolerance in mind. Reactively, systems can be equipped to identify when an error has occurred and take corrective action.

- Validation Checks: Implementing comprehensive validation checks at the input stage can prevent invalid or unexpected data from causing errors downstream.

- Fault Tolerance: Designing AI agents to continue operating effectively in the presence of certain errors is crucial. This can involve using redundant systems or fallback mechanisms to ensure continuity of service.

```
def robust_predict(model, input_data): try:
prediction = model.predict(input_data) except
ValueError as e: # Log the error for debugging
purposes log_error(e) # Use a fallback model or
method prediction = fallback_predict(input_data)
return prediction
```

Note: It's important to log errors comprehensively. This not only aids in debugging but also helps in refining the AI model by identifying recurring issues.

Mitigating Random Errors

Mitigating random errors involves designing systems that can adapt to and learn from their operational environment. Techniques such as reinforcement learning can be pivotal, where the AI agent continuously improves its performance based on feedback from its environment.

- Continuous Learning: Implement systems that can update their models based on new data and feedback. This ensures that the agent remains effective as conditions change.

Best Practices

1. Regular Monitoring and Testing: Continuously monitor AI agents for unexpected behavior and regularly test them under varied conditions to identify potential errors. 2. Diverse Training

Data: Ensure training data is as diverse and representative as possible to minimize systematic errors. 3. Feedback Loops: Implement feedback mechanisms that allow users to report errors, contributing to the continuous improvement of the AI agent.

Practical Challenge: Error Handling Exercise

To solidify your understanding, try implementing a simple error-handling mechanism for an AI agent. Create a mock AI agent that takes user inputs and responds accordingly. Introduce validation checks to ensure the inputs are within expected parameters and implement a basic fallback mechanism for when errors occur. Use logging to capture error details for further analysis.

This practical exercise will help you grasp the complexities of error handling in AI systems and appreciate the importance of designing robust and resilient agents. Through understanding and addressing common challenges, you can ensure your AI agents are not only intelligent but also reliable and effective in real-world applications.

Quality Assurance in AI Agent Development

After addressing how to handle errors in AI agents, it's essential to focus on the overarching process that ensures these agents meet the desired standards of performance and reliability: quality assurance (QA). Quality assurance encompasses a broad set of activities designed to prevent mistakes and defects in manufactured products and to avoid problems when delivering solutions or services to customers. In the context of AI agents, QA refers to a systematic process of checking to see whether a product or service being developed meets specified requirements.

Importance of Quality Assurance

Quality assurance is critical in AI agent development for several reasons:

- Ensures Reliability: QA processes help ensure that AI agents perform reliably under varying conditions, which is crucial for applications in areas like healthcare, finance, and autonomous vehicles.

- Improves Accuracy: By systematically testing and validating the AI agent's outputs, developers can improve its accuracy, leading to better decision-making.

- Increases User Trust: A well-tested AI agent is more likely to win the trust of its users, which is essential for widespread adoption.

- Reduces Development Costs: Identifying and fixing issues early in the development process can significantly reduce the costs associated with reworking and deploying updates after the product's release.

QA Techniques for AI Agents

Implementing QA in AI agent development involves several techniques:

Unit Testing

Unit testing involves testing individual components or units of the AI agent to ensure each part functions correctly. For example, if an AI agent includes a module for processing natural language input, developers should create unit tests that evaluate the module's ability to understand and interpret various inputs accurately.

```
def test_nlp_module(): assert nlp_module.parse("What
is the weather today?") == "weather_query"
```

Integration Testing

Integration testing checks the combined functionality of two or more components of the AI agent. This is crucial for validating the agent's performance when different modules interact, such as data preprocessing, model inference, and output generation.

```
def test_agent_integration(): input_data =
preprocess_data(sample_input) prediction =
model.predict(input_data) response =
generate_response(prediction) assert response is not
None
```

Performance Evaluation

Performance evaluation involves assessing the AI agent's efficiency and effectiveness, usually by measuring metrics such as accuracy, response time, and resource utilization. This evaluation is critical for understanding the agent's scalability and suitability for deployment in target environments.

Note: It's essential to use diverse datasets that reflect real-world variability during performance evaluation to ensure the AI agent's robustness.

Best Practices for QA in AI Agent Development

- Continuous Testing: Integrate testing into the continuous integration/continuous deployment (CI/CD) pipeline to automatically run tests at various stages of development.

- Realistic Scenarios: Test the AI agent in scenarios that closely mimic its expected real-world environment and usage patterns.

- User Feedback: Incorporate feedback from end-users into the QA process to identify usability issues and areas for improvement.

- Ethical Considerations: Ensure that the AI agent's behavior aligns with ethical guidelines, especially regarding fairness, privacy, and security.

Quality assurance is a vital component of AI agent development. By implementing thorough testing and validation processes, developers can enhance the reliability, accuracy, and user trust in AI agents. Following best practices and incorporating continuous feedback into the QA process can lead to the successful deployment of robust and efficient AI agents in various domains.

Chapter 17: Security and Privacy

Understanding the Landscape of AI Security and Privacy

As we delve into the world of autonomous AI agents, an understanding of the security and privacy concerns associated with these technologies becomes paramount. AI agents, with their ability to process and analyze vast amounts of data, present unique challenges and opportunities in the realms of security and privacy. This section aims to equip readers with the foundational knowledge needed to navigate these challenges, ensuring the development of secure and privacy-preserving AI systems.

The Importance of Data Protection

AI agents can only be as effective as the data they are trained on. This reliance on data, however, introduces significant privacy concerns, particularly when dealing with sensitive information. Data protection involves implementing measures to ensure the confidentiality, integrity, and availability of data.

Best Practices for Data Protection:

1. Data Encryption: Encrypt data both at rest and in transit to protect it from unauthorized access.

```
from cryptography.fernet import Fernet # Generate a
key key = Fernet.generate_key() cipher_suite =
Fernet(key) # Encrypt data text = "Sensitive
```

```
Data".encode() encrypted_text =
cipher_suite.encrypt(text) # Decrypt data
decrypted_text =
cipher_suite.decrypt(encrypted_text)
```

This simple example demonstrates how to encrypt and decrypt sensitive data in Python using the cryptography library.

2. Anonymization and Pseudonymization: Remove or alter identifying information from datasets to protect individual identities. 3. Access Rights Management: Limit access to data based on user roles and the principle of least privilege.

Note: Always be aware of and comply with data protection regulations relevant to your region or industry, such as GDPR in Europe or HIPAA in the healthcare sector.

Implementing Access Control

Access control is critical in preventing unauthorized access to data and AI functionalities. It ensures that only authorized users can perform certain actions, which is essential for maintaining the integrity and confidentiality of the system.

Techniques for Robust Access Control:

- Authentication and Authorization: Implement strong authentication mechanisms and define clear authorization rules.

```
from flask import Flask, request from flask_httpauth
import HTTPBasicAuth app = Flask(__name__) auth =
HTTPBasicAuth() USERS = { "admin": "password", }
@auth.verify_password def verify_password(username,
password): if username in USERS and USERS[username]
== password: return username
@app.route('/secure-data') @auth.login_required def
```

```
get_data(): return "You have access to secure data."
if __name__ == '__main__': app.run()
```

This Flask application example uses HTTP Basic Authentication to protect a route, ensuring that only authenticated users can access sensitive information.

- Role-Based Access Control (RBAC): Define roles for users and assign permissions based on these roles.

- Attribute-Based Access Control (ABAC): Define access rules based on attributes of the user, action, and resource.

Privacy Preservation Techniques

In the development of AI agents, it's crucial to incorporate privacy preservation from the outset. Techniques such as differential privacy and federated learning can help maintain privacy while still leveraging data for AI training.

Differential Privacy:

Differential privacy ensures that the addition or removal of a single database item does not significantly affect the outcome of any analysis, thereby protecting individual privacy.

```
import numpy as np def
apply_differential_privacy(data, epsilon=1.0): """
Apply differential privacy to a dataset. """
sensitivity = 1.0 noise = np.random.laplace(0,
sensitivity / epsilon, size=len(data))
protected_data = data + noise return protected_data
```

This example shows how to apply differential privacy to a dataset by adding Laplace noise, where `epsilon` controls the privacy-loss budget.

Federated Learning:

Federated learning allows AI models to be trained across multiple decentralized devices or servers while keeping data localized, reducing privacy and security risks.

Security Best Practices

Beyond data protection and access control, there are several best practices that should be adhered to when developing AI agents:

- Regular Security Audits and Penetration Testing: Identify vulnerabilities in your systems before they can be exploited.
- Up-to-Date Software: Ensure all software components are regularly updated to mitigate known security vulnerabilities.
- Incident Response Plan: Have a plan in place for responding to security incidents to minimize damage and recovery time.

Implementing these security measures and privacy-preserving techniques requires a careful balance between usability, performance, and protection. By integrating these practices early in the development process, AI agents can be made more secure and privacy-compliant, fostering trust among users and stakeholders.

Addressing Common Challenges

One of the most significant challenges in securing AI agents is the dynamic nature of both the threats and the technologies themselves. As AI systems become more complex, the potential attack surfaces expand, making traditional security measures insufficient. Additionally, the need to process sensitive data for training purposes can raise privacy concerns that are not easily addressed with conventional data protection strategies.

Mitigating Risks:

- AI-Specific Threat Intelligence: Stay informed about emerging threats specific to AI systems and adapt your security posture accordingly.

- Privacy-Enhancing Technologies (PETs): Employ technologies that enhance privacy by design, such as secure multi-party computation (SMPC) or homomorphic encryption.

- Ethical Considerations: Always consider the ethical implications of your AI agents, especially in terms of privacy and data usage, and strive to maintain transparency and fairness.

Practical Exercise: Implementing a Privacy-Preserving AI Agent

As a practical exercise, readers are encouraged to develop a simple AI agent that utilizes differential privacy or federated learning. Begin by selecting a dataset and an AI task (e.g., classification). Implement the chosen privacy-preserving technique and evaluate the performance of your AI agent in terms of both accuracy and privacy metrics.

This exercise will provide hands-on experience with the concepts introduced in this chapter, reinforcing the importance of security and privacy in AI development.

By understanding and implementing the principles and practices discussed in this chapter, developers can create AI agents that not only perform effectively but also respect user privacy and maintain data security. As AI technologies continue to evolve, staying informed about the latest advancements in security and privacy will be crucial for anyone working in this field.

Implementing Data Protection in AI Agents

Data protection is a more per of building and deploying AI agents. It involves safeguarding sensitive data from unauthorized access, theft, and alteration. This section outlines practical steps and best practices for ensuring data protection in your AI projects.

Encryption Techniques

At the heart of data protection lies encryption. Encryption transforms data into a format that can be unlocked only with a key, ensuring that even if data is intercepted, it remains unreadable to unauthorized entities.

- Symmetric Encryption: Uses the same key for encryption and decryption. It's fast but requires secure key management.

- Asymmetric Encryption: Uses a pair of keys (public and private). The public key encrypts the data, while the private key decrypts it, enhancing security but at the expense of speed.

Example:

```
from cryptography.fernet import Fernet # Generate a
key key = Fernet.generate_key() cipher_suite =
Fernet(key) # Encrypt data data = "Sensitive
information".encode() cipher_text =
cipher_suite.encrypt(data) print("Encrypted:",
cipher_text) # Decrypt data plain_text =
cipher_suite.decrypt(cipher_text)
print("Decrypted:", plain_text.decode())
```

Access Control Mechanisms

Access control ensures that only authorized users can interact with the AI agent or the data it processes. Implementing robust access control can mitigate unauthorized data access and manipulation.

- Authentication: Verifies a user's identity. This can be achieved through passwords, biometrics, or tokens.
- Authorization: Determines what an authenticated user is allowed to do. This is typically implemented through roles and permissions.

Best Practices

- Regularly update and patch all systems that interact with sensitive data.
- Employ principle of least privilege (PoLP), ensuring that users have only the access they need.
- Use secure connections (e.g., HTTPS) for data transmission.

Preserving Privacy in AI Systems

Privacy preservation in AI involves ensuring that an individual's data is used ethically, without compromising their anonymity or personal information. This is particularly challenging in the age of big data and machine learning, where vast amounts of data are analyzed and processed.

Anonymization Techniques

Anonymization removes personally identifiable information from datasets, making it difficult to trace data back to an individual.

- Data Masking: Replacing sensitive information with fictional but realistic data.
- Generalization: Reducing the precision of data (e.g., changing exact ages to age ranges).

Differential Privacy

Differential privacy is a framework that allows data analysis without compromising the privacy of individuals in the dataset. It adds noise to the data or queries to ensure that removing or adding a single database item does not significantly affect the outcome.

Example: Consider a database query that calculates the average salary of employees. By adding noise to the result, differential privacy ensures that the presence or absence of any single employee's data does not significantly affect the calculated average, thus preserving individual privacy.

Best Practices

- Conduct privacy impact assessments to understand the privacy risks associated with your AI agent.
- Implement data minimization principles, collecting only the data necessary for the intended purpose.
- Stay informed about and compliant with relevant data protection regulations (e.g., GDPR, CCPA).

Security Best Practices for AI Agents

Securing AI agents against threats requires a comprehensive approach that covers data protection, privacy, and the integrity of the AI model itself.

Regular Security Audits

Conducting regular security audits can help identify vulnerabilities in your AI system before they are exploited. This includes reviewing code, data handling practices, and access controls.

Secure AI Models

AI models can be vulnerable to attacks designed to steal, corrupt, or manipulate their functionality. Techniques such as model encryption and model hardening (making models more resilient to adversarial attacks) should be considered.

Incident Response Plan

Having a robust incident response plan in place is crucial for minimizing damage in the event of a security breach. This plan should include steps for identifying, containing, and mitigating breaches, as well as protocols for notifying affected parties.

Practical Exercise: Implementing Basic Access Control

Create a simple access control system for a hypothetical AI data processing service. This system should authenticate users and restrict access based on predefined roles.

1. Define roles and permissions (e.g., Admin, User). 2. Implement a basic authentication mechanism (e.g., password-based). 3. Enforce role-based access control on data processing functions.

This exercise will help you understand the basics of implementing secure access controls in an AI environment, laying the foundation for more complex security measures.

Security and privacy in AI agents encompass a broad range of practices aimed at protecting sensitive data, preserving user privacy, and ensuring the integrity and reliability of AI systems. By implementing the techniques and best practices outlined in this chapter, developers can mitigate many of the risks associated with autonomous AI agents. Remember, security is not a one-time task but a continuous process that evolves with your AI projects.

Access Control in AI Systems

Properly managing who can access what in an AI system is crucial for maintaining its security and the privacy of the data it processes. This section explores the methods and best practices for implementing robust access control mechanisms.

User Authentication and Authorization

User authentication and authorization are the cornerstones of access control. Authentication verifies a user's identity, while authorization determines what resources a user can access

- Authentication can be achieved through various means, such as passwords, biometric verification, or multi-factor authentication (MFA). MFA, in particular, adds an extra layer of security by requiring two or more verification methods.

- Authorization is typically implemented using role-based access control (RBAC) or attribute-based access control (ABAC). RBAC assigns users to roles based on their responsibilities and defines permissions for each role. ABAC, on the other hand, uses policies that evaluate attributes (user, resource, and environment attributes) to make access decisions.

```
# Example of a simple RBAC system class User: def
__init__(self, roles): self.roles = roles class
Resource: def access(self, user): if "admin" in
user.roles: return "Access granted" else: return
"Access denied" # Example usage admin_user =
User(roles=["admin"]) normal_user =
User(roles=["user"]) resource = Resource()
print(resource.access(admin_user)) # Output: Access
granted print(resource.access(normal_user)) #
Output: Access denied
```

Note: It's essential to regularly review and update access rights to ensure they align with users' current roles and responsibilities. This helps prevent privilege escalation and ensures that users have only the access they need.

Implementing Secure API Access

APIs are a critical component of modern AI systems, enabling them to communicate with other services and components. Securing API access is vital to protect sensitive data and functions from unauthorized access.

- Use API keys to control access to your APIs. API keys are unique identifiers that are passed along with API requests. They should be kept secret and only shared with authorized users or services.

- Implement OAuth for more sophisticated scenarios, especially when your AI system needs to access APIs on behalf of users. OAuth allows users to grant your application access to their data on other services without sharing their credentials.

- Always use HTTPS to encrypt API requests and responses. This protects the data in transit from being intercepted by attackers.

```
// Example of an API request with an API key
fetch('https://yourapi.com/data', { method: 'GET',
headers: { 'Authorization': 'Bearer YOUR_API_KEY' }
}) .then(response => response.json()) .then(data =>
console.log(data)) .catch(error =>
console.error('Error:', error));
```

Best Practices for Access Control

- Principle of Least Privilege (PoLP): Always provide the minimal level of access required for users to perform their tasks. This minimizes the risk of accidental or malicious misuse of privileges.

- Regular Audits: Conduct regular audits of access controls and logs to detect any unauthorized access attempts or misconfigurations.

- Separation of Duties (SoD): Divide responsibilities among multiple individuals or systems to prevent fraud and errors. This ensures that no single entity has control over all aspects of a sensitive process.

Privacy Preservation Techniques

Maintaining the privacy of data processed by AI agents is not only a legal requirement in many jurisdictions but also a matter of ethical responsibility. Here are some techniques to help preserve privacy:

Data Anonymization and Pseudonymization

- Data Anonymization removes or modifies personal information so that individuals cannot be identified, directly or indirectly, by the remaining data.
- Pseudonymization replaces private identifiers with fake identifiers or pseudonyms. This allows data to be matched with its source without revealing the actual source.

Differential Privacy

Differential privacy is a framework that ensures the privacy of individuals in a dataset by adding noise to the data or query results. This makes it difficult for attackers to infer information about any individual within the dataset.

Federated Learning

Federated learning is a technique where the AI model is trained across multiple decentralized devices or servers holding local data samples, without exchanging them. This approach allows AI agents to learn from private data without the data leaving its original location.

Implementing these security and privacy measures requires careful planning and continuous monitoring. However, the effort is well worth it, as it helps build trust with users and ensures compliance with regulations, protecting both the users and the organization.

Privacy Preservation in AI Systems

Privacy preservation is a critical aspect of developing and deploying AI agents. As these systems often handle sensitive information, it's essential to implement strategies that protect individual privacy while allowing the AI to learn from and make decisions based on data.

Techniques for Privacy-Preserving AI

Several techniques can be applied to preserve privacy in AI systems. These methods aim to enable data analysis and model training without compromising the privacy of the individuals whose data is being used.

Data Anonymization

Data anonymization involves removing or modifying personal information from a dataset so that individuals cannot be readily identified. This can be achieved through various means, such as randomization or generalization of data.

```
# Example of simple data anonymization by
generalization def anonymize_age(age): if age < 20:
return "<20" elif age < 40: return "20-39" elif age
< 60: return "40-59" else: return "60+"
```

Differential Privacy

Differential privacy is a framework for quantifying the privacy offered by an algorithm. It provides strong, mathematical guarantees that an individual's presence or absence in a dataset does not significantly affect the output of the algorithm.

```
# Example of implementing differential privacy in
data queries import numpy as np def
```

```
differential_privacy_query(data, query, epsilon):
true_answer = query(data) noise =
np.random.laplace(0, 1/epsilon) private_answer =
true_answer + noise return private_answer
```

Federated Learning

Federated learning is a technique where the model is trained across multiple decentralized devices or servers holding local data samples, without exchanging them. This approach allows AI models to learn from data without the need to store it centrally.

```
# Conceptual example of federated learning def
federated_learning(models): # Assume models is a
list of model updates from different clients
updated_model = average_models(models) return
updated_model def average_models(models): #
Averaging model weights as a simple example # In
practice, this would involve more sophisticated
aggregation techniques return sum(models) /
len(models)
```

> **Note**: While these techniques can significantly enhance privacy, they may also impact the accuracy and efficiency of AI systems. Finding the right balance between privacy and performance is crucial.

Best Practices for Privacy Preservation

Implementing the aforementioned techniques requires careful consideration. Here are some best practices:

- Understand the Data: Know what data you are collecting and processing. Identify sensitive information and apply stricter privacy controls.

- Minimum Necessary Data: Collect and use only the data that is absolutely necessary for your objectives.

- Regularly Update Privacy Measures: Privacy-preserving techniques evolve. Keep your methods up to date with the latest advancements in the field.

- Transparency and Consent: Be transparent about data usage and ensure that consent is obtained where necessary.

Challenges in Privacy Preservation

One of the main challenges in privacy preservation is the trade-off between privacy and utility. As privacy measures become stricter, the utility of the data can decrease, potentially reducing the effectiveness of AI models. Additionally, implementing advanced privacy-preserving techniques requires expertise and can increase computational costs.

Real-World Use Case: Health Care

In the health care sector, AI agents are used to predict patient outcomes, recommend treatments, and automate diagnoses. Privacy preservation is paramount, as data includes highly sensitive health information. Techniques like federated learning have been particularly useful, allowing models to learn from patient data across different hospitals without needing to centralize sensitive information.

Privacy preservation in AI systems is not just a technical necessity but also a moral obligation. By employing techniques like data anonymization, differential privacy, and federated learning, developers can protect individuals' privacy while still leveraging data for meaningful insights and advancements. Balancing privacy with the utility of AI systems remains a key challenge, necessitating ongoing efforts and innovations in the field.

Chapter 18: Ethical Considerations

Bias and Fairness

When developing AI agents, it's crucial to acknowledge and mitigate biases that can inadvertently be built into these systems. Bias in AI can manifest in several forms, from the data used to train the agent to the design of the algorithm itself. These biases can lead to unfair outcomes, discriminating against certain groups or individuals based on race, gender, age, or other characteristics.

Understanding Bias in AI

Bias in AI typically stems from the data used to train the model. If the training data is not representative of the broader population or contains historical biases, the AI agent will likely replicate and amplify these biases in its predictions or decisions.

```
# Example of biased data selection import pandas as
pd # Hypothetical dataset with an imbalance in
gender representation data = {'Name': ['John',
'Alice', 'Greg', 'Diana'], 'Gender': ['Male',
'Female', 'Male', 'Female'], 'Hired': [1, 0, 1, 0]}
df = pd.DataFrame(data) print(df)
```

This simple example shows a dataset where a hiring decision (Hired) appears to correlate with gender, which could lead to a biased AI model if not addressed.

Mitigating Bias

To mitigate bias, developers must employ strategies throughout the AI development process, from data collection to model evaluation.

- Diverse Data Collection: Ensure the training data encompasses a wide range of examples from different demographics to reduce bias.

- Bias Detection Tools: Utilize tools and techniques designed to detect and correct bias in datasets and models. For instance, IBM's AI Fairness 360 toolkit offers a comprehensive suite of metrics and algorithms to help.

- Regular Evaluation: Continuously evaluate the AI agent's decisions for fairness and bias, especially when deployed in new contexts or with new data.

  Note: It's important to involve stakeholders from diverse backgrounds in the development and evaluation process to identify biases that may not be apparent to everyone.

Transparency

Transparency in AI involves making the operations and decisions of AI agents understandable to humans. This is particularly critical in applications where trust and accountability are crucial, such as healthcare, finance, and law enforcement.

Why Transparency Matters

Transparency helps build trust with users and stakeholders by allowing them to understand how and why decisions are made. It also facilitates the identification and correction of errors or biases in the AI agent's operations.

Techniques for Enhancing Transparency

- Model Explainability Tools: Tools like LIME (Local Interpretable Model-agnostic Explanations) and SHAP (SHapley Additive exPlanations) can help explain the output of complex models in understandable terms.

```
# Example of using SHAP for model explainability
import shap import xgboost as xgb from
sklearn.model_selection import train_test_split from
sklearn.datasets import load_breast_cancer # Load
dataset X, y = load_breast_cancer(return_X_y=True)
X_train, X_test, y_train, y_test =
train_test_split(X, y, test_size=0.2) # Train a
model model = xgb.XGBClassifier().fit(X_train,
y_train) # Use SHAP to explain model predictions
explainer = shap.Explainer(model) shap_values =
explainer(X_test) shap.summary_plot(shap_values,
X_test,
feature_names=load_breast_cancer().feature_names)
```

- Transparent Design: Designing AI systems with transparency in mind, such as using models that are inherently more interpretable like decision trees or linear models.

Accountability

Accountability in AI refers to the ability to hold systems and their creators responsible for the decisions and outcomes of AI agents. Ensuring accountability is fundamental for ethical AI practices, as it addresses the consequences of AI decisions and fosters trust.

Ensuring Accountability

- Clear Documentation: Maintain detailed documentation of the AI development process, including data sources, design decisions, and evaluation methods.
- Audit Trails: Implement mechanisms to trace AI decisions back to their inputs and the logic used, facilitating review and accountability.
- Legal and Ethical Standards: Adhere to established legal and ethical standards in AI development, incorporating principles from frameworks such as the EU's Ethics Guidelines for Trustworthy AI.

Ethical Frameworks

Adopting ethical frameworks can guide the development of AI agents in a manner that respects human rights and values. These frameworks often encompass principles like transparency, fairness, and accountability.

Implementing Ethical Frameworks

- Principle-Based Approach: Incorporate principles such as transparency, justice, and non-maleficence into the AI development lifecycle.
- Stakeholder Engagement: Engage with stakeholders, including users, ethicists, and regulators, to understand diverse perspectives and values.
- Continuous Learning: Ethical AI is an evolving field. Stay informed about new research, tools, and best practices for ethical AI development.

Real-World Use Case: Healthcare AI

Consider an AI system designed to assist in diagnosing diseases from medical images. Ethical considerations might include ensuring the training data represents diverse patient populations to avoid bias, providing explanations for diagnoses to enhance transparency, and establishing clear accountability mechanisms for misdiagnoses.

```
# Pseudocode for a healthcare AI system def
diagnose(image): # Preprocess the image
processed_image = preprocess(image) # Make a
prediction diagnosis =
model.predict(processed_image) # Explain the
diagnosis explanation = explain(diagnosis) return
diagnosis, explanation
```

Best Practice: When developing healthcare AI, involve medical professionals in the design and evaluation process to ensure the system meets clinical needs and ethical standards.

Addressing ethical considerations in AI development is not just about preventing harm; it's about building systems that are equitable, transparent, and accountable. By incorporating best practices for mitigating bias, enhancing transparency, ensuring accountability, and adhering to ethical frameworks, developers can create AI agents that are both effective and ethical. This contributes to the broader goal of developing technology that serves humanity and respects fundamental human rights.

Transparency in AI Development

Transparency in AI refers to the clarity and openness with which AI systems and their decisions can be understood by humans. It is a critical factor in building trust between AI systems and their users, as well as ensuring accountability for the actions taken by these systems.

Why Transparency Matters

Transparency is vital for several reasons. First, it allows developers and users to understand how AI agents make decisions, which is essential for diagnosing errors and improving the system. Second, it provides insight into the decision-making process, helping to identify and mitigate potential biases. Lastly, transparency ensures that AI agents can be held accountable for their actions, a crucial aspect when these systems make decisions affecting people's lives.

Implementing Transparency

Implementing transparency in AI involves several strategies and techniques, focusing on making the internal workings of AI systems more understandable to humans.

- Explainable AI (XAI): XAI is an emerging field focused on creating AI models that are more interpretable to humans. Techniques in XAI aim to provide clear, understandable explanations of how AI systems arrive at their decisions.

```
# Example of a simple XAI implementation from
sklearn.tree import DecisionTreeClassifier,
export_text # Train a decision tree classifier
classifier =
DecisionTreeClassifier(random_state=123)
classifier.fit(X_train, y_train) # Generate a text
report showing the rules of the decision tree
tree_rules = export_text(classifier,
feature_names=list(X.columns)) print(tree_rules)
```

- Transparency by Design: Building AI systems with transparency in mind from the outset. This involves selecting algorithms that are inherently more interpretable, such as linear regression or decision trees, over more opaque models like deep neural networks.

- Documentation and Openness: Providing comprehensive documentation of the AI system's development process, including the data sources, algorithms used, and decision-making criteria. Open sourcing the AI model can also contribute to transparency, allowing independent verification of its behavior.

> **Note:** Transparency is not without challenges. Highly complex models, such as deep learning networks, are inherently difficult to interpret, and making them transparent can be a significant technical challenge.

Real-World Example: Transparency in Healthcare AI

In healthcare, an AI system used for diagnosing diseases from medical images must be transparent. Doctors and patients need to understand on what basis the AI made its diagnosis to trust its accuracy and make informed treatment decisions. A transparent AI system in this context could provide explanations for its diagnoses, such as highlighting the specific image features it used to identify a disease.

Accountability in AI Systems

Accountability in AI refers to the obligation of AI developers and users to take responsibility for the outcomes of AI systems.

This ensures that AI systems are built and used ethically, and any negative impacts can be addressed appropriately.

The Importance of Accountability

Without accountability, it's difficult to ensure the ethical use of AI or to rectify harm caused by AI systems. Accountability mechanisms ensure that there are clear guidelines and responsibilities for AI development and deployment, including addressing any biases or failures.

Strategies for Ensuring Accountability

- Clear Guidelines and Standards: Establishing clear ethical guidelines and standards for AI development and use. These can include industry standards, ethical frameworks, and legal regulations.

- Audit Trails: Implementing mechanisms to track decisions made by AI systems. This includes logging inputs, decision-making processes, and outputs, allowing for retrospective analysis and understanding of how specific decisions were made.

- Ethical Review Boards: Setting up independent review boards to evaluate AI projects for ethical considerations. These boards can provide oversight and ensure that AI systems are developed and deployed responsibly.

```
# Example of logging decisions in an AI system
import logging # Set up logging
logging.basicConfig(filename='ai_system_log.txt',
level=logging.INFO) def log_decision(input_data,
decision): logging.info(f"Input Data: {input_data}.
Decision Made: {decision}") # Example usage
input_data = {"patient_age": 45, "symptoms":
["fever", "cough"]} decision = "Recommend COVID-19
test" log_decision(input_data, decision)
```

Accountability in Action: Autonomous Vehicles

In the context of autonomous vehicles, accountability is crucial when addressing incidents or accidents. If an autonomous vehicle is involved in an accident, it's vital to understand the decision-making process that led to the incident. Accountability measures, such as detailed logging and ethical review processes, ensure that manufacturers can be held responsible and learn from these incidents to improve safety.

> **Warning:** Lack of accountability can lead to public mistrust and potential harm. It's essential to establish robust accountability mechanisms to ensure the ethical use of AI.

Ethical Frameworks for AI

Ethical frameworks provide a structured approach to navigating the complex moral landscape of AI development and use. These frameworks offer principles and guidelines to help developers create AI systems that respect human rights, fairness, and societal norms.

Key Principles of Ethical AI

- Respect for Human Autonomy: Ensuring that AI systems enhance, rather than undermine, human decision-making and autonomy.

- Prevention of Harm: Designing AI systems to minimize potential harm to individuals and society.

- Fairness and Non-discrimination: Committing to equity and avoiding bias in AI systems.

- Transparency and Explainability: Making the workings of AI systems as clear and understandable as possible.

Applying Ethical Frameworks

Applying these ethical frameworks involves a continuous process of evaluation and adjustment throughout the AI system's lifecycle. This includes ethical impact assessments at the design stage, ongoing monitoring for unintended consequences, and mechanisms for redress when harm occurs.

```
# Ethical Impact Assessment Example def
ethical_impact_assessment(ai_project): # Assess
potential impacts on human autonomy # Evaluate risks
of harm # Check for biases that could lead to
discrimination # Ensure transparency and
explainability of the AI system pass
```

Incorporating ethical frameworks into AI development requires a commitment to ethical reflection and action. It's about constantly asking, "Should we build this?" not just "Can we build this?" and making adjustments based on ethical considerations.

Addressing ethical considerations in AI, including bias and fairness, transparency, and accountability, requires a comprehensive approach. By implementing best practices, real-world examples, and ethical frameworks, developers can navigate the complexities of ethical AI development. This ensures that AI systems are not only technically proficient but also socially responsible and beneficial to all.

Accountability in AI Systems

Accountability in the context of autonomous AI agents refers to the principle that an AI system's actions can be traced back to human operators or developers who can be held responsible for its outcomes. This principle is paramount in ensuring that AI systems are used ethically and responsibly. It safeguards against the misuse of AI technologies and helps in mitigating any negative impacts that may arise from their deployment.

Establishing Accountability

To establish accountability in AI systems, it's crucial to implement mechanisms that can accurately trace decisions back to the entities responsible for them. This involves several key strategies:

Clear Documentation

Documenting the development process of AI agents, including the decision-making logic, data sources, and algorithms used, is fundamental. This documentation should be accessible and understandable to all stakeholders involved.

```
- **Development Log:** Maintain a detailed log of
all development stages, including algorithm
selection, data preprocessing, and model training. -
**Version Control:** Use version control systems to
track changes in the codebase and model
configurations over time.
```

Audit Trails

Creating an audit trail involves logging all actions taken by the AI system, including the inputs it received and the decisions it made. These logs should be immutable and securely stored to provide a reliable source for review if needed.

```
# Example of creating a basic audit trail in Python
def log_decision(input_data, decision): with
open("audit_log.txt", "a") as log_file:
log_file.write(f"Input: {input_data}, Decision:
{decision}\n")
```

> **Note:** Ensure that logging does not compromise user privacy or data security. Anonymize sensitive information where necessary.

Accountability Challenges

One of the major challenges in ensuring accountability is the complexity of AI systems, especially those based on deep learning. These models can act as "black boxes," with decision-making processes that are not easily interpretable by humans.

Solutions for Complexity

- Model Explainability: Use techniques and tools designed to make AI decisions more interpretable, such as SHAP (SHapley Additive exPlanations) or LIME (Local Interpretable Model-Agnostic Explanations).

- Human-in-the-loop: Implement systems where critical decisions are reviewed or made by human operators, ensuring that there is a clear line of accountability.

Real-World Use Case: Healthcare

In healthcare, AI agents are used to support diagnostic processes, treatment planning, and patient monitoring. Ensuring accountability in these systems is critical due to the high stakes involved.

- Example: An AI system designed to diagnose diseases from medical images should have a clear audit trail for each diagnosis, comprehensive documentation on the models and data used, and mechanisms for healthcare professionals to review and override decisions.

Best Practices for Ethical AI Development

To address the ethical challenges in AI, including bias, fairness, transparency, and accountability, developers should adhere to a set of best practices:

1. Ethical Framework Adoption: Adopt or develop an ethical framework that guides the AI development process, ensuring that ethical considerations are integrated at every stage. 2. Diverse Teams: Include team members from diverse backgrounds to help identify and mitigate biases that the development team may overlook. 3. Continuous Monitoring: Regularly monitor and audit AI systems post-deployment to catch and correct any unethical behavior or outcomes. 4. Stakeholder Engagement: Engage with stakeholders, including users, ethicists, and regulatory bodies, to understand the broader impacts of AI systems.

By implementing these practices, developers can significantly reduce the risks associated with AI systems and ensure they contribute positively to society.

As AI technologies continue to evolve and become more integrated into our daily lives, the importance of ethical considerations in their development cannot be overstated. By focusing on bias and fairness, transparency, accountability, and adhering to ethical frameworks, developers can create AI agents that are not only powerful and efficient but also responsible and beneficial to all.

Ethical Frameworks in AI Development

Establishing ethical frameworks is crucial in guiding the development and deployment of AI agents. These frameworks provide a structured approach to addressing ethical dilemmas and ensuring that AI technologies promote societal well-being while minimizing harm. They encompass principles such as fairness, accountability, transparency, and privacy.

Understanding Ethical Frameworks

Ethical frameworks in AI are sets of guidelines that help developers and stakeholders make informed decisions about the ethical implications of their work. These guidelines often draw from broader ethical theories and principles, applying them to the specific challenges and opportunities presented by AI technology.

Examples of Ethical Frameworks

- Asilomar AI Principles: A set of 23 principles developed during the 2017 Asilomar conference, covering research issues, ethics and values, and longer-term issues.
- IEEE Ethically Aligned Design: A comprehensive set of recommendations developed by the IEEE to ensure that AI and autonomous systems are developed and operated in ways that prioritize human well-being.

Implementing Ethical Frameworks

To effectively implement these frameworks, organizations and developers should:

1. Conduct Ethical Risk Assessments: Before deploying AI agents, assess potential ethical risks, including biases, privacy

concerns, and impacts on stakeholders.

2. Engage with Stakeholders: Include diverse perspectives in the development process, especially those who will be directly affected by the AI systems.

3. Adopt Ethical Design Practices: Integrate ethical considerations into the design and development process, ensuring that AI agents are aligned with ethical guidelines from the outset.

4. Continuous Monitoring and Evaluation: After deployment, continuously monitor AI agents for ethical compliance and impact, ready to make adjustments as needed.

```
# Example: Conducting an Ethical Risk Assessment def
assess_ethical_risks(agent_impacts): risks = [] if
'bias' in agent_impacts: risks.append('Potential for
biased outcomes') if 'privacy' in agent_impacts:
risks.append('Potential for privacy breaches') # Add
further assessments as needed return risks
agent_impacts = ['bias', 'privacy', 'transparency']
risks = assess_ethical_risks(agent_impacts)
print("Identified Ethical Risks:", risks)
```

Note: Implementing ethical frameworks is an ongoing process that requires regular revisitation and revision to align with evolving societal values and technological capabilities.

Best Practices for Ethical AI Development

- Transparency: Make the workings of AI agents as understandable as possible, not just to tech experts but also to the general public.
- Inclusivity: Ensure that AI development teams are diverse, to reduce the risk of unconscious biases being built into AI

systems.

- Collaboration: Work with other organizations, ethicists, and policymakers to share best practices and learn from each other's experiences.

Addressing Common Challenges

One of the main challenges in implementing ethical frameworks is the subjective nature of ethics itself. Different cultures and individuals may have varying views on what constitutes ethical behavior, making universal guidelines difficult to establish. Another challenge is the pace of technological advancement, which often outstrips the development of ethical standards and regulations.

To address these challenges, continuous dialogue between technologists, ethicists, policymakers, and the public is essential. Furthermore, adopting a flexible approach to ethics that can evolve with technological and societal changes is crucial.

Practical Exercise

1. Choose an existing AI agent project or concept. 2. Conduct an ethical risk assessment based on the potential impacts of the AI agent. 3. Propose mitigation strategies for identified risks. 4. Reflect on how the implementation of an ethical framework could guide the development process from the beginning.

In conclusion, ethical frameworks serve as vital tools in the responsible development and deployment of AI agents. By adhering to these guidelines, developers can navigate the complex ethical landscape of AI, ensuring that their creations contribute positively to society and do not inadvertently cause harm.

Chapter 19: Deployment and Scaling

Deployment Options for AI Agents

Deploying AI agents involves making the agent accessible to users or systems in a production environment. The deployment strategy must ensure that the agent is reliable, scalable, and secure. This section explores various deployment options and their considerations.

Cloud-Based Deployment

Cloud platforms like Amazon Web Services (AWS), Google Cloud Platform (GCP), and Microsoft Azure offer robust environments for deploying AI agents. These platforms provide essential services such as compute instances, storage options, and managed databases, which are crucial for AI applications.

- Example: Deploying an AI chatbot on AWS Lambda allows for automatic scaling based on request volume, ensuring that the agent can handle peak loads efficiently.

```
# Example code snippet for deploying a simple AI
model on AWS Lambda import json import boto3 def
lambda_handler(event, context): # AI model logic
here response = "This is a response from your AI
model" return { 'statusCode': 200, 'body':
json.dumps(response) }
```

Note: When deploying on cloud platforms, consider the network latency and data transfer costs, especially if your AI agent requires real-time interactions.

On-Premises Deployment

Some organizations require AI agents to be deployed on their own hardware due to regulatory, security, or performance reasons. On-premises deployment offers complete control over the hardware and software environment.

- Example: A financial institution deploys an AI fraud detection agent on-premises to comply with data sovereignty regulations and ensure low-latency access to transaction databases.

  Warning: On-premises deployments can significantly increase the complexity of scaling and maintenance. Ensure your team has the necessary expertise to manage these environments.

Edge Deployment

Deploying AI agents on edge devices allows for low-latency decisions and reduces the need for constant internet connectivity. This is particularly useful for IoT devices, mobile applications, and scenarios requiring real-time processing.

- Example: An AI agent deployed on a smart camera for real-time facial recognition and threat detection, operating independently of central servers.

```
# Example code for a simple edge-based AI model
processing input data def
process_input data(input data): # AI processing
logic here processed_data = "Processed data based on
input" return processed_data
```

Tip: When deploying AI agents on edge devices, optimize your models for size and performance to fit the constraints of the device.

Scaling Strategies for AI Agents

Efficiently scaling AI agents is crucial for handling increased loads without compromising performance. This section discusses various strategies to scale AI agents effectively.

Horizontal vs. Vertical Scaling

- Horizontal Scaling: This involves adding more instances of the AI agent to handle increased load. It's suitable for cloud-based and containerized environments where you can dynamically adjust the number of instances.
- Vertical Scaling: Increasing the resources (CPU, RAM) of the existing system to enhance the capacity of the AI agent. This is often limited by the maximum capacity of the server and can be less flexible than horizontal scaling.

Load Balancing

Using load balancers can distribute incoming requests across multiple instances of the AI agent, ensuring no single instance becomes a bottleneck. This is essential for maintaining high availability and performance.

- Example: Configuring an AWS Elastic Load Balancer (ELB) to distribute user queries across multiple chatbot instances.

Auto-Scaling

Auto-scaling automatically adjusts the number of AI agent instances based on the current load, ensuring cost-efficiency by scaling down during low usage periods and scaling up when demand increases.

- Example: Implementing auto-scaling policies in Kubernetes for a containerized AI model, based on CPU and memory usage metrics.

```
apiVersion: autoscaling/v1 kind:
HorizontalPodAutoscaler metadata: name:
ai-agent-autoscaler spec: scaleTargetRef:
apiVersion: apps/v1 kind: Deployment name: ai-agent
minReplicas: 2 maxReplicas: 10
targetCPUUtilizationPercentage: 80
```

Performance Optimization

Optimizing the performance of AI agents involves refining the code, model, and infrastructure to reduce latency, increase throughput, and minimize resource consumption.

Code Optimization

- Efficient Algorithms: Use the most efficient algorithms for data processing and inference. Algorithmic complexity can significantly impact performance.

- Parallel Processing: Utilize parallel processing and vectorization to speed up computations, especially for data-intensive tasks.

Model Optimization

- Model Pruning: Reduce the size of the AI model by removing unnecessary neurons, which can decrease inference times without significantly impacting accuracy.

- Quantization: Lower the precision of the model's computations from floating-point to integer, which can reduce the model size and speed up inference.

Infrastructure Optimization

- Dedicated Hardware: Use hardware optimized for AI workloads, such as GPUs or TPUs, to significantly accelerate model training and inference.

- Caching: Implement caching mechanisms to store frequently accessed data or inference results, reducing the need to recompute responses.

Maintenance and Updates

Regular maintenance and updates are crucial for the long-term reliability and performance of AI agents. This involves monitoring the system, updating the AI models, and patching the software.

Monitoring and Logging

Implement comprehensive monitoring and logging to track the performance and health of the AI agent. This can help in quickly identifying and addressing issues.

- Example: Using Prometheus and Grafana for monitoring metrics such as response times, error rates, and system resource usage.

Continuous Model Training

AI models can degrade over time as data and real-world conditions change. Implement continuous training pipelines to periodically retrain models with new data, ensuring they remain accurate and effective.

Software Updates

Regularly update the software dependencies and frameworks used by the AI agent to patch security vulnerabilities and benefit from performance improvements.

Best Practice: Implement automated testing and continuous integration/continuous deployment (CI/CD) pipelines to streamline the deployment of updates and minimize downtime.

Practical Exercise: Deploying and Scaling a Simple AI Agent

- Objective: Deploy a simple AI agent that performs sentiment analysis on user input and scale it to handle varying loads.

- Tools: AWS Lambda for deployment, AWS Elastic Load Balancer for load balancing, and AWS Auto Scaling to automatically adjust the number of instances.

1. Deployment: Package your AI model and deploy it as a Lambda function. 2. Load Balancing: Configure an Elastic Load Balancer to distribute incoming requests across multiple

Lambda instances. 3. Auto-Scaling: Set up auto-scaling policies based on the number of incoming requests to ensure efficient resource usage.

This exercise provides hands-on experience with deploying and scaling AI agents, highlighting the importance of performance optimization and maintenance in real-world applications.

Scaling Strategies for AI Agents

As your AI agents begin to handle more tasks and interact with more users, scaling becomes a critical concern. Effective scaling strategies ensure that your AI agents remain responsive and efficient, even as demand increases.

Horizontal vs. Vertical Scaling

Understanding the difference between horizontal and vertical scaling is crucial for managing your AI agents effectively.

- Horizontal Scaling involves adding more machines or instances to your pool of resources to handle increased load. This is often referred to as scaling out or in. Cloud-based deployments make horizontal scaling relatively straightforward, allowing for the dynamic addition or removal of resources based on demand.

- Vertical Scaling means upgrading the existing machines with more powerful resources such as CPU, RAM, or storage. This is known as scaling up or down. While simpler, it has its limits; there's only so much you can upgrade a single machine before costs become prohibitive or you hit technical ceilings.

Example: Scaling AI Chatbots

Consider an AI chatbot serving customer inquiries. Initially, the chatbot might run on a single server. As demand grows, response times might increase, leading to a poor user experience. Implementing horizontal scaling by adding more servers can distribute the load, reducing response times without altering the chatbot's code. Conversely, vertical scaling would involve upgrading the server's specifications, which might provide a temporary boost but would eventually require horizontal scaling for long-term growth.

Auto-Scaling Strategies

Auto-scaling is a method that dynamically adjusts the number of active servers based on the current load, ensuring that your deployment can handle peaks in demand without manual intervention.

- Cloud-Based Auto-Scaling: Most cloud providers offer auto-scaling features that can be configured based on specific metrics such as CPU utilization, memory usage, or custom metrics relevant to your AI agent's performance.

- Implementing Auto-Scaling: To effectively use auto-scaling, you must define scaling policies. For instance, you might set a rule to add a new instance when CPU usage exceeds 70% over a 5-minute period or remove an instance when CPU usage drops below 20%.

```
# Example auto-scaling policy configuration
(pseudo-code): AutoScalingPolicy: - ScaleOut:
Trigger: CPU > 70% Duration: 5min Action:
AddInstance - ScaleIn: Trigger: CPU < 20% Duration:
5min Action: RemoveInstance
```

Note: Auto-scaling introduces complexity, especially in stateful applications where instances share data. Ensure your AI agents are designed to

327

handle dynamic changes in the number of instances.

Load Balancing

Load balancing is the process of distributing network or application traffic across multiple servers. This ensures no single server becomes a bottleneck, improving responsiveness and availability of your AI agents.

- Implementation: Use a load balancer to distribute incoming requests to your AI agents evenly. Modern cloud services offer managed load balancers that integrate seamlessly with auto-scaling groups.
- Session Persistence: For AI agents requiring stateful interactions, such as conversational AI, session persistence (sticky sessions) ensures that all requests from a single session are directed to the same instance.

Performance Optimization

Beyond scaling, optimizing the performance of your AI agents can lead to significant improvements in speed and efficiency. Here are some strategies:

Efficient Algorithms

Choosing the right algorithms and data structures can drastically affect your AI agent's performance. Always look for the most efficient algorithm for your use case, considering both time and space complexity.

Caching

Caching frequently requested data reduces the need to recompute results or query the database multiple times. Implement caching at various levels (e.g., database, application, or CDN) to improve response times for common requests.

Asynchronous Processing

For operations that do not require immediate response, consider using asynchronous processing. This frees up resources to handle more user interactions while background tasks complete, improving overall throughput.

Example: Asynchronous Image Processing

An AI agent that processes user-uploaded images can immediately acknowledge receipt and process the images in the background. This approach keeps the user interface responsive, enhancing the user experience.

```
# Pseudo-code for asynchronous image processing def
handle_image_upload(image): acknowledge_upload() #
Immediate response to user
async_process_image(image) # Background processing
async def async_process_image(image): # Image
processing logic here pass
```

Maintenance and Updates

Regular maintenance and updates are essential to keep your AI agents functioning optimally. This includes:

- Monitoring: Continuously monitor your AI agents for performance issues, errors, and usage patterns. Use this data to inform scaling decisions and identify areas for optimization.

- Updating Models: AI models can degrade over time as data and user behavior change. Regularly retrain your models with new data to maintain or improve performance.

- Security Updates: Keep all components of your AI agent system up-to-date with the latest security patches to protect against vulnerabilities.

Best Practices

1. Automate Deployments: Use continuous integration and continuous deployment (CI/CD) pipelines to automate the deployment of updates, reducing manual errors and downtime.

2. Blue/Green Deployments: Deploy new versions alongside the old version to reduce downtime and risk. After testing the new version, traffic is gradually shifted, allowing for easy rollback if issues arise.

3. Feature Flags: Implement feature flags to toggle new features on or off without redeploying. This allows for safer testing and rollouts of new features.

By understanding and implementing these strategies for deployment, scaling, performance optimization, and maintenance, you can ensure that your AI agents remain responsive, efficient, and effective, even as they grow and evolve.

Performance Optimization

Optimizing the performance of AI agents is essential to ensure they can handle increased workload efficiently as part of the scaling process. Performance optimization can be approached from several angles, including optimizing the code, improving the efficiency of the machine learning models, and optimizing the infrastructure.

Code Optimization

Optimizing the code of your AI agents can lead to significant performance improvements. This might involve refactoring the code to make it more efficient, removing unnecessary computations, or leveraging more efficient algorithms.

- Example: If your AI agent processes data in a sequential manner, consider using parallel processing techniques to speed up the processing time. This can be achieved through multi-threading or using parallel processing libraries such as Python's multiprocessing.

```
import multiprocessing def process_data(data): #
Your data processing code here pass if __name__ ==
"__main__": data_segments = [data1, data2, data3,
data4] # Assume these are predefined data segments
pool = multiprocessing.Pool(processes=4)
pool.map(process_data, data_segments)
```

Machine Learning Model Efficiency

Improving the efficiency of the machine learning models used by your AI agents can also enhance performance. This might involve simplifying the models to reduce complexity, employing model quantization, or selecting more efficient algorithms.

- Example: Consider using model pruning to remove unimportant weights from your neural network, reducing its size and making it faster without significantly impacting accuracy.

Infrastructure Optimization

Optimizing the infrastructure on which your AI agents run can further enhance performance. This could mean choosing more powerful hardware, using GPUs for computation-heavy tasks, or optimizing your cloud infrastructure configuration.

- Best Practice: Utilize cloud auto-scaling features to dynamically adjust the amount of computational resources based on the workload. This ensures that your AI agents have the necessary resources during peak times without incurring unnecessary costs during off-peak times.

Maintenance and Updates

Regular maintenance and updates are crucial to the long-term success and reliability of AI agents. This involves monitoring the system for issues, updating the code and models to improve performance and accuracy, and adapting to changes in the environment or data.

Monitoring and Logging

Implementing comprehensive monitoring and logging is essential to understand how your AI agents are performing and to quickly identify any issues. This includes monitoring system performance, tracking user interactions, and logging errors.

- Tip: Use tools like Prometheus for monitoring and Grafana for visualization to get real-time insights into your system's performance.

Continuous Improvement

AI agents should be continuously updated and improved based on new data, user feedback, and evolving requirements. This includes retraining machine learning models with new data, refining the logic of the agents, and updating the code for better performance and reliability.

- Challenge: Set up a continuous integration/continuous deployment (CI/CD) pipeline for your AI agents to automate testing and deployment of updates. This ensures that your agents are always running the latest code and models.

Adapting to Changes

AI agents need to be adaptable to changes in their operating environment, which might include changes in user behavior, data distribution, or external APIs they depend on.

- Example: Implement feature flags in your system, allowing you to turn on/off certain functionalities or roll out updates to a subset of users. This helps in testing new features and quickly reverting changes if something goes wrong.

```
# Example feature flag check if
feature_flags["new_feature_active"]: # New feature
code here else: # Old feature code here
```

Warning: Always ensure that your system has fallback mechanisms in case of failure, especially when relying on external services. This could involve using circuit breakers or setting up redundant systems to maintain availability.

Deploying and scaling AI agents involves a multifaceted approach that includes optimizing performance, ensuring regular maintenance and updates, and adapting to changes. By focusing on these areas, you can ensure that your AI agents remain efficient, reliable, and effective at meeting the needs of users and the business.

Maintenance and Updates

Maintaining and updating AI agents is crucial for their long-term performance and reliability. As the environment in which the AI operates changes, so too must the AI agent. This section will cover the best practices for maintaining and updating your AI agents to ensure they continue to perform optimally.

Version Control and Continuous Integration

For effective maintenance, it's important to use version control systems like Git. Version control allows you to keep track of changes, manage updates efficiently, and revert to previous versions if an update causes issues.

```
git add . git commit -m "Update AI model parameters"
git push origin main
```

Continuous Integration (CI) tools such as Jenkins or GitHub Actions can automate the testing of your AI agents every time a change is made. This ensures that updates do not break existing functionality.

```
name: AI Agent Test Workflow on: [push] jobs: test:
runs-on: ubuntu-latest steps: - uses:
```

```
actions/checkout@v2 - name: Run tests run: python -m
unittest discover -s tests
```

> **Note:** Always ensure your tests cover a wide range
> of scenarios that your AI agent might encounter in the
> real world. This helps in identifying potential issues
> early in the development cycle.

Data Drift Detection and Model Retraining

Data drift refers to the change in the input data over time,
which can lead to a decrease in the model's performance.
Implementing data drift detection mechanisms can alert you
when the model's performance degrades due to changes in the
data.

Once data drift is detected, model retraining becomes
necessary. Retraining the model with new data ensures that it
adapts to the changes in the environment. Automating the
retraining process can help in maintaining the performance of
the AI agent without manual intervention.

```python
from sklearn.model_selection import train_test_split
from sklearn.ensemble import RandomForestClassifier
# Assuming X and y are your features and labels
respectively X_train, X_test, y_train, y_test =
train_test_split(X, y, test_size=0.2) model =
RandomForestClassifier() model.fit(X_train, y_train)
# Save your model import joblib joblib.dump(model,
'model_latest.pkl')
```

Monitoring and Alerts

Monitoring the performance of your AI agents is essential.
Implementing a monitoring system that tracks key performance

indicators (KPIs) such as response time, accuracy, and throughput can help in identifying issues early.

Setting up alerts for when these KPIs fall below a certain threshold ensures that you can quickly respond to any issues. Tools like Prometheus and Grafana are widely used for monitoring and setting up alerts.

```
alert: AIResponseTimeHigh expr:
histogram_quantile(0.9,
rate(ai_response_time_seconds_bucket[10m])) > 1 for:
10m labels: severity: page annotations: summary:
High response time detected in AI agent description:
"AI agent's response time has exceeded 1 second for
90% of requests in the last 10 minutes."
```

Warning: Be cautious of alert fatigue. Too many alerts can become overwhelming and lead to important alerts being missed. Ensure that alerts are configured for significant events.

Implementing Feedback Loops

Feedback loops allow your AI agents to learn from their interactions and improve over time. Incorporating user feedback directly into the training data can help in fine-tuning the AI agent's responses and actions.

This can be as simple as adding a feedback mechanism in the UI where users can rate the AI's response or action, and then using this feedback to retrain the model.

```
# Example feedback collection feedback =
collect_feedback() # Implement your feedback
collection X_new, y_new =
preprocess_feedback(feedback) # Convert feedback
into usable training data model.fit(X_new, y_new,
epochs=1) # Incrementally train your model with new
```

Implementing these maintenance and update strategies ensures that your AI agents remain effective and efficient over their operational life. Regular updates, performance monitoring, and incorporating user feedback are key to sustaining the relevance and efficiency of AI systems in dynamic environments.

Chapter 20: Future of AI Agents

Emerging Technologies

The landscape of artificial intelligence is ever-evolving, with new technologies emerging at a rapid pace. These advancements promise to redefine the capabilities of AI agents, making them more autonomous, efficient, and intelligent. In this section, we explore some of the most promising emerging technologies that are set to shape the future of AI agents.

Quantum Computing and AI

Quantum computing represents a seismic shift in computing power and capability. Unlike classical computing, which relies on bits to process information in a binary format of 0s and 1s, quantum computing uses quantum bits or qubits. This allows quantum computers to process complex datasets much more efficiently than traditional computers.

```
# Pseudocode illustrating a quantum operation
quantum_register = QuantumRegister(2, 'qreg')
quantum_circuit = QuantumCircuit(quantum_register)
quantum_circuit.h(quantum_register[0])
quantum_circuit.cx(quantum_register[0],
quantum_register[1])
```

Note: The above pseudocode demonstrates the creation of a simple quantum circuit that generates entanglement between two qubits, showcasing the fundamental difference in operations compared to classical computing.

Quantum computing holds the potential to significantly accelerate the training of AI models by processing vast amounts of data at unprecedented speeds. This could enhance the efficiency of AI agents, enabling them to perform complex tasks, such as real-time natural language processing or intricate pattern recognition, with much greater accuracy and speed.

Neuromorphic Computing

Neuromorphic computing aims to mimic the neural structure of the human brain, providing a new approach to artificial intelligence. By replicating the brain's architecture of interconnected neurons, neuromorphic chips can process information in a manner that's more akin to natural cognitive processes.

This technology promises to make AI agents more energy-efficient and capable of real-time learning and decision-making without the need for extensive data or pre-training. Such agents would be able to adapt to new situations with a level of flexibility and efficiency that current AI systems cannot match.

Federated Learning

Federated learning is a decentralized approach to machine learning where the training process is distributed among multiple devices or servers. This method allows AI agents to learn from data that remains stored on the local device, enhancing privacy and security.

```
# Pseudocode for a simple federated learning model
update def federated_learning_update(local_updates):
global_model = aggregate(local_updates) for update
in local_updates: global_model =
apply_update(global_model, update) return
```

Federated learning could revolutionize the way AI agents are trained, particularly in sensitive areas like healthcare or finance, by enabling them to learn from vast, decentralized datasets without compromising user privacy.

Future Applications

The advancements in AI technologies are opening up new and exciting applications for AI agents across various industries.

Autonomous Vehicles

Autonomous vehicles are perhaps one of the most anticipated applications of AI agents. With the integration of advanced AI technologies, such as computer vision and deep learning, these vehicles can navigate complex environments safely and efficiently. This technology not only promises to reduce traffic accidents but also aims to revolutionize transportation, making it more accessible and less reliant on human intervention.

Personalized Healthcare

AI agents equipped with capabilities such as natural language processing and predictive analytics are set to transform the healthcare industry by providing personalized care. These agents can analyze patient data, predict health issues before they become severe, and offer customized treatment plans. Moreover, AI-powered virtual health assistants can provide continuous support and monitoring, improving patient outcomes and healthcare efficiency.

Smart Cities

AI agents are at the forefront of turning the concept of smart cities into reality. Through the analysis of data from various sources, including IoT devices and sensors, AI agents can manage traffic flow, optimize energy consumption, and enhance public safety. These intelligent systems can predict and respond to urban challenges in real time, making cities more livable and sustainable.

Industry Trends

As AI technologies continue to evolve, several key industry trends are emerging that will shape the future landscape of AI agents.

Ethical AI

The growing capabilities of AI agents are raising important ethical questions regarding privacy, security, and the potential for bias. As a result, there's an increasing focus on developing ethical AI frameworks that ensure AI agents are designed and deployed in a manner that is transparent, fair, and respects user privacy.

AI Governance

Alongside ethical considerations, there's a trend towards establishing robust AI governance frameworks to manage the development and use of AI agents. This includes setting standards for accountability, reliability, and safety to ensure that AI technologies benefit society as a whole.

AI in Edge Computing

The rise of edge computing, where data processing occurs on local devices rather than centralized servers, is driving the development of AI agents capable of operating at the edge. This trend is particularly relevant in applications where real-time processing and decision-making are critical, such as in autonomous vehicles or IoT devices.

Career Opportunities

The rapid advancement in AI technologies is creating a wealth of career opportunities for individuals interested in working with AI agents. Roles such as AI researchers, machine learning engineers, data scientists, and AI ethics specialists are in high demand. As AI continues to permeate various sectors, the need for skilled professionals who can develop, implement, and manage AI agents will only continue to grow.

Tips for Aspiring AI Professionals

- Stay Updated: The field of AI is constantly evolving. Keeping abreast of the latest research, tools, and technologies is crucial.

- Practical Experience: Hands-on experience with AI projects, whether through internships, personal projects, or online competitions, is invaluable.
- Ethical Considerations: Understanding the ethical implications of AI and advocating for responsible AI development is increasingly important.
- Collaboration: AI is a multidisciplinary field. Collaborating with professionals from other disciplines can provide new insights and approaches.

The future of AI agents is brimming with possibilities and challenges. As emerging technologies continue to push the boundaries of what's possible, the applications of AI agents will expand, transforming industries and society in profound ways. For those entering the field, the opportunity to contribute to this exciting future has never been greater.

Future Applications of AI Agents

The potential applications of AI agents are vast and varied, reaching into nearly every sector of the economy and aspect of human life. As these technologies continue to advance, we can expect AI agents to become integral components of our daily routines, transforming industries and creating new opportunities for innovation.

Healthcare

AI agents in healthcare are poised to revolutionize patient care, diagnostics, and treatment planning. For example, AI-driven diagnostic tools can analyze medical images with greater accuracy and speed than human counterparts, leading to faster and more accurate diagnoses. Moreover, personalized treatment plans can be developed by AI agents by analyzing a patient's genetic makeup, lifestyle, and treatment history.

```
# Example of an AI diagnostic tool processing
medical images import tensorflow as tf def
analyze_medical_image(image_path): # Load the
pre-trained model model = tf.keras.models.load_model
('path_to_pretrained_model') # Load and preprocess
the image image =
tf.keras.preprocessing.image.load_img(image_path,
target_size=(224, 224)) image_array =
tf.keras.preprocessing.image.img_to_array(image)
image_array = tf.expand_dims(image_array, 0) # Make
it a batch # Predict the condition predictions =
model.predict(image_array) return predictions
```

> **Note:** The accuracy of AI predictions in healthcare relies heavily on the quality and diversity of the data used to train the models.

Autonomous Vehicles

Autonomous vehicles, guided by AI agents, promise to make transportation safer, more efficient, and accessible. AI agents process data from sensors and cameras in real-time, enabling the vehicle to navigate traffic, avoid obstacles, and make split-second decisions that human drivers might not be capable of.

Finance

In the finance sector, AI agents are transforming how companies approach risk assessment, fraud detection, and customer service. For instance, AI-driven algorithms can analyze transaction patterns to identify potential fraud, significantly reducing financial losses and increasing customer trust.

Industry Trends

As AI agents become more sophisticated, several key trends are emerging within industries that are early adopters of this technology.

Edge Computing

The integration of AI agents with edge computing is a significant trend, enabling faster processing and decision-making at the device level, without the need for constant communication with a central server. This is particularly relevant for applications requiring real-time analysis, such as in autonomous vehicles or IoT devices.

Explainable AI (XAI)

With the rise of AI agents in critical sectors, there's an increasing demand for transparency and explainability in AI decisions. Explainable AI aims to make the decision-making processes of AI agents understandable to humans, fostering trust and facilitating regulatory compliance.

Career Opportunities

The growth of AI agents is creating a plethora of career opportunities, not only for developers and data scientists but also for professionals in fields like ethics, law, and healthcare, who are needed to navigate the societal implications of autonomous agents.

AI Ethics and Governance

As AI agents become more embedded in society, the need for ethical guidelines and governance frameworks becomes paramount. Professionals in this field work to ensure that AI technologies are developed and deployed in a way that is fair, transparent, and beneficial for all.

AI Agent Development

Developers specializing in AI agent development are in high demand, tasked with designing, building, and refining the algorithms that empower autonomous systems. Knowledge in machine learning, neural networks, and data analysis is crucial for success in this role.

Data Privacy and Security

With the vast amounts of data processed by AI agents, ensuring privacy and security is a major challenge. Professionals in this area focus on developing robust security measures to protect sensitive information from cyber threats and ensure compliance with data protection regulations.

The evolution of AI agents is set to redefine our world, offering unprecedented opportunities and challenges. By understanding the future applications, industry trends, and career opportunities associated with AI agents, individuals and organizations can better prepare for the exciting advancements on the horizon.

In the final section of this chapter, we will explore the ethical considerations and societal impacts of deploying AI agents, underscoring the importance of responsible development and usage of these technologies.

> **Best Practice:** Staying informed about the latest advancements and engaging with a community of AI professionals can help individuals navigate the rapidly changing landscape of AI agents.

Emerging Technologies in AI Agents

As AI continues to evolve, several emerging technologies are shaping the future of AI agents. Understanding these technologies is crucial for anyone looking to stay at the forefront of AI development and application.

Machine Learning Enhancements

Machine learning (ML) is at the heart of AI agents, enabling them to learn from data and improve over time. Recent advancements in ML, such as deep learning, reinforcement learning, and federated learning, are significantly enhancing the capabilities of AI agents.

- Deep Learning: Utilizes neural networks with many layers, enabling AI agents to process and interpret complex data structures, leading to improvements in image and speech recognition tasks.

- Reinforcement Learning: Allows AI agents to learn optimal behaviors through trial and error by interacting with their environment. This is particularly useful in gaming, robotics, and navigation applications.

- Federated Learning: A technique for training ML models across multiple decentralized devices while keeping the data localized, enhancing privacy and security. This is increasingly important for AI agents operating in sensitive or personal domains.

```
# Example of a simple deep learning model using
TensorFlow import tensorflow as tf from
tensorflow.keras.models import Sequential from
tensorflow.keras.layers import Dense model =
Sequential([ Dense(units=64, activation='relu',
input_shape=(784,)), Dense(units=10,
activation='softmax') ])
model.compile(optimizer='adam',
loss='categorical_crossentropy',
metrics=['accuracy'])
```

Note: The code snippet above demonstrates how to define a basic neural network for classification tasks using TensorFlow, a popular deep learning framework.

Quantum Computing

Quantum computing promises to revolutionize the computational capabilities available to AI agents. By leveraging the principles of quantum mechanics, quantum computers can process information at speeds unattainable by traditional computing methods. This could enable AI agents to solve complex problems, such as drug discovery and climate modeling, much faster than currently possible.

Edge Computing

Edge computing refers to the practice of processing data near the source of data generation, rather than relying on centralized data-processing warehouses. For AI agents, this means faster response times and reduced latency, as data does not need to be sent over long distances for processing. This is particularly relevant for applications requiring real-time decision-making, such as autonomous vehicles and IoT devices.

Best Practices for Developing AI Agents

When developing AI agents, it's important to adhere to best practices to ensure their effectiveness and ethical use. Here are some key considerations:

Focus on User Privacy

With increasing concerns about data privacy, it's crucial to design AI agents that respect user privacy. Implementing features like data anonymization and secure data storage can help protect user information.

Ensure Transparency

AI agents should be transparent in their operations, allowing users to understand how decisions are made. This can be achieved through explainable AI (XAI) techniques, which provide insights into the agent's decision-making process.

Prioritize Security

AI agents are often targeted by malicious entities. Ensuring robust security measures, such as regular software updates and vulnerability assessments, is critical to protect against cyber threats.

Adopt Continuous Learning

AI agents should be designed to continuously learn and adapt to new information. This can be facilitated through techniques like online learning, where the agent updates its model in real-time as new data becomes available.

Promote Ethical Use

Finally, it's important to consider the ethical implications of AI agents. Developers should strive to create agents that benefit society and do not perpetuate biases or inequalities.

By following these best practices, developers can create AI agents that are not only powerful and efficient but also ethical and user-friendly.

The future of AI agents is both exciting and promising, with emerging technologies and advancements poised to further enhance their capabilities. By understanding these developments and adhering to best practices, developers can create AI agents that significantly impact various domains, from healthcare to autonomous vehicles. As the field continues to evolve, staying informed and adaptable will be key to leveraging the full potential of AI agents.

Industry Trends in AI Agents

The evolution of AI agents is not only shaped by technological advancements but also by the changing trends in various industries. These trends highlight the growing importance and application of AI agents across different sectors, from healthcare to finance, and beyond. Understanding these industry trends is vital for developers and businesses aiming to leverage AI agents for innovative solutions.

Healthcare

AI agents are revolutionizing the healthcare industry by providing personalized care, automating administrative tasks, and enhancing diagnostic processes. For instance, AI-powered chatbots are being used to triage patient inquiries, reducing the workload on healthcare professionals and improving patient experience. Additionally, AI agents are being employed in predictive analytics to identify potential health risks and recommend preventive measures.

```
# Example: AI Agent for Patient Triage class
PatientTriageAI: def analyze_symptoms(symptoms): #
Implement logic to analyze patient symptoms pass def
recommend_action(): # Based on analysis, recommend
next steps pass
```

> **Note:** While AI agents offer significant benefits in healthcare, developers must prioritize privacy and data security to protect sensitive patient information.

Finance

In the finance sector, AI agents are transforming the way businesses and consumers manage finances. From personalized investment advice to fraud detection, AI agents are at the forefront of financial innovation. An example includes AI-driven robo-advisors, which provide investment management services with minimal human intervention, making financial advice more accessible and affordable.

```
// Example: Basic AI Agent for Fraud Detection
function detectFraud(transaction) { if
(transaction.amount > threshold && transaction.type
=== 'unusual') { alert('Possible fraud detected'); }
}
```

Retail

AI agents in the retail industry are enhancing customer experiences and operational efficiency. From personalized shopping recommendations to inventory management, AI technologies are being integrated into various aspects of retail. For example, AI chatbots assist customers in finding products, thereby improving engagement and sales.

Transportation

The transportation industry is seeing the advent of AI agents in autonomous vehicles, route optimization, and traffic management. AI agents are critical in processing vast amounts of data from sensors and cameras to make real-time decisions, enhancing safety and efficiency on the roads.

Career Opportunities in AI Agent Development

As AI agents continue to permeate various industries, the demand for skilled professionals in AI and machine learning is surging. Career opportunities range from AI research and development to specialized applications in healthcare, finance, and more.

Skills Required

- Programming: Proficiency in programming languages such as Python, Java, or C++ is crucial.
- Machine Learning: A strong foundation in machine learning algorithms and data analysis techniques.
- Problem-Solving: The ability to design and implement solutions to complex problems using AI.

Roles and Responsibilities

- AI Research Scientist: Focused on advancing AI technologies and developing new approaches to AI agents.
- Machine Learning Engineer: Specializes in designing and implementing machine learning models for AI agents.
- AI Application Developer: Builds and integrates AI agents into applications tailored for specific industries.

Navigating the Field

To excel in the field of AI and AI agents, continuous learning and staying updated with the latest research and technologies are key. Engaging with the AI community through forums, conferences, and collaborative projects can provide invaluable insights and opportunities for growth.

Challenges and Considerations

While the future of AI agents is promising, developers and businesses must navigate challenges such as ethical considerations, data privacy, and the potential for job displacement. Balancing innovation with responsibility is essential for the sustainable development of AI agents.

By understanding the current industry trends and preparing for the future, individuals and organizations can harness the power of AI agents to create innovative solutions and drive progress across various sectors.

Career Opportunities in AI Agents

The burgeoning field of AI agents is not only transforming industries but also creating a wealth of career opportunities for those skilled in artificial intelligence, machine learning, and software development. As AI continues to evolve, the demand for professionals who can design, build, and implement AI agents is on the rise. This section explores the various career paths available in the realm of AI agents, offering insights into the skills required and the roles that are shaping the future of technology.

Emerging Roles in AI Development

AI Agent Developer

An AI Agent Developer specializes in creating intelligent agents that can perform tasks autonomously or assist humans in decision-making processes. These professionals need a strong foundation in programming languages such as Python or Java, along with a deep understanding of machine learning algorithms and data structures.

```
# Example of a simple AI agent code snippet in
Python class AIAgent: def __init__(self,
knowledge_base): self.knowledge_base =
knowledge_base def make_decision(self, input): #
Implement decision-making logic based on the
knowledge base pass
```

AI Systems Architect

AI Systems Architects design the overall structure of AI systems, ensuring that the hardware and software components work seamlessly together. They must understand the requirements of different AI models and how they can be integrated into existing IT infrastructures.

> **Note:** A strong background in systems engineering and experience with cloud platforms like AWS or Azure is essential for this role.

Machine Learning Engineer

Machine Learning Engineers focus on developing algorithms that enable AI agents to learn from and adapt to new data without being explicitly programmed. They work closely with data scientists to understand data patterns and implement models that can improve agent performance over time.

Skills Required for a Career in AI Agents

- Programming Proficiency: Expertise in programming languages such as Python, Java, or C++ is crucial.
- Understanding of AI and Machine Learning Concepts: A solid grasp of AI principles, machine learning models, and neural networks is necessary to build effective AI agents.
- Data Analysis and Processing: The ability to work with large datasets and perform complex data transformations is

essential.

- Problem-Solving Skills: Developing AI agents often involves tackling unique and challenging problems that require creative and efficient solutions.

Navigating the Career Path

1. Education and Training: A degree in computer science, artificial intelligence, or a related field is typically required. Additionally, online courses and bootcamps can provide practical, hands-on experience with AI technologies. 2. Build a Portfolio: Demonstrating your skills through projects or contributions to open-source AI initiatives can be a powerful way to attract potential employers. 3. Stay Updated: AI is a rapidly evolving field. Keeping abreast of the latest research, tools, and technologies is crucial for success.

The field of AI agents offers a dynamic and exciting career path for those interested in the forefront of technology. By acquiring the necessary skills and staying engaged with the latest developments, aspiring professionals can find rewarding opportunities in developing the intelligent systems of the future. Whether you aim to specialize in AI development, systems architecture, or machine learning, the journey towards becoming an expert in AI agents promises to be a fulfilling one.

www.ingramcontent.com/pod-product-compliance
Lightning Source LLC
LaVergne TN
LVHW022333060326
832902LV00022B/4016

* 9 7 9 8 2 8 2 2 8 6 7 4 8 *